African Women

First Published in 1939 and reissued with a new preface in 1965, *African Women* presents a study of the Ibo women of Nigeria. The originality of the book lies in the fact that practically all the information is obtained from women and that throughout, customs, laws, circumstances and happenings are described from the women's point of view.

Divided into four major parts, the book discusses important themes like the Aba riots; linguistic description of Owerri province; missions and native organization; women in Nneato; women in Nguru; women in transition in Owerri Town; sophisticated women in Port Harcourt; education and other western developments; and the future of Ibo women. This is an important historical reference work for scholars and researchers of African Studies, African history, and women's studies.

African Women

A Study of the Ibo of Nigeria

Sylvia Leith- Ross

Routledge
Taylor & Francis Group

First published in 1939 by Faber and Faber Ltd.
Reissued 1965 by Routledge & Kegan Paul Ltd.

This edition first published in 2024 by Routledge
4 Park Square, Milton Park, Abingdon, Oxon, OX14 4RN

and by Routledge
605 Third Avenue, New York, NY 10017

Routledge is an imprint of the Taylor & Francis Group, an informa business

© Sylvia Leith- Ross, 1939, 1965

Publisher's Note
The publisher has gone to great lengths to ensure the quality of this reprint but points out that some imperfections in the original copies may be apparent.

Disclaimer
The publisher has made every effort to trace copyright holders and welcomes correspondence from those they have been unable to contact.

A Library of Congress record exists under LCCN: 39006672

ISBN: 978-1-032-88958-0 (hbk)
ISBN: 978-1-003-54053-3 (ebk)
ISBN: 978-1-032-88959-7 (pbk)

Book DOI 10.4324/9781003540533

AFRICAN WOMEN

★

*A Study of the Ibo
of Nigeria*

★

Sylvia Leith-Ross

Sometime Leverhulme Research Fellow

★

With a foreword by
Lord Lugard
G.C.M.G., C.B., D.S.O.

LONDON
ROUTLEDGE & KEGAN PAUL LTD.

First published 1939
by Faber and Faber Ltd.
Reissued 1965
by Routledge & Kegan Paul Ltd.
Broadway House, 68-74 Carter Lane,
*London, E.C.*4
Printed in Great Britain
by Lowe & Brydone (Printers) Ltd.
*London, N.W.*10

Foreword

Some thirty years ago Mrs. Leith-Ross first came to Nigeria as the bride of an official of exceptional organizing ability and initiative whose early death was a great loss to the country. Through the subsequent years, as she truly says, Nigeria has been a part of her life. First as a student of the Fulani language among the Moslems of the North, later in the Education Department in the South where the Europeanized Africans of Lagos contrasted with the illiterate tribes of the interior, and then once more to the North to study the problem of women's education, she had acquired a unique experience when in 1934 she accepted a Leverhulme Research Fellowship for the study of the conditions of life of the women of Iboland.

The Ibo tribe which occupies a region in the southeast of Nigeria is estimated to number some three million souls, and with their affinities have even been assessed at nearly double that number. Their social organization, still in the primitive stage of the family, the 'extended family' and the 'kindred,' offers to the administration a very complex problem in the application of 'Indirect Rule'. The exceptional difficulty of acquiring their 'tone' language—intensified by the number of quite distinct dialects—accounts for the paucity till lately of knowledge regarding them.

Leaving to others the complex politico-religious tribal organization, our author avoids any review of the steps taken by the British Government to get into closer

touch with the indigenous social system, and devotes
herself to a study of the daily life of the Ibo women and
their reactions to the changes brought about by contact
with the outside world, a task for which she is eminently
well qualified.

In the first fifteen chapters the picture is presented
from four different standpoints. At Nneato, secluded in
'the bush', there had been but little contact with foreign
influences; Nguru, though little less remote, still showed
the psychological effects of the 'Women's Rising' at Aba
(in which it had participated) by an attitude half of
frustration and self-defence, half triumphant. Owerri, a
township partially sophisticated, showed the results of
increasing Western contacts on morals and the marriage
institution, though even here the land remains the
predominant interest. Finally at Port Harcourt, a commercial centre on the coast, we are introduced to the
Ibo woman in fashionable dress and high-heeled shoes,
probably professing one or other of the different religious
sects, of which we hear there were fourteen variants in
a single street.

Here environment has had its effect, but the essential
characteristics of Ibo womanhood are little changed. She is
'ambitious, courageous, self-reliant, hardworking and independent'. Her interests are centred in love of her yam-
field coupled with a passion for trading and the desire to
grow rich—97 per cent are 'women-farmers'. She claims
full equality with the opposite sex, and would seem indeed to be the dominant partner. The Women's Councils
(approved and trusted by the men) enact laws for the
protection of the crops, and enforce them by suitable
penalties—including ridicule.

A ruling characteristic of men and women alike is
their great desire for children and their affection for
them—which no change in conditions can alter. They
share too an indifference towards old customs and beliefs
—except polygamy and 'bride-price'. The alacrity with

which they will abandon old ways for new is evident
in the popularity of the hospitals, courts of law, schools
and post offices, and though they show little deference
towards Europeans, they are intensely eager to obtain
the education which Europeans have brought, as a
means of getting rich. For this they will profess Christianity, or even spend the money due as bride-price, so
that marriage is deferred, with bad consequences. It is
a curious revelation of the Ibo point of view that the
substitution of African scenes for the allusions to snow
and robins and water-taps in the old text-books is un-
popular as seeming to deny to the African what is good
for the European!

Since there is no surplus food to sell, trade consists in
the purchase of a selection of imported goods—a few
pence-worth at first, and eventually perhaps of large
quantities on credit from merchants—and their barter in
a distant market where slightly higher prices are to be
got. We hear of one overseas deal when a local disease
destroyed the poultry in Fernando Po, but the native
traders shrewdly exported only cockerels lest the pur-
chasers should restart breeding!

The last five chapters are devoted to a discussion of one
or two of Africa's problems not primarily relevant to Ibo
women. The author is puzzled why a race so virile, ambitious, and adaptable has never risen to a higher plane,
and she wonders what its future may be when it has
become more sophisticated, and the population has
increased by the saving of infant life. The density in the
Nguru district was estimated at 1,000 to the square
mile, but the people are unwilling to migrate.

She has much of interest to say about Mission-work
and the effect of conversion to Christianity. The churches
—one of which cost £3,000—are full to overflowing with
eager worshippers, some of whom come great distances.
They chant hymns not a word of which they understand, and appear to be unconscious that various pagan

practices are wholly incompatible with their new vows. The result is farcical and the motive generally mercenary, especially in the case of the 'mass of fancy religions, which fills the country with bishops and prelates'. The C.M.S. bride-training institution—later extended to teaching pagan wives to read as a necessary requisite for baptism—is popular, practical and useful, but the responsibilities and obligations of Christian marriage are not understood. A devout convert urged that marriage should be by native custom with a simple church service as blessing, and that the Christian marriage service should be deferred for five years, when if the union was not childless it could take place.

Our author's appreciation of what the dance means to the African is expressed in terms more understanding and more vivid than I have ever read elsewhere. No one who has watched the intense absorption, the almost hypnotic oblivion to fatigue or any other distraction, can fail to agree with her that 'there is no European equivalent which gathers up into a single activity every possible range of thought and emotion'. It is, she says, as integral a part of the African's existence as the air he breathes.

Nor should the reader omit to take note of the extremely interesting description of the *Mbari* 'house' erected at a cost which must entail sacrifice on a poor community. Upon its architectural and mural decoration and indeed upon the clay figures it contains, the highest skill has been expended, and there is the greatest pride in the results—a combination of Madame Tussaud's and obscenity which yet represents a craving for artistic expression.

To those who value the first-hand impressions of a very competent observer, extended over a considerable period of time, Mrs. Leith-Ross's book may with confidence be recommended as an eminently readable record of research in a field hitherto but little explored.

20 *August* 1938.   LUGARD

Preface to the Second impression

Though time and the immense leap into independ-ence have brought many changes, I think the broad background of *African Women*, drawn in 1936-38, has little altered.

The Province of Owerri with which this study is concerned no longer exists as an administrative entity[1]. Local Government has taken the place of the British Administrative Officers. Palm oil is no longer the only economic mainstay. Hospitals and schools have multiplied. The narrow paths I knew are lorry-ridden roads. The people are better off, more clothed, more educated, more politically minded, yet daily life remains much the same.

The past history of the Ibo is still scarcely known though the potential richness of that past, which I had obscurely sensed, has been partly revealed by such finds as the Igbo-Ukwu bronzes and the further excavations by Professor Thurstan Shaw. The Ibo language, thanks to the studies of Ida Ward, Miss M. M. Green, and the Rev. G. E. Igwe, is now seen to be a highly developed and sensitive instrument[2]. The people themselves show no lessening of their intense vitality, as characteristic of them today as it was when I first knew them. The women, heads held high, move as fearlessly through the complexities of modern life as they did, years ago, through the gloom of the palm belt.

[1] The maps, therefore, as far as their provincial boundaries are concerned, are no longer up to date.

[2] Its orthography has been revised since this book was written.

The acknowledgments I made in the first edition of *African Women* must be repeated here: to the Leverhulme Trustees for making my return to Nigeria materially possible and for the generous confidence they placed in me; to the Nigerian Government and especially to the then Chief Commissioner for the Southern Provinces, Sir William Hunt, for allowing me complete liberty of action; to the Missions for their continuing and broad-minded kindness; to my African friends for teaching me increasingly to comprehend and appreciate our common humanity; to my brother, the late Major F. H. Ruxton, C.M.G., for the value of his example and never-failing encouragement. Lastly, I remember with thanks and deep admiration the officials of every degree who made me welcome and allowed me to feel that, as they did, I belonged to Nigeria.

S.L–R.

Acknowledgements

My indebtedness is so great that I hardly know where my acknowledgements should begin or end. In the first place, I have to thank the Leverhulme Trustees not only for the means which made my return to Nigeria materially possible, but even more for the generous confidence they placed in me, though the very generosity of that confidence made it all the more difficult to live up to. In the second place, I have to thank the Nigerian Government, and especially the Chief Commissioner for the Southern Provinces, Sir William Hunt, for allowing me entire liberty of action and for the facilities granted me; the Missions for their constant kindness to, and patience with, an often argumentative visitor; my African friends, for having taught me evermore to comprehend and appreciate our common humanity; to my brother, Major F. H. Ruxton, for the value of his example and of his never-failing encouragement.

To the officials of every degree, I would like to express not only my thanks but my admiration, both to the living, whose welcome made me feel I still belonged to Nigeria, and to the dead, who made Nigeria worth belonging to.

As this book admittedly deals only with one aspect of one portion of Iboland, it should be read in conjunction with Dr. C. K. Meek's *Law and Authority in a Nigerian Tribe;*[1] Dr. Basden'd *Niger Ibos;* and Miss

11

Acknowledgements

Margery Perham's more general *Native Administration in Nigeria*. My thanks are due to Miss Perham and to the publishers, the Oxford University Press, for permission to quote substantial extracts from the latter book in my first chapter. The very important language question is discussed in an article by Miss M. M. Green in *Africa*, Journal of the International Institute of African Languages and Cultures, vol. IX, No. 4.

For purposes of comparison, Miss Monica Hunter's *Reaction to Conquest* should be read; and Mrs. Hilda Thurnwald's rapid but shrewd survey of East African women in her *Die Schwarze Frau im Wandel Afrikas*. In a different category, but as giving the most profound and sensitive study of the black man in contact with the white, so deep-sighted that for once it could almost be said that it was a portrait of 'the African' in general, I would recommend Leland Hall's *Salah and his American*.

[1] Dr. Meek's work was not yet published at the time I was taking the notes on which my own book is based. Later on, I was able to see the typescript, but I have not taken any information from it, though I was encouraged to see how often our findings agreed.

Contents

13

Contents

14

Contents

Woman in Transition—in Owerri Town

Sophisticated Women—in Port Harcourt

III. MEN AND WOMEN

Contents

Illustrations

I

Introduction

---

*General aim and limits of investigation. Importance
of accurate knowledge concerning women's rights and
responsibilities in primitive communities and special importance of such knowledge in dealing with the Ibo. The
Aba Riots.*

In writing a book about the Ibo women, the first question that arises is: why the Ibo? The answer is:
Because in Nigeria, the most populous and potentially
the most important of our Crown Colonies, the Ibo-
speaking people are the most numerous, the most
adaptable, the most go-ahead, the most virile, and at the
same time the most primitive.[1] In the process of adaptation to modern life, this last fact is of inestimable advantage. Starting at scratch, they have nothing to unload:
no institutional religion, no traditions, no caste or other
hide-bound social system. Possessing intelligence, potentially equal to the average European, the Ibo is ready to
plunge forward into Western civilization—even as he
has already begun to do. And the women, economically
and politically, are at least the equal of the men.

Speaking in general, the women of Nigeria are seldom
of the chattel type and correspond little to the widely held
idea of the downtrodden slave or unregarded beast of
burden. The Ibo women in particular, by their number,
their industry, their ambitions, their independence, are
bound to play a leading part in the development of their

[1] I use the term 'primitive' only in a relative sense.

19

country. Their co-operation will be as valuable as their enmity would be disastrous. The women who could organize in a few days a movement as original and as formidable as the Aba Riots, known to them as 'The Women's War', which necessitated the calling in of military forces before order could be restored, and the subsequent appointment of a Commission of Inquiry, cannot be disregarded in future plans and policies. I have therefore tried in the following pages to give an account of the Ibo woman in the ordinary round of her daily life, stressing the situations which seem most likely to raise future difficulties, attempting to gauge her comprehension of and attitude towards those same difficulties, and her inward and outward reactions to the fast-changing world around her. It has been my aim to present her as an individual, with her own personal opinions, tastes and scales of value, living a life of her own, in theory dependent upon man but in practice surprisingly independent of him. I have endeavoured to show, not only by contrast of differing habits and customs but also by the contrast of character, that even within one race there is no standardization, there is no typical portrait one can draw and then say: 'This is an Ibo'. How much less then can one say, as is so often done, 'This is an African' or 'African women do this' or 'The women of Africa think that'?

The only originality of the book lies in the fact that practically all the information is obtained from women and that throughout, customs, laws, circumstances and happenings are described from the women's point of view. This necessarily limits the scope of the book and renders it often superficial. Origins and history are left aside; religion is only studied in so far as it impinges on the life of the women; tribal organization is only gone into because it gives the frame into which the picture must fit. Economics play a larger part as they are almost more the women's province than the men's; the judicial system touches both, as do health problems and education. It is of course as impossible to sunder the lives of the women from those of the men in an uncivilized community as it would be in a civilized one, but the emphasis has been deliberately laid upon the feminine aspect of all questions. This stress has obviously many disadvantages. On the other hand, an accurate knowledge concerning women's rights and responsibilities in primitive communities, some idea of their thoughts and the trend of their opinions, are important, especially so to the European legislator, administrator, and educationalist. We have perhaps until recently received our information too exclusively through men, whether acting as investigators or as informants. Even with the highest degree of trained discernment, it is difficult for a male investigator to get an accurate impression of what goes on in a woman's mind when it is revealed to him by another man; and with all possible goodwill, it is difficult for that man not to be biased by tradition, vanity, or self-importance. He will probably, and often unconsciously, make out that the woman is of little account, that her whole life is in his hands, that she has no will, no means, no property, no power, nor organization, nor means of redress. He upholds the accepted view that the husband is lord and master and that the woman is his property, and does not mention the safeguards with which custom surrounds her, the weight of feminine opinion, the independence of her economic position, the power she wields by the mere fact that she holds the pestle and the cooking-pots. Judging from my own experience among various peoples of Nigeria, I am inclined to believe that their women, because of their economic importance both as mothers, farm cultivators, and traders, have rather more power than is generally thought and that therefore they must be taken into account in the framing of new legislation, or the introduction of new methods of trade or husbandry, or the creation of new social or economic situations.

Whether this is so or not, it is certain that amongst

the Ibo, as has already been mentioned, the women do play an influential part, not only by native custom but because of their inherent vitality, independence of views, courage, self-confidence, desire for gain and worldly standing. More than the men, they seem to be able to co-operate, to stand by each other even in difficulties, and to follow a common aim. The men, except when they are among strangers in a distant place, do not seem to have any common link which goes beyond their immediate town and one cannot easily imagine any situation which would overcome their mutual suspicion and unite them in a common impulse or incline them to acknowledge the leadership of a 'stranger', even though that stranger lived but a few miles away. Yet, among the women, there seems to be something—perhaps merely the bond of sex—that links them up over wide areas so that a woman's call to women would echo far beyond the boundaries of her own town. The fact that the men generally live in their own home towns while their wives often come from other towns—Owerri Town, for example, is strictly exogamous—emphasizes the difference. The women are thus already members of two towns: their husband's, in which they live, their parents', which they often visit. Their marketing takes them far afield, as do visits to their married daughters; but beyond these tangible factors there does seem to be an intangible communion, normally latent and without visible organization, but so profoundly felt that the slightest stir sets the whole body trembling.

This has been exemplified on three occasions, in those dramatic and curious happenings known as the Spirit Movement, the Dancing Women,[1] and the Aba Riots. The records of the first two are confusing and not very full and though the facts were known and to a certain

[1] A succinct account of these two Movements, which took place in 1927 and 1925 respectively, will be found in Annexure 1, paras 56 et seq. of the Report of the Aba Commission of Inquiry, 1930.

extent the motives also, one suspects that through lack
of time and staff, the administration may not have been
able to investigate them as fully as would have been
expedient in view of the fact that they spread over such
large areas. The third, and the most recent, has been the
subject of much careful inquiry but here again the student is left with the unsatisfied feeling that he has
lighted on something the understanding of which is of
vital import to the future of the country, but that he
does not rightly know what it is.

The clearest account of the confused happenings known
as the Aba Riots is contained in Miss Perham's *Native
Administration in Nigeria*, from which I have her permission to quote the following extracts:

'At the end of 1929, just when the Government was
congratulating itself upon the success with which the
difficult task of introducing direct taxation into these
provinces had been accomplished, rioting of a serious and
unusual kind broke out in Calabar and Owerri. These
riots must be discussed in considerable detail. In a study
of this nature there is at least one good reason for this
detailed treatment. People who do not know how to com-
municate or even to formulate their sense of grievance
in constitutional terms may resort to violence as the
only effective way in which they can show their dissatisfaction with their conditions. The "Aba Riots", as
they are generally called, may be regarded as a comment
upon the administration of the past; while the lessons
they taught have largely governed subsequent policy.

'The events will first be summarized as far as possible
without comment, for their significance was only revealed by later investigations.[1] In Owerri Province, in the

[1] Miss Perham states in a footnote: 'The following account, in so far
as it has not been derived from information supplied direct to the
writer, is based upon the Reports of the two Commissions of Enquiry,
Sessional Papers of the Nigerian Legislative Council, Nos. 12 and 28
of 1930, and to the *Minutes of Evidence* issued with the latter, *Gazette
Extraordinary*, 7 February 1930.'

heart of the Ibo country, where a particularly dense population inhabits the palm forest, there is a place called Oloko. Here a Warrant Chief, Okugo, under instructions from the District Officer, was making a re-assessment of the taxable wealth of the people. In this he attempted to count the women, children, and domestic animals. A rumour at once spread among the women that the recently introduced taxation of men was to be extended to them. All through this densely inhabited forest country, at intervals of a few miles, are markets where many thousands, mostly women, collect to do petty trading, sell palm-oil to the small middlemen, and gossip with each other. The rumour thus ran through all the locality in a few days, spreading anger and dismay which were all the more intense because at this moment the price of palm-produce was falling, and new customs duties had put up the cost of several imported articles of daily use. They were seriously perturbed. "We depend upon our husbands,[1] we cannot buy food or clothes ourselves and how shall we get money to pay tax?" They decided to combine. "We women", as one of them stated afterwards in her evidence, "therefore held a large meeting at which we decided to wait until we heard definitely from one person that women were to be taxed, in which case we would make trouble as we did not mind to be killed for doing so. We went to the houses of all the chiefs and each admitted counting his people."

‘Okugo, continuing reluctantly[2] to carry out his orders, sent a messenger to count some of his people. This man entered a compound and told one of the married women,

---

[1] As will be seen when discussing Ibo women's economic situation in later chapters, this statement is only partially true.

[2] Another version given me was that Okugo himself purposely went beyond the District Officer's instructions so as to stir up strife, hoping for personal profit if he did so. Several picturesque tales were told to prove this but I deliberately refrained from questions as it was both useless and inexpedient to re-open a matter which had already been officially dealt with.

Nwanyeruwa, who was pressing oil, to count her goats
and sheep. She replied angrily, "Was your mother
counted?" at which they closed, seizing each other by
the throat. A meeting of women was called and
Nwanyeruwa's excited story was told as confirmation of
the rumour. A palm-leaf, which, it appears, is at once a
symbol of trouble and a call for help,[1] was sent round to
all the women of the neighbourhood. From the whole
country-side women poured into Oloko and proceeded
according to custom to "sit" upon the man who had tried
to assess Nwanyeruwa. All night they danced round his
house singing a song quickly invented to meet the situation. Growing hourly more excited, they went on to
Okugo's compound where his own people tried to defend
him with sticks and bird arrows. The crowd mobbed
him, damaged his house, demanded his cap of office, and

---

[1] In spite of many efforts, I was never able to get definite evidence
of a palm-leaf being sent round as a symbol of trouble or as a call for
help. All the examples given me of the use of palm-leaves (other than
when the leaves were connected with medicine) were bound up with
the idea of victory or rejoicing. When women have 'sat' successfully
upon a man, they may bind palm-leaves round waist and head and
dance round the market; or if a spirit has demanded the sacrifice of a
cow from a certain family, when the sacrifice has been accomplished
its members will wear palm-leaves and sing: 'We are free! we are
free!' (from the trouble the spirit was causing); or if a man wins a
case in court, he will also wear palm-leaves. Newly married girls will
do likewise when, as in Eziama, they are led singing round the market, rejoicing that their husbands were wealthy enough to have been
able to pay the full dowry and that they themselves had been found
virgins. In the same place, I was told also that a 'yellow' palm-leaf
(a dry leaf in contradistinction to the young leaves which are generally used for the purpose of personal decoration(?)) would be held aloft
as a flag of truce, supposing two villages were at war while a third
one was trying to make peace between them.

In the actual Riot areas which I visited, even the most indirect
questioning concerning the symbolic meaning of palm-leaves brought
forth no replies of any worth, the women immediately thinking that
I was trying to obtain fresh evidence regarding the Riots themselves.
The only palm-leaves I saw used in these parts had taken on a completely modern symbolism, being tied to the handlebars of second-
hand bicycles to indicate they were for sale!

charged him with assault before the District Officer of Bende. The latter arrested him and brought him into the station. "The women," said this officer, "numbering over ten thousand, were shouting and yelling round the office in a frenzy. They demanded his cap of office, which I threw to them, and it met the same fate as a fox's carcase thrown to a pack of hounds. The station between the office and the prison . . . resembled Epsom Downs on Derby Day." The women continued to camp in thousands round the District Office until Okugo was tried and sentenced to two years' imprisonment for assault. (The second Commission afterwards recommended him for a free pardon.) But this was not the end. The women, for a reason which we shall consider later, refused, in spite of all the assurances of chiefs and Administrative Officers, to believe that women, "the trees which bear fruit", were not to be taxed and this even after a deputation of fifty had taken train to provincial headquarters at Port Harcourt to question the Resident. From Oloko women went out in all directions, beyond the boundaries of the province and even into the neighbouring Ibibio country, spreading the rumour, and from a wide area subscriptions began to come in to Nwanyeruwa, who had become a figure of womanhood rising up against oppression.

'The trouble spread in the second week of December to Aba, an important trading centre on the railway. Here there converged some ten thousand women, scantily clothed, girdled with green leaves, carrying sticks. Singing angry songs against the chiefs and the court messengers, the women proceeded to attack and loot the European trading stores and Barclay's Bank, and to break into the prison and release the prisoners. The mobs were to some extent checked by the police supported by a hastily raised force of European traders and Africans, among whom the Boy Scouts worked hard on the side of law and order. After two days of rioting troops arrived and

dispersed the crowds without any serious casualties. More
or less successful attacks followed elsewhere upon "factories" and other buildings at railway stations and trading centres, but the women were far more interested in
destroying the Native Courts and mobbing the Warrant
Chiefs than in looting. It is impossible to follow the
details of such diffused disorder, but one or two incidents
are worth picking out.

'During the second week of December the movement
spread from the Ibo divisions of Owerri and Aba to the
Ibibio peoples of Calabar. At much the same time as the
elaborate form of re-assessment, which the women connected with female taxation, was being undertaken in
Oloko, the Resident of Calabar had issued instructions
for a similar kind of enumeration in his province. This
was zealously enacted in one district by a cadet in the
administrative service. In some villages, the people
cleared into the bush at his approach, taking their small
stock and chickens with them; here, however, he counted
the houses, there being generally one to each woman,
and the tethering pegs for the goats and sheep. These
animals, we may notice, were often the personal possessions of the women. In the neighbouring district the
chiefs protested vigorously against these house-to-house
visitations, though they professed themselves ready to
parade all the men of each village in the central square.
Another cadet, in Opobo district, to the south, met with
determined opposition from the chiefs as well as from
the people who were already in touch with the women
of Owerri. The women followed him about wailing and
cursing; palm branches, doubtless reinforced with magic,
were tied across paths and doorways, while on one occasion it was grimly pointed out to him that he was actually
standing on a grave where a white man like himself was
buried. Finally, he was assaulted and his tax register
taken. At the neighbouring centre of Ukam he and two
senior colleagues were powerless to check the women, on

this occasion accompanied by men, who opened the lock-up, destroyed the Native Court, and cut the telegraph wires. At Utu-Etim-Ekpo appeared crowds of women scantily dressed in sackcloth, their faces smeared with charcoal, sticks wreathed with young palms in their hands, while their heads were bound with young ferns. It is interesting to note that no European understood the exact significance of these last symbols, though nearly all the native witnesses assumed that they meant war.[1] They burned the Native Court and sacked and looted the "factory" (European store) and clerks' houses. They declared that the District Officer was born of a woman, and as they were women they were going to see him. Police and troops were sent and as, on two occasions, the women ran towards them with frenzied shouts, fire was opened with a Lewis gun as well as with rifles, and eighteen women were killed and nineteen wounded.

'The following day an even more serious collision occurred at Opobo. Mobs of women passed shouting and singing about the town, "What is the smell? Death is the smell." They beat upon the iron trading stores with their sticks and threatened the traders. To one, Mr. Butler, a merchant, they shouted derisively, "All right, Bottle, no fear morning time five o'clock we go come for you," and the next day, "We'll get our Christmas clothes out of you to-day." In order to calm their excited fears, the District Officer agreed to meet the seven leaders at the District Office the following day. Palm-leaves were sent round to all the neighbouring clans, and when the time came not seven but several hundred arrived at the District Office, armed with stout cudgels and dressed only in loin-cloths and palm-leaves. In front of the District Office was a light bamboo fence, beyond that the road and, almost immediately beyond that, the river. The District Officer, with a military officer and a platoon of

[1] The symbolic use of ferns may be confined to the Ibibio. I have not myself come across it among the Ibo.

troops, parleyed with the women from inside the fence. The leaders asked him to make notes of the discussion and then asked to see his notes. They consisted of the statements that the Government will not tax women and that the women did not want the men to be taxed; that known prostitutes were to be arrested (though there was some doubt afterwards as to whether it should have been "not to be arrested"), that there should be no payment for licences to hold plays, that the local chief should be removed, and various other requests. They demanded, out of their half-knowledge of legal forms, that he should sign the document; that the signature should be witnessed by the interpreter and the office clerk and stamped with the office stamp. They next demanded six typewritten copies, one for each section of the women present. While these were being made, they began to complain about the state of trade and the way in which the firms were cutting out their position as retailers and middle-women.

'All this time the meeting was becoming rowdier. More and more women were streaming up, until the numbers were estimated as being about fifteen hundred. When the copies were handed out, various other demands were made, such as that they must be put into envelopes, that they must have two-shilling stamps attached. They made threatening and obscene gestures against the troops, called them sons of pigs, and said they knew the soldiers would not fire at them. At last they struck at the District Officer with their sticks. The Lieutenant caught the blows, made signs to the District Officer as to whether he should fire (for it was impossible to make himself heard in the uproar) and, just as the fence began to give way before the rush of women, shot the leader through the head with his revolver. Two volleys were then fired on the crowd, which broke and fled, leaving thirty-two dead and dying, and thirty-one wounded.

Introduction

'This shooting was on the 17th December. Trouble continued sporadically in various parts of the disturbed area, but by the 20th the situation was completely in hand, and the rest of the month was taken up with pacification by means of patrols, and punishment under the Collective Punishments Ordinance. The disturbed area covered about six thousand square miles and contained about two million people. Attacks were made upon Native Courts in sixteen Native Administration centres, and most of them were broken up or burned.

The Behaviour of the Women

'When the character of the riots themselves is reviewed, the overwhelming impression is of the vigour and solidarity of the women. Men occasionally make a flickering appearance in the background, but they seem, with a few exceptions, to have stood completely on one side, passive, if consenting parties, to the extraordinary behaviour of their wives. Such a movement is almost unthinkable among the more docile stay-at-home women of the greater part of eastern and southern Africa, but the West Coast women, at least in those parts where neither strong measures of conquest nor Islam have tamed them, seem to be made of sterner stuff. The traveller from East Africa must be struck at once by the huge crowd of strenuous, excited women who fill the markets and stream along the roads in pursuit of trade, and whose manner is markedly free both towards himself and their fellows. To push through one of these dense crowds in a market glade of Owerri Province, with the women struggling, shouting, and laughing around you, is to realize how dangerously this excited good humour could change its character. Their organization into societies and age groups—of which Administrative Officers knew, and still know, all too little—their concentration in markets and wide dispersal

30

along the trade routes, are factors which may help to account for their rapid mobilization over two Provinces.

'The women surprised their rulers, surprised their own people, and, probably, themselves. All the male witnesses, both Europeans who had been long in the country and Africans, insisted that they had never seen anything like this before. "I am an old man", said one witness, "and have been a chief a long time. . . . In all my life I never saw the women carrying on in this fashion before. I never saw the women flinging sand at their chiefs or white men or attacking them with sticks. . . ." The Africans particularly remarked as ominous the garnishing with wild fern and the complete absence of children;[1] they were surprised, too, to see so many strange women from distant parts collected together. The rioters themselves, who readily gave evidence, even volunteered to do so, explained how they sent round the palm-leaves to rally their comrades, and how those whose business it was beat the drums. "We always obey these messages." Unwilling women, encountered on the road, or haled out of their houses, were forced to join by the threat of having their property destroyed. One woman with her daughter-in-law, who was killed, was forced to join a crowd, and she testified to the impression made upon her by the rioters.

'"We met a crowd of women heading to Utu-Etim-Ekpo. The women stopped us. There were plenty too much women, a very large crowd. They were coming along the road and beating their laps and lifting their hands towards the sky and waving their sticks. All had sticks; big sticks. I was afraid of them. They took away my basket and forced me to join them. . . . 'You are a woman, you must join us.' They looked quite different

[1] The absence of children does not seem to me so surprising, at least in so far as the Ibo are concerned, as Ibo women do not take their children about with them to farm and market as much as, say, the Yoruba. The drums referred to here must be the small light women's drums such as I have described on p. 106.

31

from any other crowd of women I have ever seen. They had *nkpatat* (wild fern) round their heads. There were no children with them. As they had no children with them that also made me afraid. I do not know where any of the women came from. I was very much afraid of them and did not look at their faces."

'Once on the march, their resolution was extraordinary. They are repeatedly quoted as having said they were prepared to die. In one instance, after having been fired upon with loss of life, the crowd came on again. The first Commission, in excusing the firing, spoke of "the savage passions" and ferocious demeanour of one of the mobs, while one of the military officers, who had considerable experience of mobs in India and Ireland, told the Commission that "he had never seen crowds in such a state of frenzy or so much out of hand".

'It is therefore surprising that very few people were mishandled by the women, and no one seriously injured either among those whom they singled out for special attack, or those who barred their way, though in numerous cases they had them at their mercy. It is clear that on some occasions the leaders, even at their own risk, were counselling moderation. When the original rioters, the Oloko women, heard of the looting at Aba they sent the following telegram to the District Officer there: "Please inform our women friends there stop such they are doing thats not our objects the tax matter is settled to our satisfaction nothing like houses destroying at Oloko where tax matter first started." At Ikot Expene a fearless and sensible missionary was able to push his way through a crowd of some three to four thousand of the peculiarly intractable Ibibio women. He found their leader, and persuaded her to call up the headwomen of the fifty-nine "towns" represented and to parley with him in the church. He obtained from the District Officer fifty-nine typed slips settling their grievances, which were distributed and which "they keep to this day".

The Aba Riots

Again in Ahoada the District Officer was confronted by a crowd of two thousand women at one of the Native Courts. When the crowd attacked and fired the court, the women leaders put a guard on the District Officer in his rest house. "They said that they had no complaint against the Government and that I was a stranger and they did not consider it right that I should suffer in any way." The story may also be quoted of one military officer who ordered his men to sling their rifles, cut sticks from the bush, and beat the women along the road. When the mob suddenly increased to about fifteen thousand they used the butts of their rifles and drove them into a market-place. "I told them that they had already had a taste of what they might get and I told them not to make idiots of themselves. I gave them five minutes to sit down and if they did not obey I would fire on them. I told them as each minute went by and when I said "half a minute to go" suddenly the whole crowd sat down. I was flummoxed then to know what to do with them. Anyway, we got the headwomen from each group and I made them come and sit under a tree." Here he harangued them. "They went back and addressed their various groups and they brought in fourteen Warrant Chiefs' caps and laid them at my feet. . . ."

'In considering the behaviour of the women there is one further fact to be mentioned. They seem to have been convinced, in spite of rhetorical assertions that they were prepared to die, that no harm would come to them. What was the basis of their confidence? Perhaps they remembered that in the fighting which accompanied the occupation of the country, the women had, as far as possible, been left unharmed. We may notice, however, that other African movements, notably the Maji Maji rebellion in German territory, have been accompanied by the insurgents' belief in their immunity from physical injury. Only so, perhaps, can primitive people break the spell in which their fear of their powerful and

33   B

mysterious white rulers binds them. There is no evidence
that the Nigerian women had protected themselves with
any special magic, but in embarking upon their extreme
course of action they had certainly armed themselves
psychologically with a sense of security. They reiterated
in some cases up to the moment before a volley, that
soldiers would not fire on women; that the soldiers had
no bullets or that women were never killed in war. They
called themselves vultures, which in Ibibio are called
the "Messengers of God". One woman explained this in
her evidence:

'"I was surprised to see the soldiers fire as we were
women we call ourselves vultures as we did not think
soldiers would fire at us. Vultures go to market and eat
food there and nobody molests them nobody will kill
vultures even in the market, even if it kills fowls. We
only fling sticks at them if they take our chop and so we
thought soldiers will not harm us what we may do."

'They called themselves Oha Ndi Nyiom, which appears to have an abstract meaning and may be rendered
in English "women's world" or "the spirit of womanhood", and their demeanour on this occasion (i.e. the
destruction of a court house) tended to show that they
believed themselves to be possessed of the spirit of
womanhood and therefore inviolable. It was certainly
necessary to dispel this dangerous sense of immunity.'

Miss Perham then goes on to describe the Commissions
of Inquiry: 'Early in January 1930 a Commission, consisting of the Administrator of Lagos Colony and the
Crown Counsel, was appointed to apportion the responsibility for the loss of life where firing had taken place.
They reported at the end .of the month, completely
exonerating those responsible for the firing. It was
generally felt, however, that the serious nature of the
disturbances warranted a more representative Commission with wider terms of reference. Such a Commission
was appointed in February. . . . The Commission toured

34

the disturbed areas, holding public sittings from March until May, and reported in July. They examined 485 witnesses, including many of the rioters, and all the available officials and soldiers concerned in the event; were addressed by seven counsel, African and European, and studied an immense number of memoranda and other documents. Their Report, with its Annexure and Minutes, runs to two bulky volumes.

'To this second Commission the women are not merely an unruly mob endangering the King's peace and deserving severe treatment. Their intimate and sympathetic investigations take us, as it were, into the heart of the mob, reveal the fears and misunderstandings which moved the women and point to the administrative errors and difficulties from which these arose. The presence of Africans on the Commission and in Legislative Council, and the need of satisfying a large literate African public, undoubtedly promoted this sympathetic handling of the rioters' case. Whatever view is taken of the findings of the Commission, its activities probably helped to prevent a wedge of bitterness and distrust being driven between the Government and the people.

'. . . The Commission found that the main cause of the rioting was the widespread belief that the Government was about to tax women. A cardinal administrative error accounted, in their view, both for this conviction and the absolute refusal of the women to believe the reiterated assurances of Administrative Officers that it was unfounded. In the very part of Owerri where the trouble began, the real reason for the numbering of men in 1926—namely taxation—had been deliberately concealed from the people. In order to avoid obstruction, they were left to think it was only a census count. When, therefore, the Government began to count women, with the small stock and poultry which they regarded as peculiarly their own, they naturally concluded that this meant taxation for themselves, and as naturally rejected all

35

assurances to the contrary. If their reaction was extreme beyond all that might have been expected, it was because they were still resentful at the recent and, to them, unprecedented taxation of men, and because the economic situation had recently changed for the worse. We must understand that the women persuaded themselves that they were not only the victims of outrageous oppression but faced with absolute ruin.

'The Commission found that discontent with the Native Court members was an important contributory cause of the outbreak. Released in their excitement from all fear, the women certainly showed what they thought of the system by which they were administered. In many, though not in all the disturbed areas, their animus was directed against the Warrant Chiefs and the Native Courts. Demonstrations in front of chiefs' houses, the seizure of the chiefs' caps, and the rough treatment of their persons, resulted from a belief that the chiefs had betrayed them to Government. The lesser Native Administration employees, court messengers and clerks, were also singled out for obloquy. Clearly there was no recognition that these people were the leaders or the servants of the people, any more than when they destroyed the court houses there was any recognition that these buildings were their own, even though they had been built and maintained by themselves. When the women were called upon to give evidence, they uttered a flood of criticism against the corruption and injustice of the chiefs and courts which merited and received careful attention, though its value was obviously that of second thoughts, as a measure of such abuses is generally taken for granted by Africans. . . .'

In reviewing the Riots, Miss Perham says: 'It is an encouraging feature of this unhappy incident that the responsible authorities in Nigeria, as in England, should have been so ready to face the fact that it resulted largely from defects in their Government. Here the Aba riots

The Aba Riots

point a moral that is applicable far beyond Nigeria. The difficulties in this region. . . . were exceptionally great. But beneath the peculiar local symptoms lies a pathological condition common to the whole of negro Africa. It is produced by the sudden strain thrown upon primitive communities by the strong, all-embracing pressure of European influence. There are examples in various parts of the world of primitive peoples unexpectedly rebelling after years of acquiescence in European rule, and their conscious purposes often draw strength from what is at bottom an unconscious cultural protest. The reaction may not be expressed in this form. Some tribes endure the stress of change so quietly that their rulers do not observe their difficulties. One relief for the desire for reassertion is found in the formation of secret societies or of quasi-Christian bodies independent of white control, whose proceedings express at once European influence and an anti-European attitude. The Watch Tower movement in Southern Africa, with its apocalyptic hopes of the fall of Christendom, "Satan's organization", clearly belongs to this category.

'Among other evidence supporting this view of the Aba riots is the wildness and variety of some of the women's complaints. At Owerrinta, for instance, some Native Court members reported upon their attempts to argue with the women.

'"They said they would go to Owerrinta to demolish the Native Court; they did not want the Native Court to hear cases any longer, and that all white men should go to their country so that the land in this area might remain as it was many years ago before the advent of the white man. We told them, 'Do you want this done? Don't you realize that Government is doing good things for you all?' We also pointed out to them that in the old days before the advent of Government people killed one another without redress. . . . We also pointed out to them the advantages of the railway, that they could go to Aba or anywhere else by paying five shillings. They said that after driving away everybody they would remove the rails." A string of reckless complaints was uttered by women witnesses before the Commission. "We said that we thought the white men come to bring peace to the land." "Our main grievance is that we are not so happy as we were before," and again, "Our grievance is that the land is changed—we are all dying."

'In south-eastern Nigeria, a relatively sympathetic Government was dealing with one of the least disciplined and least intelligible, of African peoples. If this Government held itself ultimately responsible for the riots, the presumption is that the Governments of southern and eastern Africa would be even more responsible for outbreaks among their more tractable people. The evidence of the anthropologists shows that most African tribes *within their social groupings* were naturally, perhaps exceptionally, law-abiding people; and in view of the disturbing character of our intrusion it is our obvious duty to study both their old organization and the strains to which we are subjecting it. I would go so far as to say that, under present circumstances, Africans cannot be held responsible, in the widest sense, for outbreaks of disorder or rebellion. This is no academic question. It entails that when such disorders occur, even though in the interests of both sides their immediate suppression may necessitate strong measures, they should be regarded as almost certain evidence of administrative shortcomings on our part, and should be subjected to full, sympathetic, and, as far as is humanly possible, impartial investigation, the results of which should be published. There will almost certainly be revealed either misunderstanding of our intentions on the part of the people, or what in their eyes are real injustices and hardships. There will also, in all probability, be revealed an improper functioning of those native authorities to whose guidance the people would naturally look and who should be acting as liaison between them and our Government. The agitator, too often the scapegoat of inefficient administration, finds no foothold when the system is healthy. The gap that lies at present between Africans and the ever-shifting Administrative Officers who represent to them the British Government, can only be bridged by knowledge, and over that bridge it is we who have to go, three-quarters, or more, of the way to meet them. It is here—as the Aba riots abundantly showed—that expert sociological investigation must play its part. Yet such research is still regarded as a luxury which can be indulged in only when there is time and money to be spared from other enterprises, none of which can succeed apart from the human factor.'

These last paragraphs of Miss Perham's are an added justification of the attempt I have made in the following pages to go at least a little way across the bridge towards a knowledge of 'one of the least disciplined, and least intelligible, of African peoples'.

II

Introduction

Previous experience and methods of work. Advantages and disadvantages of being a free-lance investigator; of being a woman investigator. Difficulty of nomenclature. Exceptional situation created by exceptional density of population. Generalization impossible. Only possible to describe certain areas as most typical of transition stages.

At the International Congress of Anthropological and Ethnological Sciences of 1934, a speaker, Miss E. J. Lindgren, said: 'The observer of social psychological phenomena needs to adapt himself as completely as possible to his human surroundings, and his own physical and mental characteristics will therefore largely determine his degree of success', and another speaker, Mr. Gregory Bateson, on another occasion, advised: 'In all publications the type to which the investigator belongs should be stated and the general tone of his behaviour described.'

These speakers were surely right. At the risk of appearing fatuous, an investigator should give the reader some idea of his own character and outlook, his preparation for the work in hand. Even though he keep stern watch, personal reactions must occasionally influence his judgment, his personal likes give a quicker understanding of one race, his personal dislikes raise a barrier between himself and another. It seems better to admit the human factor at once than to pretend to a complete

40

absence of personal bias and, for my part, in work such
as I have been doing, of which the success depended almost entirely on my capacity for adapting myself 'as
completely as possible to my human surroundings', I
was conscious all the time that there was a danger of mis-
statement, of mis-interpretation due to the fact that my
'type' did not fit in with the Ibo 'type'. This knowledge
made me of course all the more careful not to pass light
judgments nor take anything for granted, but it prevented that spontaneous and mutual understanding
which sometimes flashes between two women, giving a
momentary but unforgettable vision of what each other's
worlds are like.

Nigeria has always been part of my life. One of my
earliest memories is that of hearing my father talk of
West Africa—he was in command of a sloop at the taking
of Lagos—and the first poetry he taught me was the
grim old sailors' rhyme:

> *The Bight of Benin—the Bight of Benin,*
> *Few come out though many go in.*

My brother, Major F. H. Ruxton, served with the
Royal Niger Company and then under the Colonial
Office as Resident both in the North and in the
Cameroons until his retirement late in 1928, after having been Lieutenant-Governor of the Southern Provinces. I myself first came to West Africa in 1907. After
the early death of my husband, who was Chief Transport Officer of what was then known as Northern Nigeria, I returned twice more to the country, with the
approval of Lord—then Sir Frederick—Lugard, for the
purpose of making a study of the Fulani language, the
results of which were published by the Nigerian Government. In 1925 a post was offered me in the Education
Department and I spent a year and a half at Lagos and
in touring round the Southern Provinces. Later, I was

41

asked to investigate the possibilities of educating Mohammedan girls in the Northern Provinces, and spent nearly
a year at Ilorin. Later still, I was asked to start a school
for girls at Kano, where I spent another fourteen months
and then had to resign on account of health.

It will be seen that most of my experience lay in the
North where conditions were almost the exact opposite
of those in the South, more especially of those in the Ibo
country. Space, colour, a wide sky, horsemen, walled
cities, kings—that was the conservative North as I knew
it. A glimpse of a few feet only between palm-trees,
teeming life of brown bodies seen in the green gloom,
little huts, not even a village chief, but on the other hand
numberless schools, roads, lorries, that was the go-ahead
South as I got to know it in Owerri Province. Nevertheless, the time I had spent in Lagos was some sort of preparation for this contrast. It gave me an acquaintance
with an urban population, long in contact with Europe,
and ranging from slum-dwellers through dock labourers,
skilled artisans, clerks in Government or commercial
offices, to doctors and lawyers, bishops and pastors.

The educated women in Lagos were Yoruba, or of
Sierra Leone descent. The older ones had a mid-Victorian sternness often flouted by the younger ones, who
wished to run long before they had learned to walk. I do
not think either generation was very happy, balanced
between two worlds, and though few consciously felt the
strain, it must have given them a sense of doubt and insecurity. The women of Ilorin, though Yoruba too, were
very different. Their clash of cultures had come long ago,
somewhere about 1817 when Afonja of Ilorin, a pagan
as were then all his people, invoked the aid of Malam
Alimi of Sokoto and his Mohammedan friends against his
suzerain, the Alafin of Oyo. The help was efficacious but
proved disastrous in the end to Afonja, who was killed in
1831 by his former allies. The population had to submit
to the rule of strangers, whose religion they were forced

to adopt. Whatever the strain the women had gone through then, they had long got over it and walked sedately to and fro between farm and market and town and farm, the garment of their new religion sitting lightly if still a little strangely on their comfortable shoulders, half asleep and in no wise demanding to be awakened. They were quite willing to be friendly once they had made sure who and what I was, but, industrious, self-sufficient, content, they had little to say or to ask. On the other hand, they were quite willing to show me their crafts and I had good practice in watching various kinds of weaving and the making of the most admirable pottery which served me later as a basis of comparison. And above all, I gained experience of those endless and seemingly aimless conversations, I got used to the measuring eyes, I learnt to study the polite stiff faces which, according to my own behaviour, might or might not relax and lighten.

During my stay at Kano, I saw little of the women, but I had the opportunity of comparing the Kano I had known in 1912, which was, wall and lane and gateway, almost exactly as Barth had seen it in 1854, with the Kano of to-day with its railway, warehouses, water supply, and electric light. If conservative, aristocratic, and Mohammedan Kano could show such a transformation in the space of twenty years, how could I be surprised when I got to Owerri to find that go-ahead, democratic, semi-Christian Ibo-land should show even greater changes in an even shorter time?

When, as a Leverhulme Research Fellow, I came to Nigeria again in 1934, my colleague, Miss M. M. Green, and I, went straight to Owerri, the headquarters of the Owerri Division of the Owerri Province. Owerri is close to several densely populated areas and, on the whole, seemed a suitable base. Our original plan was to settle in a native village for a year or more and to work together, supplementing and checking each other's information and sharing the work so that one would always be available for watching any local cycle of work or play while the other would be free to go to any special ceremony or event. For various reasons, we decided to modify this plan and though we returned at intervals to Owerri as our base, we worked in separate areas, meeting at Owerri to compare notes and discuss progress.

Having more experience of the native than scientific training, I had decided with the approval of Sir Donald Cameron, then Governor of Nigeria, and others, that I would limit myself to a study of the daily life of the Ibo women and that especially in certain areas of the Owerri and Okigwi Divisions of the Owerri Province. Apart from the general interest such a study could have, it might be, if properly carried out, of some importance to the administration as these Divisions had been the scene of the beginnings of the Dancing Women's Movement and of the Aba Riots, to which reference has already been made. As my colleague was planning a more comprehensive study of Ibo social life in a section of that same area, it seemed that our studies might supplement each other.

The method to be pursued was not easy to think out. Belonging neither to Government nor Mission, how was I to explain myself to the people, how account for my presence, my insatiable curiosity? In the North, it had been easier. Some knowledge of the Koran, of local history, a big book under one's arm, and one was accepted as a wise woman in the tradition of those of Djenne and Timbuctoo. But among the Ibo there was no such tradition of scholarship. Knowledge for its own sake was an idea they could not grasp. Nor could they grasp that a scientific body existed which sent out men and women to gather such knowledge. Where in Ilorin people had spontaneously come forward to show me some object made in 'olden times', some specially well-built house or some well-carved stool, the Ibo remained indifferent. When told of the book that would be written about them, of the British Museum, where specimens of their crafts would be sent, of the need for their co-operation, they looked incredulous or blank, or hinted that co-operation could only be had for money. Only once did I see sudden apprehension of something which was world-wide and beyond price: Mary, one of my interpreters, an intelligent but scarcely educated woman, noticed that I used a centimetre tape measure instead of the yard measure she vaguely knew. I explained that the metric system was more widely known than our own and therefore it was used in taking all scientific measurements. Reverently she took the tape from me, passed it slowly through her fingers. Then she looked up: 'Scien-ti-fic measurements . . .' she whispered to herself, with precision and with awe. From that moment she seemed somehow to understand my aim, but, except for a few highly educated men, she was the only one.

On the other hand, my neutral position gave some advantages. Information had not to be arranged to suit me, there was no fear of angering the Government official nor of shocking the missionary. Often I felt I had not learnt as much as either of these would have done; but very occasionally I felt I had learned more—or rather that I had seen things from a new angle which might possibly be a little nearer the native's own angle. Having neither souls to save nor taxes to collect, I could move easily among the people and their problems; nevertheless, it would have been unforgivable if I had ever forgotten to walk carefully, or had ceased to realize that for good or evil, the native sees the white man as a whole, bearing equally the full responsibility of each other's words and deeds. And whatever the disadvantages and difficulties of being a free-lance investigator, at least I had the advantage of being a woman. And I think this was a real one. Black or white, we were secretly leagued

Introduction

together. Behind our respectful references to men ran
the same glimmer of laughter, the same good-humoured
tolerance. Of laws and institutions we spoke with the
same shrug of the shoulders, discussed women's burdens
with the same philosophical acceptance, dandled the
children with the same satisfaction and bent over the
cooking-pots with the same appraising look. I always
stressed the fact I had come all the way from England
solely to learn about the Ibo women, that they were the
only people I wanted to talk to, that none of the men's
doings were my affair. This statement was of course too
wholesale but, as had already happened at Ilorin, it
sometimes gave the women a pleased sense of importance, of nearness of interest, of similarity of experience,
of my being their exclusive possession whom they could
approach at any hour. They naturally took advantage of
this at every turn, but if in the meantime I had got the
information I wanted I could not grudge them their
own small victories.

The language question presented serious difficulties.
Ibo is a tone language which very few Europeans have
mastered. I knew I would never be able to speak it sufficiently well to be able to talk freely, so I was obliged to
do all my work through interpreters. Great as is the disadvantage, it is perhaps not quite so great as it sounds,
especially in Nigeria, where, more especially in the
North, it is the custom for a chief to speak through a third
party. The native sees nothing strange in this and indeed
might more easily talk through someone of his own
colour than direct to the white man. On the other hand,
one loses all the precious information to be gathered
from conversations overheard, from the calls of women
going to the market, from the remarks of passers-by,
from scolding mothers and playing children. I can only
be thankful that my own two interpreters were as good
as they were so that I did not lose even more than I
did.

My Interpreters

One of them, Mary Anderson (her native name was Mbafɔ Uhoaku, daughter of Aduku of the Umuwere family) was a middle-aged woman catechist attached to the Methodist Mission. I had met her years before when staying with Mrs. Grainger, then Miss Leggatt, a missionary doing admirable work amongst the women and girls in the Okigwi Division, and had always remembered her keen bright face and quick understanding. She remembered me also and when she offered to give up her holidays so that she might come and interpret for me, the Mission kindly allowed her to do so. Although so long in contact with the Mission, she was not detribalized, was friendly with Christians and pagans alike and was an exceptionally shrewd, courageous and understanding woman. Her English was strange but vivid, she knew how to draw the women out and her own comments were full of truth and humour. I enjoyed nothing so much as, at the end of the day, going through my notes with Mary beside me explaining and supplementing. Work over, we would gossip about the village, the conduct and character of the people we had met, discuss the problems of marriage and education and religion which were already confronting her people, or, best of all, sit in the dusk, all gulfs bridged, capping each other's slightly scandalous stories.

My other interpreter, Salome Njemanze, was the granddaughter of the late Chief Njemanze of Owerri Town, an outstanding man to whom reference will be made again later. She did not of course have the experience and worldly wisdom of Mary but she was observant, curious, frank, and when she talked freely about her own home and childhood, intensely interesting. She never quite understood what I had come for and her patience sometimes gave out, but she liked the changing life we led and her own importance.

Of their reliability, either as interpreters or as informants, I was never quite sure. As Mary knew the women

47

so well, it was often wisest to leave the wording of a difficult question to her and when she avoided pressing for an answer, I guessed it was because she thought it best not to do so. I thus deliberately chose to put myself in her power, trusting to her loyalty to me as a friend of Miss Leggatt (here as elsewhere in Nigeria one's most valid passport is friendship with a man or woman the natives have loved), and knowing that alone amongst these people whom I understood so little, I might make endless and dangerous mistakes. In the case of Salome, I do not think she ever wilfully misinterpreted me and was often as curious as I was to obtain some piece of information but when she got tired or bored—for a young girl, the strain on her attention was considerable—she was useless. Her great value lay in the fact that she would make friends with other girls, less on the defensive than the adults, and I would get glimpses of home life which I could not have obtained otherwise.

As to the information they themselves gave me, that of Mary was, on the whole, trustworthy. Although so long a Christian, she remembered her pagan childhood, kept a sane balance and seldom rushed to the convert's extremes of condemnation. With Salome, there was the fear that, rather than humble her pride, which was a lively one, by admitting that she did not know, she would invent some satisfactory answer, but as a matter of fact, in every case where her information could be checked, it was found to be accurate.

And now I come to the question which presented even greater difficulties than that of language. I had always worked on the assumption that no fact should be put on permanent record until it had been checked at least three times. But in a society as fluid, as individualistic as that of the Ibo, how check anything except over an area so minute that it would not be of any interest? Every law and custom, ranging from exogamy to the rotation of crops, from prohibited foods to the payment of dowries, varies from village-group to village-group. Indeed, the whole Ibo nomenclature of towns, villages, quarters, kindreds, families, is still so little understood that my colleague and I have been obliged to use arbitrary English terms which only partially fit the facts. One is inclined to say the Ibo thinks in human, not in geographical terms. A town would not be a piece of land covered with dwellings but the residence of such and such families. He would not, so to speak, see the ground for the people. To him, the British Isles are not islands with coasts and bays and inlets, actual masses of soil which would be there whether we inhabited them or not, but merely the home of the British people. I doubt whether he could visualize a world unrelated to the idea of family. A teacher, who had a notion of the size of London, asked me whether all the inhabitants were related to one another. This position of thinking in terms of people, and especially in terms of family, rather than in terms of soil is a perfectly tenable one but it is made even more complicated for the white man by the fact that there may be several groups in a Province all bearing the same name and yet totally unrelated to each other. Added to that is the difficulty that everyone speaks in different terms: there are administrative areas, and Native Court areas, and Mission areas, and language, or rather dialect, areas, and none of them correspond. You may be told that it is only eight miles' march from your camp to Owerri. You look surprised, knowing that it must be at least fifty-three miles. You say: 'But that cannot be. I have just come from there. Owerri is not in this area at all.' 'Oh yes, it is,' and you find out there is another Owerri and though it is not in the same administrative area, which is what you were thinking of, it is in the same Mission area, which is what your Christian guide was thinking of, while if you asked a pagan he would probably have said this same Owerri was in a different area altogether as he would be thinking in terms

49

of Native Court areas. In addition, maps are scàrce and poor, with names spelt according to various orthographies so that the bewildered newcomer does not know whether Awlu is the same as Orlu, Onitsha as Onica, Igni as Nyi.

But more bewildering than anything because so rare in Africa, is the exceptional density of the population. Accurate statistics are still lacking but in certain districts it is said to be 1,000 per square mile,[1] and it is often six to seven hundred. This exceptional density creates exceptional situations and also, unfortunately, greatly increases the difficulty of the investigator's work. It may be possible to take as a unit a village of some 500 souls, to get on friendly terms with all of them, watch their doings, grasp their relationships and follow up their kindred ramifications. But this is no longer possible when your smallest unit is a widespread town (or 'village-group' as we prefer to call it) sheltering some 5,000 inhabitants. Nor is the population at all homogeneous: some 'clans' are predominantly farmers, others traders, and within the same 'clan' one finds all degrees of development from the juju priest to the Standard VI schoolboy, from the old medicine woman muttering over her dog skulls to the mincing young lady in satin frock and high-heeled shoes. No generalizations are possible. No statement can be made unless it is immediately qualified by a warning that this statement may probably only be true as regards one family in one village, and the more one learns the more one sees how endlessly shifting is the Ibo scene, so that the Western onlooker cannot, as yet, descry a pattern or even recognize what is warp and what is woof in this immense and crowded tapestry.

Given these conditions, how could I best fulfil my mission, seeing that I could not conscientiously make any statement regarding the Ibo women as a whole? To write

[1] The latest estimate (1937) of the population of Orlu in the Okigwi Division gives the surprising figure of 1,300 to the square mile.

50

with anything approaching scientific accuracy, one would have to write a monograph on each village-group in turn. To write with even enough accuracy to make the work worth while, I would have to find certain limited areas which could be taken as fairly typical of the various stages of transition. Even so, when heading a future chapter, say 'Primitive Woman', I must be careful to add 'in Nneato' for I might find she was a very different being forty or fifty miles away. In heading a chapter 'Woman in Transition', I must add 'in Owerri Town' for the same phase of transition might take quite another form in Aba or Onitsha. This is discouraging to reader and writer alike. We are always walking along narrow lanes. We never reach a hilltop from which a broad view can be obtained, helping us to understand the general lie of the land and main features of river and mount, farm land and forest. But were I to attempt any generalizations or pretend that whatever I have found out has a wider application, I know that my account would be misleading.

The choice of areas was not easy to make. Thinking it over, looking at this vigorous, ambitious, avid, and numerous race, it struck one at once that their future was of sole importance, not their past. Here, at any rate in so far as I was concerned with the women, there was no object in looking backward, in searching out the strange and intricate ways in which a custom comes into being, the fragile but unbreakable bonds that keep an untouched native society together. They themselves look forward. 'Is it not the young who lead us now?' as one of them said, and they race forward with such speed that we must think and decide and act quickly if we are to keep ahead of them, guiding them when necessary, and giving them a goal which will be worthier of them than the Golden Calf which is all that most of them now seek.

Yet the future must depend upon the past—though one feels this strangely little when dealing with the Ibo

Introduction

—and if it was my aim as stated in my first chapter to study the Ibo woman's inner and outer reactions to a changing world, then it was advisable to know what she was like before she began to come into contact with this changing world and to look for her under the most primitive 'bush' conditions. From there I would have to follow her to a spot in which, while still living under purely native and agricultural conditions, she would nevertheless have more frequent contact with the outer world as exemplified by Missions, teachers, middlemen, roads, and lorries. The next phase would be to watch her in a semi-urban life where she would consider herself more civilized than her bush sister and even see a few Europeans, where her husband might be a clerk in Government service and her brother the driver of a daily lorry to the coast town and all that that stood for in the way of wealth and opportunity. Lastly, she would have to be looked for in the coast town itself, where, divorced from all her natural environment, she would sink or swim according to whether Christianity, education, example, had added to or detracted from her natural worth.

III

Introduction

Short geographical, historical, and linguistic description of Owerri Province. Population; resources. Administration; Missions. Native organization. Form in formlessness.

Ibo-land can be said very roughly to be that huge mass of land which is enclosed on the north by the Benue River, chief tributary of the Niger, on the south by the sea, on the west by the Niger and on the east by the Cross River. The country inhabited by the Ibo-speaking people is mainly included in the two great provinces: Onitsha Province to the north and Owerri Province to the south. They also occupy about half of the sparsely populated Ogoja Province and large groups are found in Warri and Benin Provinces.

The boundary between the Onitsha and Owerri Provinces is more or less arbitrary, fixed sometimes for geographical and sometimes for political reasons. The land rises steadily from the coast to the north. First come the creeks and waterways, the mangrove swamps and waterlogged land of the coast, then as more and more dry land appears the mangroves give way to oil palms, interspersed with a few forest trees. We are now in the palm belt, flat, monotonous, hot and dim, which stretches mile upon mile till, north of Owerri Division, it thins out a little, forest trees grow more numerous, bare grassy hills appear, the air grows drier, lighter, streams run clear. The road swings up and up, through terraced farms, patches of light forest, over bare uplands, then down again to Enugu, the capital of the Southern Provinces and residence of the Chief Commissioner,[1] from whence one sees, ridge upon ridge, the low hills beyond which lies the Benue.

Ethnographically, its inhabitants are Negro, but within this broad classification, they show considerable variety of physical types.

Of its history, little can be said at present. Talbot, Meek, Jeffreys, each make their contribution. Intelligence Reports contain small items of information. Local ancestries go far back but vary with each telling. The old men sit in the meeting-house, telling old tales, squabbling and contradicting. The young men are content to have no past so long as they can have a future. No buildings survive; no writings exist even in an alien script like the Hausa tales written in Arabic. Of course, in time, more information will be obtained, especially, I think, from various places in the Onitsha Province and from Aro Chuku, home of the Long Juju, whose power was broken by a British expedition in 1901. A better understanding of the people's religion will also give clues and a closer study of their crafts, in the comparatively few places where they have any, may reveal unsuspected outside influences. At present, in Owerri Province at least, one has the impression that 'history' was never more than the struggle of a teeming population to gain land to till, then the swaying to and fro of masses without individual leaders, through which cut, every now and then, purposeful and swift, the Aro raiders. These Aro, whether as raiders, settlers, traders, slave dealers, seem to have permeated the whole of the country and, wherever they went, to have imposed themselves upon

[1] The title of Chief Commissioner was substituted for that of Lieutenant-Governor in 1935.

the imagination of the people by their ruthlessness, their capacity for amassing riches, and the prestige of the oracle of the Long Juju.

Nevertheless, every now and again, one has a sense of an older culture lying behind what one now sees, long forgotten by the people themselves, grown so faint that it is only in certain lights that one catches a glimpse of it, but the glimpse is of something so rich, so vital, that the present sinks into insignificance beside it. I heard it twice in a woman's song, saw it once in a woman's dance, once in a ritual gesture of embrace, once in the shape and decoration of a water-pot, once in the mural decoration of a *mbari* house. Of course, it may have been pure fancy but when, as among the Owerri Ibo, one lives in a world so curiously lacking in any sense of the past, the faintest echo of lost centuries strikes upon the ear like thunder. Useless as such speculations are, one cannot help wondering whether the Ibo had a former civilization, then sank into a period of lethargy rather than of decadence, and are now once more arising. (I am now speaking solely of the Ibo people I know myself, not of the Ibo of Onitsha Province, to whom Dr. Jeffreys has already assigned a history and a civilization transmitted from Egypt.) With no written words, no permanent buildings, proofs are hard to come by, yet it seems almost incredible that a race so virile, so active, so eager as the Ibo should never have risen above the exceedingly primitive conditions in which the white man found him. I am not referring to his political organization, which, on the contrary, seems always to have been highly developed along its own unique lines, but to his living conditions, the paucity of his implements, the poorness of his utensils, the almost complete absence of art or craft, the lack of ingenuity in home or farm or fence or trap or water storage. Sporadic manifestations there are but the general level of material culture is the lowest I have seen[1] and

[1] I do not know the creek tribes of the Southern Provinces.

the contrast is all the more striking in that the general physical and psychological level of the race is so high.

No expert has yet been able to give the exact meaning of the word 'Ibo'. As the people recognize no tribal bond, it is certainly not their own word for their tribe or race or land. The people themselves, before the advent of the white man, had not got beyond calling themselves by the name of their village-group. It seems probable that the term was originally one of contempt applied by those of a village-group to others not of their village-group. To-day the people apply the word to their language and, secondarily, to other Ibo-speaking people but only in talking to a white man would a native refer to *himself* as an Ibo.

Although the same language is spoken throughout the country, the dialects vary so much that in extreme cases an Ibo from one district cannot make himself understood in another. In ordinary cases, both sides purposely drop the most 'local' parts of their speech and so find a common, if limited, medium. To meet the difficulties caused by these wide variations of dialect, the Protestant Missions, about 1913, introduced what is known as Union Ibo, based upon the Owerri type of dialect but including some of the commonest words of the Onitsha dialect. The translation of the Bible is in this Union Ibo, as are a number of school readers, and it is taught in all the Mission schools. On the other hand, the Roman Catholic Mission makes no use of it, and its schools use the dialect of their respective Provinces, Owerri or Onitsha.

The few but influential Government schools teach either dialect and employ the orthography as laid down by Professor Westermann.[1] This the Protestant Missions have not adopted (though the Roman Catholics

[1] Professor Westermann was invited by the Government to visit Nigeria in 1929 for the purpose of advising on the subject of vernacular literatures and orthographies.

have), probably on account of the expense of re-casting so much type, but it is unfortunate that yet one more factor of diversity should be added to the already chaotic language situation.

Ibo, which belongs to the Sudanic family, is a rich, flexible, and adaptable language but the fact that it is a tone language, depending upon fine distinctions of sound for the meaning of its words and the grammatical construction of its sentences, makes it so difficult for the average European with no training in phonetics nor special gift of ear, that it will never be commonly spoken amongst white and black as is Hausa in the North. It is likely, therefore, that the spread of English will be rapid, even amongst those who do not actually go to school. They will learn from each other, pick up phrases from lorry drivers and court messengers, hear a few words at some Mission church. Indeed, it is already rare not to find someone even in the remotest village who cannot at least say 'Yes, sah!' or 'morning-o!' and the native himself is only too anxious to learn, realizing that any job with the white man largely depends upon it.

All the same, one cannot agree with those who think the Ibo language will disappear within fifty years and that English will have become the common tongue. Quickly as it seems that English will spread, it is likely that it will be reserved for what one might call public dealings, especially with the white man and frequently also with members of another tribe, while Ibo will naturally remain the language of private dealings, of home and farm and market, and most emphatically of the women.

The ultimate future of the language must lie in the hands of the Ibo himself. It will greatly depend upon (*a*) whether his desire to preserve his mother tongue is great enough to make him take the trouble to forge a written language capable of expressing the wider thought of his future out of a spoken language that has only had to serve the narrower outlook of his past; (*b*) whether he will change his attitude to the teaching of vernacular in schools.

As regards (*a*), the literate men or women, if they wish to read, are practically forced to turn to English literature, either in the shape of books, or of newspapers, which, though edited locally, are written in English. Even the reports of, say, some local club composed entirely of Africans are written in English, although the discussions may have been in Ibo, and even those who have only a smattering of English nearly always correspond in that language. I am told that even love-letters between the more sophisticated boys and girls are written in English! An ex-schoolgirl whose English was just good enough for her to act sometimes as my interpreter admitted that she 'no know how write Ibo' and was obviously incapable of writing down even the simplest name or sentence. Her correspondence, and all Ibo are enthusiastic correspondents, was done in English, and she told me all her girl friends would do the same. It is true that since she was at school, rather more attention has been paid to the teaching of Ibo composition, but even so the existence of the two orthographies, the 'old' one and Professor Westermann's 'new' one and the many variations of dialect, do not yet allow any sort of standard spelling to be set up. The result is that the adult frankly admits that it is easier for him to write in English than in Ibo, and were two passages put before him, one in English and one in Ibo, he would unhesitatingly choose the English one, 'as being so much more easy to read'.

As regards (*b*), the Ibo parent is so keen for his child to learn English that he grudges the time spent on instruction in the vernacular. He considers that the school fees he pays, often with real inconvenience to himself, are wasted if the teaching given only enables the boys or girls to read and write in their own tongue. In spite of the dictum of many authorities that instruction, if it is to be properly absorbed, must, at least in the first years, be given in the mother tongue, the native parent has never been convinced of the value of such education and has only seen in it a specious pretext for keeping the native in his place as 'hewer of wood and drawer of water'. The controversy seems less acute now and the general principle that the vernacular only should be taught in the infant classes for the first year and that thereafter it should remain as the medium of instruction, with English as a 'subject' up to Standard IV, has been accepted, but parents would be indignant if, after this period, full emphasis were not laid upon the teaching of English and English alone.

A school manager of experience confirmed my supposition that even if a school were known to give advanced teaching under the best conditions but in the vernacular, it would not be patronized. If the pupils could not learn English, other learning was useless. Several Africans agreed. As one said: 'The people do not yet see education as food for body and soul but only as a means of obtaining employment.'

According to the census of 1931, as quoted in the *Nigerian Handbook* of 1936, the total number of Ibo is put at 3,172,789, but it is probably far greater. In comparison, the Hausa in the Northern Provinces number 3,604,016; the Fulani, 2,025,189; the Yoruba in the Provinces west of the Niger, 3,166,154.

Owerri Province, with which this book deals exclusively, has an area of 9,970 square miles and a population approximately of 1,616,000, but once again this number is probably underestimated. As much of the southern and south-western part of the Province is uninhabitable or inhabited only by small fishing communities, the large population has to congregate on a relatively small area and thus one finds a density per square mile unequalled anywhere else, although the average density for the whole Province works out at only 154·22. Statistics are still so uncertain that the figures are admittedly only approximate but Intelligence Reports often give local densities of 700 and 800, and one wide stretch of country is always spoken of as 'the thousand belt'. When it is remembered that Great Britain has an average of only 505 to the square mile, one can imagine what it means to have more than twice that number living on one square mile of African bush.

Scattered among the indigenous population are a few Yoruba, clerks or middlemen, whose wives do petty trading; a few Hausa living in special quarters in the towns who trade in cattle brought down from the North, beads and trinkets; some Calabari from the coast, great buyers of palm-oil and kernels; a very few Syrians established only in such towns as Aba and Port Harcourt.

The proportion of women to men seems to be about equal except in places like Aba and Port Harcourt, where there is an artificial influx of men.

Infant mortality, except in a few towns,[1] cannot even be guessed at. In the few cases when I have been able to obtain by indirect means some indication of the number of deaths in any given family, I have been surprised to find the proportion was not high, but these statistics are on such a small scale that they have no real value. On the other hand, in certain districts, according to the Lady Medical Officers who visit the villages in rotation, mortality is undoubtedly high, though strangely enough neither mortality nor incidence of disease seems to bear any relation to the poverty or over-crowding of the districts in question.

The Ibo is primarily an agriculturist. Even those groups which are regarded by other Ibo as traders all hold and cultivate land. Even the wives of Government clerks in a Port Harcourt office two or three times a year

[1] In Port Harcourt, in 1934, it was 249 per 1,000 under 1 year.

go back to their husband's house, change their city frocks for kirtle and head-tie, seize hoe and basket and go forth to farm. This bond with the land may unfortunately come to be forgotten by the new generation of boys now attending school. If it were forgotten by the girls also, as appears likely to be the case, it would be a disaster.

Neither horses nor cattle, except those belonging to one special breed,[1] can live in Ibo-land on account of the tsetse fly; game is scarce; fishing is only on a very small scale except on the coast and along the bank of the Niger;[2] the only mineral so far exploited is coal from the Udi coal-mines near Enugu; the forests supply a little iroko and mahogany.

The main export from the country is palm-oil and to a lesser degree, palm-kernels. The oil palm grows wild practically throughout the country but more especially in the Owerri Province. Seedlings are distributed by the Agricultural Department and efforts are being made to induce the farmers to plant them in properly tended plantations so that the yield per palm may be increased and the quality of the oil improved. This, however, depends largely on the way the oil is pressed out of the nuts, work which in the Owerri Province it is customary for the women to do in their own homes.

A few oil-presses have been set up and will certainly multiply, especially if the introduction of co-operative schemes which are now being talked of succeed. With their coming, a new factor will be introduced into many women's lives, the invidious one of leisure.

The oil is sold to European firms, who ship it home in casks for the manufacture of soap, candles, margarine, etc., while the kernels are shipped in bulk and have their

[1] The 'Pagan' or West African Shorthorn.

[2] Apart from the comparative scarcity of streams in many parts, fish are often considered the 'children' of the local stream-spirit and can therefore not be killed.

oil extracted later for use in soap, cattle food, lard substitutes, etc.

In much of the Owerri Province, this palm-oil trade
dominates the whole situation. It is the native's chief
means of obtaining cash to pay his tax, to buy European
goods for his wife to retail in the up-country markets, to
purchase for himself such luxuries as a singlet or a pair
of shorts, a bicycle, a cloth cap. It forms one of the chief
topics of conversation; the rise and fall of its price is
watched as we watch the Stock Exchange, and the
slightest variations are instantly known as well in the
tiny bush market held where four tracks meet in the
shadow of the forest as in the yards of the big factories,
hot with sun and noise and the clang of lorries. In the
boom period, the price rose as high as 10s. a tin, i.e. a
4-gallon kerosene tin. The natives have never forgotten
this nor understood why they are not getting it still.
They make little distinction between trade and Government and so think Government is keeping the price
down, and, worse still, accuse England of refusing to buy
their palm-oil while ready to buy vast quantities of
whale-oil from foreigners. This deal in whale-oil, which
took place about October 1934, was known immediately
throughout the country, and in the remotest bush I have
been asked to explain it and to give the reason why
Government allowed it. It is a delicate matter, this entry
of the nearly untutored savage into the world market
without preparation, without economic education. It is
of course excellent that he should be the grower and the
seller of his own produce, grown on his own land, that
he should deal directly or almost directly with the European buyers. He is shrewd enough to know how to protect his immediate interest fairly adequately but not yet
enough developed to appreciate the intricacies, the financial and technical problems of world trade. They bewilder,
frighten, or anger him and at present he has no one to
teach him, no one to explain to him these mysterious

happenings that occur thousands of miles away and yet
have power to raise him up or to cast him down without
warning and apparently without reason or justification.

Apart from the palm-oil, all other cultivation is for
home consumption and even in the case of the oil palm,
a good deal of the oil produced is used locally, as it forms
the basis of the sauce eaten with pounded food, and is
also used for frying sliced yams, coco-yams, plantains, etc.

The food crop is much the same throughout the
Owerri Province, although a foodstuff will be more popular in one district than in another. It consists mainly of
yams in their many varieties, cassava (manioc), coco-yams,
maize, beans, a few ground-nuts, and a variety of garden
produce such as peppers, native tomatoes, pumpkins, okra,
etc. To these must be added as articles of diet: dried fish,
either smoked or sun-dried (the smoked is preferred as it
keeps longer, but the sun-dried is considered to have a more
delicate flavour) which is added as a relish to the palm-oil
sauce eaten with the customary *fufu*, i.e. pounded yam or
cassava or coco-yam; and the numerous kinds of leaves
picked in the bush and also used as flavourings for this
same sauce. The quantity of meat eaten, beef, mutton,
goat's flesh, pork, or an occasional antelope varies constantly but is never very great. Meat is preferred to fowl
and there is a certain prejudice against eating the fowls
reared in one's own house, except in an emergency as when
an unexpected guest arrives. Fowls are looked upon ' a little
as one's own children' though no care is taken of them
beyond shutting them up for the night,[1] and they will be
sold in the market without compunction. Eggs are rarely
eaten and then only hard boiled. Milk is never seen, as
to milk a cow or goat would be considered as 'abomination'. Bananas, plantains, and bread-fruit trees are
grown near the houses; wild fruits are more numerous

[1] At Ugueme, a village in the Awgu hills north of Okigwi, a dance or
feast or a mere visit would last until 'it was time to shut up the fowls'.
This was a recognized closing hour: '*on se couche avec les poules. . . .*'

than one at first realizes though their taste is disappointing; acclimatized fruits such as oranges and mangoes are eaten with enjoyment but do not form part of the staple diet even though the oranges are in season throughout the year. Palm-wine is obtained by tapping either the wine palm (*Raphia vinifera*) or the oil palm.

On the whole, diet has been surprisingly little affected by Western contact. In the bush, one does not see a vestige of European tinned food; bread and unsweetened biscuits are increasingly popular in places where there is some slight European contact but nothing else has entered into the daily life of the people. Perhaps the only important advance has been a greater readiness to use tinned milk in those cases where the mother has died or is too weak to nourish her child. As has been seen, the Ibo consider it an 'abomination' to milk either cows or goats, so the motherless baby had small chance of survival before Missions and Government hospitals introduced feeding with tinned milk or milk powder. Though the Ibo knows quite well that his child is drinking cow's milk, the fact that it comes out of a tin and is 'white man palaver' presumably de-abominates it.

Tobacco in leaf form can be bought in any market. It is used either for chewing or smoking, or, when ground, as snuff. A 'head' of tobacco consisting of five or six leaves is worth about sixpence and forms a very acceptable present among men and women, especially among those of the older generation. Cigarettes are filtering in but have not yet reached the bush.

The sale of sugar is also on the increase and some of it no doubt finds its way to the illicit distilleries that abound, in spite of all precautions, in some parts of the Southern Provinces, though they are not so frequent among the Ibo. Indeed, on the whole, one can say that the Ibo are a temperate race. Palm-wine, when fresh, is no more intoxicating than cider and even when fermented makes one more often quarrelsome or fuddled

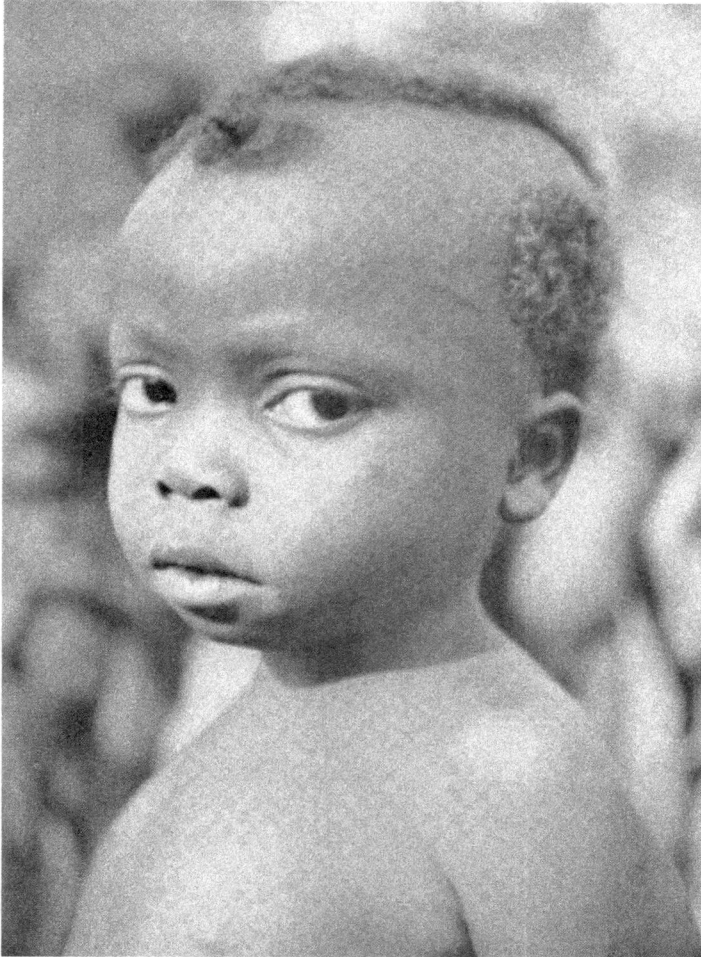

CHILDHOOD

PREPARING PALM OIL

SALOME

than violent. Very heavy duties make the price of imported spirits so high that few can afford to buy them except in the shape of an occasional bottle of gin on some ceremonial occasion.

Although their meals sound monotonous to us, they are not so to the Ibo, who is probably more of a gourmet than many of his neighbours. There are several ways of varying the pounded foods and all sorts of flavourings (including caterpillars, locusts, and mushrooms) can be added to the sauce. Real interest is taken and imagination exercised and the native will describe with enthusiasm the preparation of a good dish. The word 'tasty' will be included in even the most limited vocabulary and will have the same connotation as in a Whitechapel back-kitchen. Unfortunately, with this laudable appreciation of good food goes a fussiness about its nature: this man will not eat cassava, coco-yams disagree with that one; one only likes 'chewing food', the other only 'swallow food'. Poor Mary Anderson, used to the meat of Okigwi, wrote me pitiful wails when reduced to the fish diet of Oron; my own servants insisted on carrying vast quantities of food with them whenever we moved for fear that in the next place 'they no find proper *gari* for chop'.

As neither animal nor chemical manure is available,[1] the farmer must let his land lie fallow between each crop. This all-important factor in the agricultural situation will be dealt with again in subsequent chapters when we come to describe individual areas.

Now, against this broadly sketched-in background, what do we see of the white man, Government, Mission,

[1] Slight attempts at using animal manure are made in some parts. Coarse grass or leaves are put down as bedding in the little enclosure where the goats or sheep are kept and are subsequently strewn upon the farm. In one tiny garden where the eldest daughter of a widow had made use of every inch of space, I noticed she had conscientiously and exactly placed five fresh goat droppings upon every little heap of earth drawn round the newly sprouted maize.

or trader? Owerri Province is divided into six Divisions (Owerri, Ahoada, Okigwi, Degama, Bende, and Aba), subdivided into Districts. In charge of the Province is the Resident with headquarters at Port Harcourt but spending much of his time on tour. In charge of each Division there is nominally a District Officer with two or three Assistant District Officers and Cadets under him. One officer is generally left in charge of the station while the others tour the Division, but owing to officers going on leave or being invalided, it often happens that a large Division such as the Owerri one is left in charge of two officers only.

At each station, that is to say, at the headquarters of each Division, there is a European or, very occasionally, an African doctor who, besides being responsible for the health of the Europeans, supervises sanitary work in the station and native town, runs a native hospital and visits bush dispensaries.

The Missions in Owerri Province include the Church Missionary Society, the Roman Catholics, the Methodists, the Niger Delta Pastorate, which is affiliated to the Church Missionary Society, the Second Day Adventists, the Salvation Army, the African Church, largest of purely native churches, nominally Christian on Church Missionary Society lines but permitting polygamy, and a host of minor bodies founded by Africans and often encouraged, even financed, by sects in the United States. The larger Protestant Missions agreed some time ago to keep fairly well-defined spheres of influence. The Roman Catholics, however, recognize no limit to their sphere, and the smaller churches spring up everywhere they can find a few adherents. Except for a very few Government and even fewer native-owned private schools, all education is in the hands of the Missions. All teaching, however, must be given according to the Government Education Code and many schools receive Government grants. There is an intense desire for education amongst the Ibo,

Native Organization

but, owing perhaps to the consequent great influx of pupils, the lack of well-trained teachers and of sufficient European supervision, the standard is not high, the pronunciation of English being especially faulty even when the knowledge of the language is good.

Trading firms in charge of European agents are only found in the bigger towns such as Enugu, Aba, Port Harcourt, and at the old-established trading-centre of Oguta, which dates back to about 1890.

As there are no settlers[1] and practically no casual travellers, the European population is small,[2] thus Nigeria is spared many of the problems which confront the Administration in other parts of Africa.

It is outside the scope of this book to give any detailed account of British administration in the Eastern Provinces.[3] It is well known that Nigeria set the example of indirect administration, that is to say, administration through existing native institutions with the minimum of change or interference. The experiment was first tried in the North and was then extended to the South. In the Eastern Provinces, its application was more difficult than anywhere else as tribal organization appeared at a first glance to be practically non-existent and the people themselves, dubious of Government's intentions, gave little information. So natural did it seem to find autocracy in some form or other wherever one went in Africa that it was impossible even to imagine a democracy so absolute as that of the Ibo, and thus excusable but unfortunate misunderstandings arose: the organization which did actually exist, tenuous and intricate, was not recognized and wrong men were pushed forward, often by the

[1] All the lands in the Southern Provinces of Nigeria belong to the people themselves. They cannot be alienated except on short lease with the approval of the Governor.

[2] The total European and Syrian population for the whole of Nigeria was only 5,442 according to the 1931 Census.

[3] For an admirably lucid study of this subject, Miss Margery Perham's *Native Administration in Nigeria* should be read.

67

natives themselves, and given an authority to which they had no right and often ultimately abused. The old system of direct administration had really been better for the people than an indirect administration working through channels which the Government believed to be indigenous but which in reality were as foreign as those they were meant to supplant.

Though a thorough reorganization has taken place, these years of mutual misapprehension have left a certain legacy of suspicion and mistrust that it will take some time to overcome, especially as the Ibo is by nature only too ready to believe the worst of everyone, even of his nearest neighbour.

I cannot help thinking that even now we may not have grasped the genius of the Ibo people, that we still look for the solid signposts we find along other paths of African life and the solid structures that carry the weight of tribal existence. It would almost seem as if we had to get rid of all Western conceptions of what makes, vitalizes, and keeps together a community and try instead to accept the possibility that there may be form in formlessness, structure in very lack of structure. We tend to solidify what is in solution, to tabulate what is constantly shifting, to give recognizable names to a system of thought and government which we are as yet incapable of grasping. It is perhaps not so much ignorance that keeps us far from the Ibo as our incapacity to perform the mental feat of seeing life as he sees it. But the Ibo is so adaptable, so ambitious, so little attached to his past so long as he can look forward to a future, that this lack of comprehension on our part does not perhaps matter so much as it would with other people.

If the assertion were not far too sweeping, and in a sense too cruel, one would say that of all African people, they are the most ready to enter the modern world on equal terms, with no regrets, nor strains nor conflicts, having nothing of their own to lose.

Part II
Women

IV

Primitive Woman—in Nneato

Reasons for choice of Nneato area. What a purely farming community looks like. How one lives in it. What the women do in it.

My reasons for going to Nneato were twofold. In the first place, from what I could hear, the district was as 'bush' as I was likely to find, thickly populated and purely agricultural. In the second place, I had an introduction in the person of Mary Anderson, my interpreter, whose home it was and who was willing to accompany me. I knew that through markets and church meetings she would send round the word that I had been a friend of 'Ma Leggatt' and with the further guarantee of her own presence I would be well received. This was important, as though I could count upon perfect safety everywhere and reasonable facility in getting food, water and carriers, it would take months to get into touch with the people or make them understand who one was and what one had come for. I went there twice, once in December and once in April, so that I saw the life of the people both in the non-farming and the farming season.

Nneato, in the Okigwi Division,[1] is the name given to a district containing three village-groups linked together

[1] The area of the Okigwi Division is given as 842 square miles with a population of 455,464, representing a density of 540·931 to the square mile. (*Nigerian Handbook*, 1936.)

71

by ancient ties of kinship and known as Akabo, Ubaha, and Eziama. I use the term 'village-groups' as being slightly more descriptive than the word 'town' which is generally used in Government reports. The latter necessarily suggests an agglomeration, something that has shape, bounds, streets and lanes, market and meeting-places, something that strikes one at once as an entity, as having almost a personality. In the North and in the Western Provinces, towns of this sort, that is to say towns in the ordinary English sense of the word, are frequent. Among the Ibo, except in a few instances, they are unknown. What the reports and the English-speaking natives themselves call 'towns' are widespread 'garden cities', formless and, to the unpractised eye, without beginning and without end. These garden cities are composed, sometimes of walled compounds, sometimes of houses surrounded by a fence or standing open to the path. The dwellings are often out of sight of one another, with small stretches of forest or farmland in between. It is possible to be in the heart of a 'town' and not to see one vestige of habitation. Only when one stands listening does one become aware of an intense and hidden stir of life muffled by the high-growing trees and the hot damp air. That is perhaps one of the most characteristic, and one might almost say alarming, experiences that one meets with in Ibo-land: the realization that what seems solitude is filled with people, that what seems silence is a continuous human murmur, that what seems an empty land teems with active life.

In the Nneato district, all dwellings are built within mud-walled compounds. Generally, several large compounds close together form a 'village' of the village-group in question. Ubaha has six such villages, Eziama five. The villages can be as much as a mile or so distant from each other and yet everyone knows they belong to the same village-group. In between lie forest, fallow land reverting to secondary bush, and farmland under

72

cultivation. Here in Nneato there is no shortage of land so a farm can lie fallow four or five years, during which time the bush regains possession of it and so quick is its growth that a four-year-old fallow looks almost like untouched forest. Nearly always the larger trees are left standing and even when the land is under crops it is not always easy to distinguish at a first glance where forest ends and farm begins. Once more the English word, although commonly used, is misleading. A 'farm' generally denotes house and out-buildings, pasture and cultivated fields. Here it means nothing but small patches of land, sometimes of an acre or so but often much less, with no, to the white man, visible boundary, no particular shape. The hoe-made ridges or rows of mounds bend in and out among the tree-trunks, make way for an ant-hill, or cease by a heap of fallen timber. The word 'field' would be equally misleading as it gives the impression of fully cleared land, of a certain amount of space, of light and air and a clear-cut boundary. There is nothing of this kind—indeed the only open spaces I know are unfertile lands covered with high coarse grass and small scrub. The forest reigns supreme, forms the background of every scene, is the factor that must always be reckoned with, and homes and gardens and farm and live-stock must learn to live and flourish beneath its shade. Nevertheless, here is no longer the dull palm belt of Owerri, the forbidding gloom of Aba: palms are fairly plentiful, especially in the deep and narrow valleys, but the general impression is that of magnificent forest trees rising out of a light undergrowth of brush and saplings, with all the varied greens, straight clean tree-trunks and noble branchings of a European forest. Some of the paths, sunk between red banks, fringed with fern, and dappled with light and shade, might belong to an English woodland. The country is broken into long ridges, forest covered save where a sandy path leads out to an open stretch of sun-bleached grass. Streams are numerous, the air at dawn clean-washed, birds call. The soil, except for patches of sand and outcroppings of laterite, is good. The water supply is good also, coming often from fern-hung grottoes from whose roofs diamond-bright water drips into shallow pools. The dry season lasts roughly from the beginning of November to the end of March, with another short spell in August between the rains. The average rainfall at Owerri is ninety-seven inches; in the Okigwi Division, it is slightly less.

There is but one road running from Okigwi, headquarters of the Okigwi Division, to Nneato Native Court, which stands on a bare hill-top in the centre of the village-group. It is negotiable by a car of high power and a driver of unflinching purpose. Apart from this road, communication is by a network of paths only a few feet wide and kept clear by the various villages. A stream may be bridged by a single tree-trunk flung across, round and slippery. If the bridge is high above the stream and the stream especially turbulent, a second tree-trunk and a rail of twisted creeper are added. Travelling is done on foot, though a few of the younger men have now been able to purchase bicycles. Men and women are beautiful runners and walkers. They take comparatively short steps, moving smoothly even over the roughest ground. The loads they carry on their heads, generally packed in long-shaped baskets, can weigh anything up to a hundred pounds or more but generally speaking the loads are lighter and the distances between the local markets smaller than in other parts of Nigeria.

In the Nneato area, there are two kinds of trade, long-distance trade carried out exclusively by men, local trade carried out by men and women but especially by women. The long-distance trade is not on a very large scale. It goes (*a*) north-west to Onitsha where men exchange their bags of woven grass, very strong and handy, or the mats made by the women, for much-prized dried fish or European cloth; (*b*) south to Owerrinta, Aba, or Itu on the

Local Trading

Imo River, where the men sell their tins of palm-oil or bags of kernels to native middlemen or direct to the European agents. Goods are always sold for cash, i.e. coins of the British West African currency, or cowries.

The local trade is between the markets of the neighbouring village-groups. It is intensive and dominates the life of the people to an amazing degree. There seems to be some subtle relationship between the spirits, the days of the week (the Ibo week is of four days), the sites of the markets and the days on which the markets are held, which I do not pretend to have understood, but it seems clear that markets are owned by spirits and it is the priests of these spirits who manage the markets as a bailiff would manage for his master. For example, the much-frequented market of Eziama is owned by Iyeke, sometimes called the husband of Ajala, the earth spirit; his drum stands in the place of honour in the market and the market is held on the day of the week called Eke. It is the priest of Iyeke who assigns a pitch to each vendor, who in turn presents him with a fowl or some palm-wine, part of which is sacrificed to the spirit. No further rent is charged nor are there any tolls. All disputes arising in the market-place used to be settled, and still are, though to a lesser degree, by the priest.

These markets, especially when one finds them miles from the beaten track, strike one as almost incredible. On my first visit to Eziama, I had walked over from Ubaha with Mary Anderson, following a tiny, winding, many-branched path through forest sometimes dense, sometimes opening out to make room for little farms. As we went, a few women and men joined us, then a few more, carrying loads of mats or foodstuffs. The path seemed to get narrower, fainter, the tree-trunks higher, the roof of branches thicker, the quiet more intense. The world was a remote memory, our silent-footed companions and ourselves, the only souls alive. As the path straightened out into a dark tunnel leading slightly upwards, there was a murmur as of the far-off approach of wind or rain. It rose into a mysterious tempest of sound and as I turned quickly, and indeed almost nervously, towards Mary, the path suddenly flung us out on to the edge of an immense open space ringed with forest, the huge drum of Iyeke uplifted beneath its thatched shelter on the farther side, and filled with clamour, as of a stormy sea beating against the banked trees, which rose from a crowd so dense that it seemed only able to sway and ripple where it stood. Every moment, fresh buyers and sellers poured in from numerous side paths, while others on the edges began to drift homewards, so that it was impossible even to guess at the number actually present: three thousand, four thousand, more perhaps, and that would not include all those still coming or already going along the network of shadowy paths. Often as I went to this particular market, it was never without a thrill that I caught the first murmur of sound, mounting higher and higher above the tree-tops, and came into the sudden blare of light beating down on the mass of tight-locked naked bodies. Yet, when one got to know the technique, so to speak, of shopping in Eziama market, it was not so difficult after all. All the goods and foodstuffs were set out in their appointed sections and lanes were somehow kept open between them. It is true that one had to pick out the needed pot from between ten pairs of legs and pull out the desired mat from under twenty garrulous women; fowls were passed from hand to hand over the heads of the crowd till they reached their purchaser and a sudden shriek would tell one a foot had inadvertently stepped into a cherished pot of palm-oil, but good temper reigned supreme, and even if a quarrel did arise it was quickly smothered by the laughter of the onlookers.

Housing is poor but seems sufficient for the people's needs. The usual type of dwelling is rectangular, built of mud and floored with mud. The roof consists of a framework of bamboo covered with a thatch made of overlapping palm leaves. Small openings are cut in the mud walls to serve as windows or, when the cooking is done indoors, as chimneys for the smoke. Often as I visited the compounds, I was never able to perceive any uniform plan in their lay-out, and the descriptions given me seldom tallied with what I saw. Generally speaking, the main, sometimes the only entrance, led into an inner court on which gave the *obi*, that all-important if unimposing structure which served as a meeting-place, reception-room, workroom and, on special occasions such as a feast or the entertainment of passing strangers, as eating-room. The *obi* varied in style and size but was generally a low-roofed, three-walled shelter, mud walled and floored, palm thatched, with two low mat-covered mud couches on either side. Sometimes it stood isolated, sometimes a low door at the back led to the inner courtyards. The compound itself was a maze of small courtyards divided from each other by palm stem or bamboo fences over which one climbed at certain lowered points and which each contained one or several houses, kitchen, and store. A 'big' man would have a house of his own roughly in the centre of the compound or of his section of the compound if it was a very big one, with his wives in neighbouring houses. The 'small' man with only one wife would have a house, of which the following diagram gives the general type:

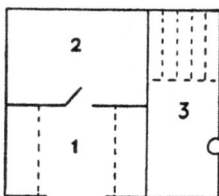

(1) veranda with two mud couches;
(2) kitchen;
(3) children and chickens;
(4) bamboo shelf for children to sleep on;
(5) hole in wall a few inches above ground level by which chickens can go in and out.

Women

In attempting to understand Ibo domestic architecture, it is important to locate at once the 'hole for fowl' as this appears to dominate the whole situation and to be the one stable feature, giving a sure clue to the whereabouts of the sleeping-room, from which one can generally deduct the whereabouts of the other rooms.

In a house of this type the parents sleep on one of the mud couches in the veranda. A small door leads into an inner room where the children sleep for safety (this is probably a relic of the days when child-stealing by the Aro was common). They have either a kind of shelf made of bamboo poles let into the wall and supported by vertical sticks, which constitutes their bed, or mud couches like their parents. I do not remember seeing any movable bamboo beds like those seen in Owerri and elsewhere. The room in all cases is very small and ventilation is practically nil. Boys and girls sleep together until about the age of nine or ten; then the boys go and sleep on the veranda on a couch opposite their father and mother. If the latter has her period, or is suckling a child, or is near delivery, she will sleep in an inner room with the small children and her daughters of any age. When a boy grows up but before he is married, he moves into a 'single house', that is to say, a house consisting of a veranda with an inner room which he either uses as his personal storeroom or in which, so my informant explained, he sleeps 'until he perspires', when he comes out on to his veranda, which is also fitted with a mud couch. One can recognize a 'single house' by the absence of any kitchen but there may be a small extra room for fowls and goats. These houses stand alone or are semi-detached with a low wall separating the two verandas.

The girls sleep in their own homes until they go to their husbands for good. There is no special sleeping-hut for girls between puberty and marriage.

There are practically no traces of decoration except an occasional rough design in black and white of serpents or

78

crocodiles on the outside walls of a house (I think this is more likely to be a fashion imported from Onitsha Province than an indigenous one), and in a priest's house there were interesting designs deeply traced in the mud of the back wall of his *obi*. He was proud of his handiwork, which indeed was excellent, but declared the designs had no meaning and were only 'to please his eye'.

Considering how closely the people live together, that the neighbouring stream is their only washing-place and that their compounds may be swept but never cleared of the accumulated litter, it is surprising how little they smell. Absence of clothing is a great advantage; constant employment in the open air is another. Latrines, in the shape of a simple trench, are sometimes found at a little distance from the dwellings; more often, any spot, public or not, will serve so long as it is not within the compound.

As for live-stock, a few cattle (the little black-and-white 'Pagan' breed that is immune from tsetse) roam about, a few goats butt at each other in a clearing, a few sheep or chestnut-coloured pigs wander down the path, fowls and dogs and babies cluster by the compound door. Much of the scavenging is done by these horrible little dogs which infest every house. They are much smaller than the 'pi' dogs of the North, white with patches of fawn or black, bloated, covered with disease, and more repulsive than any animal I have known. The Ibo eat them with relish. It is a common sight to see two or three leashed together being dragged to a market to be sold for five shillings or more. A slightly larger species, rather of the whippet type, is occasionally used for hunting, but the Ibo seem singularly incapable of developing any intelligence in animals.

In appearance, the men are stocky and thick set with magnificent backs and shoulders. Many of the faces indicate a far higher intelligence than one actually finds. The women are slimmer, and even when they age

79

never run to the heavy fat of the Yoruba. Except for the free movements of their unclothed limbs and an occasional gravity of face and brow, they are not beautiful. Both sexes range in colour from the darkest to the lightest brown but the dark colouring is the most frequent. They are of negro type in so far as they have crinkly hair, flat noses, and thick lips, but, more especially among the men, one sees some quite startling diversity of features. Apart from some of the Christians, the people ordinarily wear no clothing beyond, for the men, a narrow blue or white strip fastened round the waist and brought up between the legs, and for the women, after puberty, a scanty kirtle round the waist barely reaching to the knee. The men cut their hair short. The women do theirs in innumerable twists bound with black thread and sometimes wear a head-tie of bright European cloth. The weapons are an occasional bow and arrow, an occasional Dane gun, and the ubiquitous matchet, i.e. a long straight blade used for all purposes, whether hacking down a tree or an enemy, splitting open a coco-nut, clearing a path, peeling a yam, or for gently scratching the back to keep off the midges. Their utensils, whether in home or field, are few and poor. No well-carved stools, no elaborately-ornamented calabashes are found here as in the North and in parts of the Western Provinces, though strangely enough carved wooden doors are often seen of excellent design and workmanship and of two distinct periods, one much older than the other.

Nneato is in the area of the Methodist Mission, which has a church at Ubaha and a church and vernacular school at Eziama. Both are under the supervision of the white Superintendent at Ihube.

Having made sure of securing the services of Mary Anderson, I left Owerri on the 3rd of December 1934, with my two servants and the lightest of camp kit, and went by lorry to Okigwi, a distance of thirty-seven miles, mounting slowly from the palm belt to the more open country of Okigwi. Three miles farther on stands the Methodist Mission of Ihube, where I picked up Mary and motored on a few more miles until the road degenerated into a switchback and the lorry at last refused to proceed. The remainder of the nine miles was done on foot and at dusk we arrived at Ubaha where I was to camp in the Mission church, the only accommodation available. These churches are built in native style with mud walls and mud benches, palm-thatch roof, small openings in the walls for windows, and no furniture beyond a table and chair for the teacher or catechist who leads the services.

The present church was full of people when I arrived, church members who had come to greet both me and Mary with presents of yams or fowls or eggs. Mary did most of the talking while the audience stared at me, their eyes bright in the semi-darkness of the church. When it was their turn to question, the 'church-leader' especially wanted news of the outside world and soon got on to the subject of which I was to hear so much, that series of questions that was to be repeated again and again: 'Why had the price of palm-oil fallen? Why was there no money? Was it true the whole world was poor? Why had England bought whale-oil instead of buying more of their palm-oil? Why did not the Government do something?' Even when I was able to give an answer, the questioner hardly listened and certainly was not convinced. He and his people had a grievance and they were not going to allow it to be reasoned away. Behind their intelligent faces, there was a wall of obstinacy which one did not know how to break down, nor could one easily distinguish what were legitimate and possibly remediable complaints and what was querulous and very vocal self-pity. Certainly when, later on, Mary took me to a compound where she was lodging, the scene was of a peaceful gaiety which belied the pessimism to which I had listened. The door in the compound wall was open. Close by it, against the stars, rose a high ɔba, the ingenious structure on which the store of yams is hung, loaded full with the recent harvest. A wide courtyard ran down to the three-walled shelter where the men were sitting. Shadowy figures passed to and fro with pots and platters of food. Wood smoke rose straight, there was a hum of quiet talk. Some boys wrestled in the dust with sleepy laughter. Then movement slackened, sounds died down. A few bell-like notes tinkled quickly, slowed and stopped. Work over, hunger satisfied, the household turned towards the night and slept.

I stayed a week at Ubaha and then moved on to Eziama, four or five miles farther up the road, which now dwindled to a narrow path, passable only for carriers. Here again I stayed in a Mission church which also served as a school. It stood in a cleared space surrounded by high trees between which paths radiated in every direction. It was an excellent observation point as one could watch the streams of people on the big market days, the coming and going of the villagers, the work done on the farms; and illuminating contrast, all night one could hear the thud of the men dancing in Ajala's near-by sacred grove, and all day the drone of the school children learning the alphabet and the multiplication table.

Mary's family and friends received me well; I was able to do a little simple medical work for the people and felt free to question and watch as much as I liked. Nevertheless, I missed one valuable opportunity after another: even Mary did not always realize what would be of vital interest and would only tell me afterwards of some social event that had taken place; even a willing informant would soon tire or be confused by some ill-timed question on my part. And above all, there was always the fact of numbers to contend with: how work out relationships when the family could not be disentangled from the crowd of two or three hundred onlookers who had gathered round the moment my inquiry commenced? How understand the living arrangements of a compound when the entire village swarmed in and out, blocking every doorway? How question a woman about her craft when her answers were drowned by forty voices raised in voluble explanations? And it was not possible to order them away as one could have done elsewhere. Not only, as Mary said, were they in their own homes but they had none of the almost superstitious awe of the white man as such that used to exist in the North. Though never for a moment insolent, they were hail-fellow-well-met and it was evident that one would have to accept their rather casual treatment and apparent lack of ceremonial. That they had a code of manners of their own, there could be no doubt, but it was a singularly modern one.

After I had been a few days in Eziama I decided, rightly or wrongly, to concentrate on seeing what I could of ordinary daily life rather than on watching ceremonies, dances, special festivities, important as these are and bound up with the inmost life of the people. But a limit had to be fixed somewhere and it seemed that, as I could not follow both lines of inquiry with any degree of thoroughness, I had better make use of the fact that I was a woman and confine myself to doing what a man could not: that is to say, sitting about as little noticed as possible, among the babies and the cooking-pots. The result is the following attempted reconstruction of woman's life in an agricultural community, based on information obtained from the women themselves, from Mary acting, so to speak, as show-woman, and from personal observation.

For the Ibo man there are two distinct periods in his year: the farming season from about late February to November and the slack season from November to

Women

February. For the woman, apart from those of her duties that are also seasonal, there is the continuous round of her household duties and her regular visits to the neighbouring markets. This is an average woman's day during the late autumn, that is to say, when the farm work is over: she rises just before sunrise and while her husband goes out to get the palm-wine which during the night has been dripping into gourds tied to the wine palms, she immediately gets a little food, generally some *fufu* left over from the night before, for the younger children. These would probably have fallen asleep before the last evening's supper and therefore would not have had food for some time. 'Being the weakest, they must be fed first.' She then washes her baby if she has one, sweeps the house with her daughters' help, and about every other day smears over the floors with a handful of leaves dipped into 'black man's paint', that is to say, a mixture of dung, ashes, and a little water so as to consolidate the earthen floor. A careful housewife will also fill in and smooth over any cracks or ant-holes in the floor, and if she is house-proud she will rub over the walls and the low couches with a little liquid red clay, which gives them a polish as of polished stone. Indeed I have seen some of these couches that might have been made of pink-red marble, so smooth and glossy was their surface.

By this time her husband will have come back and while he sells his palm-wine to buyers at the door, she will have begun to prepare the breakfast. This consists again of *fufu* and is eaten between eight and nine. After breakfast, the husband goes off to his *ɔba* where he continues tying up, one by one and according to size and kind, the yams that have recently been brought in from the farms, or he stays in the compound to repair a roof or patch a wall or to build a new hut for an about-to-be-married son. The woman takes her basket and goes to the farm to harvest her own coco-yams or, if this

84

has already been done, goes to the enclosure in which stands the ɔba, where the heaped coco-yams need to be picked over frequently to prevent them rotting. She may also have to go for wood and water if her children are not old enough to do so, though what Mary called a 'loving' husband might often do this for her. There must have been a number of such husbands in Eziama for it was a common sight to see men coming back from fetching their palm-wine with an extra gourd of water for the house or at evening to meet them returning along the twisting paths, a load of firewood or a single heavy branch upon their heads.

At two o'clock there is another small meal quickly prepared, after which the women turn to their mat-making, fetch more water or what not and about five-thirty begin to prepare the evening meal. If the *fufu* is to be made of yam, it does not take so long, but cassava has to be peeled carefully and then scraped into fine shavings with a small native knife. This work is done by the women and girls, and so mechanical does it become that they can do it walking or sitting or standing, in the doorway of the kitchen, on the fallen tree-trunk by the path side, watching a dance, listening to my gramophone, in the dark and at dawn. It seems to soothe and occupy them very much as knitting does a white woman. The evening meal is eaten at varying times. There is a saying that an early-rising moon eats a poor man's dinners while a late-rising one eats a rich man's dinners, which seems to indicate that late hours are not confined to the fashionable society of the West. The fact that the bush Ibo have no lights beyond the home-made 'candle' of sticks rolled in the short 'hairs' of the palm-nuts and impregnated with palm-oil, or a flaring torch also dipped in palm-oil, or a small stick wrapped round with rag and stuck into a recipient equally filled with palm-oil, is of no importance. Like all natives, the Ibo sees in the dark and his possessions and utensils are so few that they are easily found.

Bedtime for children or adults is elastic. On the whole I should say the Ibo takes exceptionally little sleep. The children are up and about long after dark, the boys playing, the girls helping their mothers. After supper, the sounds of chattering and story-telling go on and on within every compound wall (though I do not remember ever meeting the professional story-teller as found in the North). Should there have been a wedding or a death or a birth or a 'second burial', the singing and dancing, the drumming and the wailing do not cease till far into the night. Moonlight brings out the whole village. Special festivals last all night. It is only during the rains, when the water lashes down upon hut and forest that the people get a full ration of sleep. They are not quite such early risers as those of the North, but also they take no rest during the day. There is a good deal of sitting about and talking, especially among the men, but though the women may also appear to be dawdling around, they will have their cassava basket with them, and their ever-busy scraper. Unfortunately, contact with the white man is beginning to breed in the Ibo the conviction that an afternoon siesta is of paramount importance. After having made me laugh with an innocently malicious description of rest-time at a Mission station when 'we girls who sit for compound', and she huddled herself up, finger on lip, frightened eyes glancing, 'we all sit so', even Mary would go off for a two-hours' sleep, although she knew I disapproved! Doubtless the amount of sleep required varies with race and climate but one cannot help thinking that the Ibo adult would benefit by a longer period of silence and that the children would not pass through the almost universal phase of physical debility which follows babyhood if they had a rational amount of rest at night.

On market days the women have a busy time. Some

markets are held in the morning, about nine, others at
midday, others in the early afternoon. Much farther
south, round Aba, the usual market time seemed to be
about four or five, but I never found an evening market
like the great King's Market held after sunset at Ilorin,
dimly lit by hundreds of tiny lamps. Whatever the time,
nearly the whole day is spent in getting ready, walking
the two or three or six or ten miles to the nearest market-
place, disposing of the goods, buying others, walking the
long way home and then preparing the evening meal and
seeing to the children. One would think this practice of
visiting different markets two or three times a week with
all its attendant bustle and fatigue, would be gladly dis-
pensed with, especially as the trade done, except in some
special instances, consists of the traders taking in each
other's washing. The fowls are sold so as to buy yams, the
yams are sold so as to buy palm-oil, the palm-oil is sold
so as to buy peppers, all of which could have been done
without stirring from the women's respective villages.
It is only when they need to buy non-local products such
as pottery, tobacco, salt, dried fish, or small European
goods, that they really need to go to a market, but the
market is more to them than a mere shopping-centre.
More perhaps than their homes, it is the centre of their
own individual lives, it is their battlefield, their opportunity, their channel of expression; it is their club and
their theatre, their newspaper and their post office. Here
in fierce bargaining and quick calculation, they can show
what stuff they are made of, here they can talk and
laugh and shout and chaffer to their heart's content,
here they meet friends and relatives, visitors from other
villages they may not have seen for months, they can
hear the news and gossip of the whole Province and,
most important, they can send messages to right and
left, immediately passed on from woman to woman,
from one market to another. One hears over and over
again the remark: 'I will speak of it in the market,'

exactly as we would say: 'I will take this telegram to the post office.'[1]

In the farming season, the arrangement of a woman's day depends upon the stage the farm work has reached and the distance to the farm. Sometimes the whole family will go out together, taking their food with them, and not return till dusk; other times, if the farm is close, the woman will go out for a few hours and hurry home to cook the food, though the times of meals are necessarily uncertain and often she merely leaves a bowl of food ready for the men to eat at whatever time they get back from their work. It will be seen that the woman's day is full and sometimes heavy but it must be remembered that she is not often alone to do the work but is helped by her co-wives, 'mates' as they are called in pidgin English, by her children, and by the elderly female relations of her husband.

What strikingly differentiates the Ibo from the Hausa or the Fulani of the North is the fact that meals are in common, husbands, wives, and children eating together. In Nneato at any rate this custom prevails though exceptions occur, as, for example, if a woman has her period she eats in her own hut with her daughters while the sons eat with their father. If there is only one wife, she, her husband, and children all eat out of the same pot and dip the lumps of *fufu* into the same sauce. There are no rules of precedence though one is expected to eat in a seemly fashion, without grabbing and especially without wasting the sauce. The model husband puts the best pieces aside for the others and perhaps picks out a tasty morsel to give to a child whom he is teaching to eat properly. If there are several wives, say four, they each bring the pot in which they have separately prepared food and

[1] This point is important, as the fact that even in normal times and with no need whatever for urgency, news can travel with such speed disposes of the theory advanced after the Aba Riots that the women must necessarily have some powerful and intricate organization with means of communication known only to themselves.

place it before the husband. He tastes the contents of all
four and eats of the one he finds best, together with the
wife who has cooked the food, and her children. The
other wives eat from their own pots together with their
children, the hurt to their vanity slightly compensated
by the fact that they get more to eat than the wife who
has had the honour of sharing with her husband.

Even if the husband's mother lives in the compound,
she does not eat with her son. On the other hand, friends
and even strangers, male or female, would join the
family circle, the husband 'being proud too much to
show how many wives, how many pots he get' and only
embarrassed if his children do not behave properly or if
his wives fight among themselves. If they show themselves too quarrelsome and strangers come, they are told
to eat apart while husband and visitors eat together; although my informant added, her eyes twinkling, 'some
husbands like having quarrelsome wives; he say: 'me
plenty big man, me fine fellow, all women make palaver
about me'.

Division of labour as between the sexes does not seem
so clear cut among the Ibo as among other tribes. In the
home, the boy may sweep the yard, even the house 'if
he be good boy and want to help his mother', he may
possibly help to pound the *fufu* but he would never cook,
nor have I ever seen one washing or scraping cassava.
The girl helps in all domestic work, including the cooking, and both boys and girls fetch wood and water,
though on the whole it is more usual to see the boys
doing outdoor work while the girls are more use at home.
The man does all the building work, even to sewing together the palm-leaves that constitute the thatch. Yet
this work is not actually taboo for a woman, as is proved
by the fact that if a widow has no son and her male relatives neglect her, her daughter will make the thatch herself. She may be laughed at by her companions for
undertaking man's work but it will bring no discredit

upon her. Similarly, I have seen a boy making a mat, which is purely women's work, for his sick mother.

In agriculture, division of labour is strict in theory, variable in practice. The yam crop is the main one and here the man is supposed to do the preparing of the land, the burning of the cleared grass and brushwood, the hoeing of the ground, the planting of the 'men's' yams, and later on the cutting of stakes and the tying up of the yam tendril to the stakes. Just before the harvest, he builds a new *ɔba* or repairs last year's, clears the ground around it, and sees the wall or fence is adequate to keep out live-stock.

The harvest finished, it is he who strings up the yams on the *ɔba*, a square staging of bamboo poles, some eight or ten feet high and five or six feet across. The spaces between the bamboo poles allow free circulation of air, a small thatched roof keeps off the hottest sun and protects the yams from rain. The women plant the 'women's' yams, do all the weeding, which is generally done twice, and help to bring in the yams from the farms when the crop is ready. In practice, one will see women firing the undergrowth, men weeding, men planting both 'men's' and 'women's' yams, and vice versa. Broadly speaking, 'women's' yams are those that are planted first and in consequence ripen first. They are smaller than the men's yams and do not keep so well. There are at least five varieties of yams, easily distinguished by the natives, and having each its own period of planting and of growth, its method of cooking, and its market value.

Apart from his share of work in the cultivation of the yam crop, the man collects the clusters[1] of oil nuts which grow sometimes fairly close to the base of the oil palm but more generally some twenty or thirty feet from the ground. To do this, he passes a raffia rope round his waist and levers himself up till he is able to hack off the

[1] These 'clusters' are called *banga* in Ibo and as there is no English equivalent, the vernacular word is always used.

clusters with his matchet. Apart from the danger of the occupation, no woman would be permitted to climb a tree nor even a native ladder, nor to mount upon a roof. This taboo is so strict that when a rich man fell ill, his sickness was attributed to the fact that his wives went up the stairs to an upper floor of the mud-block house he had built for himself in his own village.

Once the man has carried the clusters home, the preparation of the oil is in the hands of the women, though in Eziama I saw two young men who were pounding the nuts in the hollowed-out section of a log which served as a mortar. Though the women prepare the oil, and often sell it if it is only a small quantity, the price of it goes to the husband; on the other hand, the palm-kernels are the perquisites of the women.

Men also collect the palm-wine, and as far as I know, only men sell it. The woman, besides doing her share of the work in connection with the yam crops, has crops of her own which she sometimes plants apart, sometimes on the same land as the yams, for, apart from the regular farm often a little distance away, the women of the compounds have their own gardens close by, either within the compound wall or just outside. These little gardens with their fences of sticks or palm branches, are often models of neatness and care. In them or on the farm, she plants cassava, coco-yam and, on a smaller scale, beans, maize, pumpkins, okra, pepper, etc. The pepper can be planted either in the woman's garden as already described or on the farm along with the main crop: for example, pumpkin is sown on the heap of soil that covers the newly planted seed yam while okra and maize are sown between the heaps. Or coco-yams and yams can grow together; but the planting of yams and cassava together is strictly forbidden as it would be an insult to Njoku, the yam spirit.

All the above-named crops, perhaps not in theory but in practice, are the women's own property. She is bound to use them for her family's sustenance when the annual supply of yams is getting low, i.e. from middle April to July and even before that a wife who does not give her husband a dish of cassava from time to time is accused of meanness, but anything left over from the household wants can be sold in the market. The money thus earned is kept by the woman, who can spend it as she pleases, possibly on something for herself or her children, more probably on goods or foodstuffs she knows she can get cheaply in one market and sell at a profit in another. Her knowledge of local prices even over a wide area is surprising and her joy is great when having bought a fowl in Ngodo for sixpence she can, after having walked fourteen miles, sell it in Eziama for sixpence halfpenny.

Even the ill-defined rules regarding the division of labour, as sketched above, fall to the ground when the woman is a widow or when her husband is absent. Provision for such cases is made by native law and custom, carefully and sensibly made, but does not always operate.

For example, Mary's mother, an elderly widow who had also become a Christian, had three daughters but no son. Her eldest daughter, who was Mary, contributed to her maintenance from out of the salary paid her by the Methodist Mission; her second daughter, Christina, a tall buxom girl, lived with her at home; her third daughter, sixteen-year-old Dinah, had been sent, again with Mary's help, to a Mission boarding-school. The mother and Christina lived in her late husband's family compound in a small three-roomed house with a yard round it in which was a tiny plot of corn and a tethered goat. The autumn I was there, they were going to farm some land immediately opposite, allotted to the mother presumably by the senior male member of her late husband's family. Strictly speaking, this land should have been cleared for her by her male relatives-in-law and the heavy hoeing should also have been done by them. Whether they had refused to render her this customary service or whether she had not wished to be beholden to them, I could not discover. The fact remained that, once more helped by Mary, she had hired labourers from Ngodo, which is a very poor district, paying them at the rate of three halfpence a day with three meals or three-pence a day without meals, to do the clearing of the bush. As usual, the land in question had lain fallow three or four years. The land once cleared, Christina had her-self hoed it—I remember noticing how well this had been done and what good soil it was—and she and her mother had planted the various kinds of yams. With the cassava, corn, and coco-yams which Christina had also planted, Mary said proudly her mother's store was as well filled as a man's 'because she had a strong daughter'.

Another woman came to see me: she was also a widow and a Church member, but older than Mary's mother. According to her looks and the few dates that Mary could pick up from her conversation she must have been about seventy. Although barren, she had been her pagan husband's favourite wife. When he died, she was inherited according to native law and custom by the son of another wife. This man, Abraham, was now a Chris-tian and the local 'church leader' so could not marry her, though in any case she was beyond the age. Abra-ham had a large family of his own and though he had been good to her, he was not able to do much for her, and, too old to do more than the lightest gardening, she often went hungry. I insisted that her husband's rela-tives were morally bound to support her though perhaps only Abraham was 'legally' responsible for her. She and Mary agreed but said that 'times had changed': her late husband's brothers were indifferent, Abraham's brothers did nothing; the younger generation, though rebuked, did nothing either. The old woman, curiously like an old grandmother among our own poor in her philosophy and tolerance, did not blame Abraham: 'A man would be glad to inherit a young and pretty wife but not an old

93

woman like her. If she had anything to leave, it would have been different, but she had nothing.' Mary angrily remarked that if a man wanted to inherit property, he must also be ready to inherit poverty, and sternly went off to talk to the church members and see what could be done in the matter.

It is true that in both these cases the widows were Christians and had thereby put themselves to a certain degree outside the family circle with all its reciprocal rights and obligations. Though actual persecution of Christians, even in a mild way, is rare, it could not be expected that a pagan family would consider itself quite so responsible for a member who had deserted its common faith, and more especially its common ancestor worship. But even in purely pagan families one found, for one reason or another, more married or widowed women on their own than one expected. When asked what they lived on, Mary said serenely that they 'managed' and expressed no surprise at nor commiseration with their solitary state.

The only woman's craft is that of mat-making. These mats are made from strips of the long narrow leaf of the screw pine (*pandanus*). The screw pine grows in damp places, near streams, and has sometimes 'stilt' roots like a mangrove. The mats are mostly self-coloured though sometimes one will be seen with strands of red or yellow raffia woven into it in a simple pattern or just round the edges. The best of these mats are very good indeed, wonderfully strong and supple and almost silky to the touch.

There is also a form of art practised by the women which would repay further study: it is that of painting designs on the body with a dark bluish-brown juice (*uri*, or *urit* as K. C. Murray spells it). This body-painting is widely spread: the finest examples I saw years ago at Aro Chuku, but actually in the Okigwi Division it was in Eziama that I found the best designs, even bolder and more striking than those illustrated in 'Body Paintings from Umuahia' by K. C. Murray.[1]

Hairdressing and the shaving of the hair into patterns on the heads of young children is also women's work, and here again they show taste and skill. As soon as a girl's breasts begin to form, she starts dressing her hair, or more generally it is dressed by a friend, at first simply then more and more elaborately. She is supposed to adopt a new style every year for a period of eight years. In the last stages, the coiffures become most intricate affairs. The hair is smoothed with palm-oil and stiffened with antimony, innumerable twists are looped together over the ears or gathered into a tight-fitting helmet shape, and small pearl buttons or brass studs brought from Onitsha are fastened into the twists. At the time of my visit to Nneato, small silver medals of His Holiness the Pope were in great demand for the same purpose.

As said before, no cloth is woven by men or women. Before the introduction of European cotton goods, the women's scanty kirtle was woven of raffia on looms by men. Nowadays in Nneato the industry has died out and only survives in the making of large and small raffia bags, also by men.

[1] *The Nigerian Teacher*, vol. i, no. 4, 1935.

V

Primitive Woman—in Nneato

What the women say of marriage, birth, and widow-hood. Their pagan councils and Christian meetings.

When we turn from the small daily happenings of the Nneato woman's life to the more important incidents in her career, we find the same absence of any hard and fast rules. For example, marriage, on the surface, seems a straightforward affair yet as soon as one starts to ask questions regarding concrete examples, one finds one can no longer piece together an account which is not full of contradictions and inconsistencies. I will not attempt to describe the various customs which go to form the 'legal' aspect of marriage, the visits, the presents, the reciprocal duties between the two families, the various stages of the dowry payments, etc. I will only give a few glimpses of the part played by the bride herself.

A girl, while she is still at her mother's breast, can be affianced, that is to say, her parents can begin to receive payments of her dowry, although a local saying, 'he who pays threepence at birth puts his money into water' or 'he pays dowry for a wife who wets his cloth', i.e. who is still a baby, shows that general experience recognizes the disadvantages of such early 'engagements'. All the same, informants agree that about four times out of ten, the payment of dowry begins while the prospective wife

96

GIRL DANCERS, EZIAMA

MALE DANCERS, EZIAMA

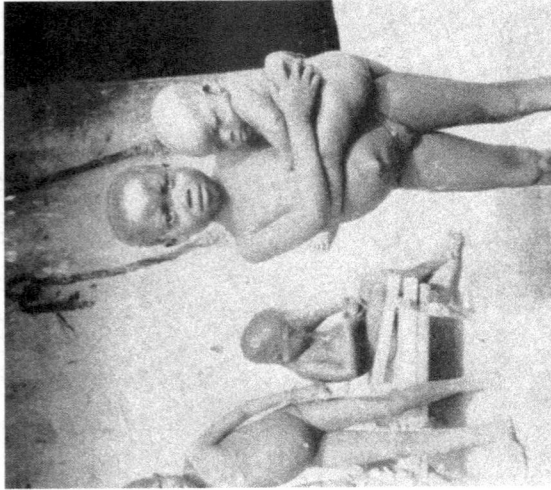

THE NURSEMAIDS

is still an infant. As she gets older, she goes to and fro
between her home and her fiancé's compound, still helping her mother but at the same time getting used to her
future husband's ways and the fashion of his house and
of her future mother-in-law. Should she have intercourse with her fiancé or at any rate conceive by him
before the proper time, i.e. about four years after her
first menstruation and before she has reached her eighth
style of hairdressing (see p. 95), she would be looked
down upon by her companions 'who would make her a
song'. This 'making a song', i.e. bringing shame and
ridicule on the victim by means of more or less ribald
improvisations concerning his or her personal appearance, character, and conduct, is a popular and very effective form of Ibo punishment. But cases have been known
where the man himself has had to bear the reproaches
of the girl's parents and the weight of public disapproval
for having violated a too young bride.

Although both families try to get the full sum paid
up before the marriage is consummated, it is permissible
for a girl finally to go to her husband as soon as the larger
portion has been handed over. In Nneato, if the dowry
has not been paid up before a year and a half after the
birth of the first child has elapsed, the parents can recall
their daughter and the husband has no redress, but I
have never actually known of such a case. On the other
hand, payments may be spun out indefinitely, either
because of the young man's inability to pay or because
of the rapacity of the girl's parents. Indeed, as an elderly
woman put it with a sigh: 'There is no end to marriage
in this country. . . .' Yet, when I tentatively asked, seeing how clearly the women realized all the complications
inherent in the dowry system, whether they had ever
thought of doing without it, they looked at me in
shocked astonishment: 'But if no dowry were paid for
us, we should be harlots. . . .'

Before going finally to her fiancé's house, the girl is

'cut', a ceremony which takes place in her parent's compound and which I was able to see: the girl lay on two banana leaves spread on the ground, her head between the thighs of a young man (her future brother-in-law, I was told. It must be a near male relation, and in this case the girl may not have had brothers of her own), her hands above her head and the arms held down by the same young man. Her only clothing was a skimpy kirtle; her body was freshly decorated with *uri* marks and she had some medals in her hair.

The 'cuts' were already marked out in white chalk: three rows from the base of the throat to the pit of the stomach and two rows half-way round the waist. An oldish man performed the operation with a native knife rather like a scalpel but with a slightly broader blade. With it, he lifted the skin by making a small cut and when the requisite number of cuts were made, he lightly rubbed powdered charcoal over them. The girl then rose up and went to her hut to wash herself. When she came back, he smeared the cuts with oil while an old woman rubbed her body with yellow powder. She was then allowed to rest, given some food, and spent the afternoon receiving visitors.

While the operation was going on, some twenty women, old and young, crowded round, singing loudly a kind of chorus and making a curious sound at the back of their throats like an animal's growl, or a very deep hum. The sound was so peculiar and so regular that for some time I thought it came from some new kind of musical instrument. The girl herself joined in the song all the time. Children were also present and a number of young men, friends of the future husband, come to see whether the bride was courageous or not. When the cuts are healed, they have the appearance of small oval blisters. No solemnity was attached to the ceremony and, whatever its original significance may have been, it seems now to have been forgotten and all the explanation

Marriage

I could get was that the 'cuts' were 'for pretty'; though one informant added, rather improbably, that the blisters served as money in the next world, a blister being picked off every time a purchase had to be made and whoever had not been 'cut' in this world would find herself very poor in the next!

When the girl is considered ready to conceive and consequently ready to take up her permanent abode in her fiancé's house, a feast takes place at which the fiancé kills a goat to be eaten by both families and presents another goat to his fiancée's family. The fiancée, usually accompanied by a bevy of other girls who have reached the same stage at the same time, goes round the market-place followed by a small girl from her own family bearing the skin of the killed goat, another carrying a three-pointed stick upon which the fat of the goat is placed (to show how rich an animal had been chosen for the feast) and a third bearing a bowl into which are put small gifts of money for the bride 'for honour of being able to conceive'. She will also be followed by women from her fiancé's family, singing songs in her praise, and the fiancé's men friends will let off their Dane guns with much noise and smoke.

There is, as far as I could tell, no actual marriage ceremony: indeed I do not know at what point the Ibo considers the girl as his 'wife', whether it is when she first goes to his compound, or when the marriage is consummated, or when she first conceives, or when the full dowry has been paid.[1] Marriage is more probably a process in his eyes than a single act. This attitude is not uncommon among the Ibo; if there is *unity* of process, he cannot divide the process into sections or points of

[1] The term *munye*—wife—is applied to the girl during the whole of this period so it seems likely that the pair are considered to be 'married' from the moment the first instalment of dowry has been paid. To lessen confusion, I have used the terms 'betrothed' or 'fiancée' in all cases where the girl has not yet gone to her future husband's home for good.

time. For example, he will say 'the evening meal is at
five o'clock' when actually the preparation begins at
five o'clock and the meal itself is not eaten till seven-
thirty, but the preparation of the food being part of the
process leading up to the eating of the meal, he looks
upon the hour of five as the moment when the meal
really begins. In the same way, he will tell you it takes
a certain time to reach a man's house. At the end of the
time, you have only reached the fringe of the man's
town and have still half an hour's walk in front of you.
You are annoyed, but to your guide, the reaching of the
town is the beginning of the process of reaching the
man's house since that house is one with the town and
his mind refuses to sub-divide the process.

When the wife has her first child, both families are
very pleased. For a lunar month after the child's birth,
the mother is confined to her own hut where only her
husband and mother or very near relatives may visit
her. The baby must have been delivered in the little yard
outside the hut; should it have been inadvertently delivered inside the hut, it would be 'abomination' and
the baby would be thrown into the bush. Even if the
woman were alone and tried to conceal the fact, she
would sicken and die, probably out of sheer fright.

The placenta is buried outside in a deep hole. Should
a wife run away to another man and have a child by
him, the placenta must be sent back to the husband for
burial, thus admitting his ownership of the child, even
though he is not its father. When the mother comes out
of her seclusion, the child is named by three names, one
given by the husband's family, one by the mother's, one
by the *dibia* who has been called in to divine what male
or female ancestor has entered the child and names it
accordingly. A feast is then made which is partaken of by
the two families, the blood of the goat or the fowl and a
small piece of the meat being sacrificed to the ancestor.
The child's mother must not eat of the meat as it would

Birth and Reincarnation

come into her milk and thus the ancestor would eat twice of it, once in the spirit world (through the sacrifice) and once in the human world (through the child whose body it has come to inhabit). If the *dibia* has announced the return of an ancestor who was popular, the latter is welcomed and the baby, in whom he now resides, made much of; but should he have left unpleasant memories, the *dibia* is quickly told to try again, or the family goes off to another *dibia*, hoping for better luck.

In the neighbouring Ngodo district, a man who had been much plagued by women during his lifetime, might wish to be re-incarnated in a woman 'so as to be able to get some of his own back'. In Eziama, a woman might be re-incarnated in a man but not vice versa: 'indeed, it would be very foolish for a man to wish to become a woman,' remarked my informant, a middle-aged woman of the world. Some women present said frankly they would like to become men, but I could not get them to explain themselves fully. This is to be regretted as I had occasionally caught glimpses of some peculiar conception of sex or of a thread of bi-sexuality running through everything (yet I think hermaphrodites are 'abomination')—or of a lack of differentiation between the sexes—or of an acceptance of the possibility of the transposition of sex—which it would have been interesting to study. (Yet the facts of paternity have, according to several informants, been always known, even in the most backward parts. Incredulous giggles met my suggestion that the knowledge was not universal.)

On the death of the husband, the widow or widows shave their heads and go about in rags for a year. They may go to market but not to their own local market; they may farm, but they will be careful to go to their farms a little time after the others have gone out, as men do not care to meet a widow too early in the morning, lest the same fate befall them as befell the widow's late husband. Before every feast, big or small, they burst into tears and

101

lamentations, remembering the happy times they have had—'even if they hadn't,' cynically added Mary. Those that are still young, are inherited by any of the husband's sons by another wife; or failing sons, by his brothers; or failing these also, they can go back to their parents, but if they marry again, the dowry must be paid to their late husband's family, not to their own parents.

In the Nneato area, at the present time, the dowry for a girl would be as low as £5 to £10; but for a widow or for a woman who had left her husband, it would have to be as much as £15 or £20 to compensate for the dowry which was originally paid for her when dowry rates were high. At that time, if the dowry was, say £20, the father of the girl would have kept about £15 and £5 would have gone to the girl's mother; if the dowry was £10, the father would have kept £7 and £3 would have gone to the mother. Nowadays the proportion is smaller still but it will be seen that the mother's share is a recognized thing and shows once more that the Ibo woman is as much her husband's partner as his chattel. However, in considering this question of dowry, it must be remembered that the money is not pure profit to the parents; a certain portion of it is expended on the bride's outfit, that is to say, on the cooking-pots and the seed yams, the baskets, mats, and cloths she takes with her to her new home.

The question of a married woman's or widow's property is a nebulous one. One is constantly being told a woman has no property yet one is equally constantly being shown 'my' farm or hearing of a woman who has gone to court about 'her' oil palms or 'her' share of a dowry. From all the numberless inquiries I made, in Nneato and elsewhere, I could get no clear idea or recognize any general and accepted practice. This is all the more unfortunate as the question, in view of the increase in marriages under the Ordinance or 'Christian' marriages, is important.

102

Divorce

Should the husband desert the wife or die, the Christian wife is left far more solitary and unprotected than under the old pagan régime. She will refuse to be inherited by any of her husband's family; she may find it difficult to go back to her own, perhaps pagan, family. She may have children whose school fees she has had to pay and who, going to school, will not be able to help her in home and farm. No one is responsible for her and, unless she is able to inherit from her husband, her case is a hard one.

Divorce exists according to native law and custom. The procedure varies a little with each locality but the general rule holds good that a marriage can be dissolved by either party, providing the dowry is repaid to the husband either by the wife's family, or her prospective second husband, or herself. Only in a few cases can the wife regain her full freedom without this repayment of dowry. It seems that at the moment more wives ask to be divorced from their husbands than husbands from their wives, although the latter know that, should they have had any children, they will have to leave them with their father, even should he have been the guilty party. This tendency is delightfully explained in a letter written to a Nigerian paper: 'Women being of soft tendency cannot tolerate peevish and feverish act of husband meted to her from time to time she is in this way feeling tired of staying any longer with her husband and will consequently seek way to divorce such husband', though I cannot think the excuse of a 'soft tendency' would apply to the stalwart wives of Nneato!

Marriages 'under the Ordinance', whether they have taken place in church or in the District Office (which here would correspond to a Registry Office) can only be dissolved through legal proceedings in the British Courts.

It will have been seen that children always belong to the husband, whether he is their actual father or not, and whether he has completed the full payment of dowry

103

or not; but if a girl is entirely free, that is to say, if not even the smallest instalment of dowry has been paid, then, if she bears a child, that child belongs to her parents 'but they think shame'.

I could find no trace of any systematic education either of boys or of girls, except the home training by imitation of the adults; no puberty rites nor initiation ceremonies.

Circumcision of girls as well as of boys takes place generally a few days after birth; when a girl menstruates for the first time, her parents rejoice as it proves she is normal (if she were not, she would have been given (not sold) to a passing Aro to be sold as a slave), but there are no special ceremonies; the facts are told her by her mother and when she goes to her prospective husband's house, old women of his family supplement this information. Nevertheless, the care of babies is instilled into them at the earliest age, for an Ibo mother hardly ever takes her child to farm or market as among the Yoruba, where the baby practically lives all day on its mother's back. Among the Ibo, if carried at all, the infant is carried on its mother's hip but nearly always it is left at home, sometimes in the care of the grandmother but more often in that of an elder sister or, failing a sister, an elder brother or cousin.

These children take their position as nursemaid very seriously; even the small boys will be seen wiping the baby sister's nose with the utmost care and quickly twisting a little grass together so that it should not sit down on the bare ground. One of the most attractive features of Ibo family life is this affection, shown not only by the proud father lifting an ecstatic baby on to his shoulder, but by the younger children, patiently hushing a tiny form to sleep, sitting motionless and cramped, a tiny head in the crook of their own tiny arms.

This brief account of some of the incidents in a woman's

family life presents no very original features; on the other hand, her public life seems to strike a new note.

Remembering the Aba Riots of 1929, the extraordinary rapidity with which these thousands of women had mobilized, their organization and discipline (except on those occasions when hysteria broke through), one could not help wondering whether there was not some vast network of secret societies binding the women together and to some central authority.

Nneato itself had taken no part in the Riots, although invited to do so, but it lay on the very fringe of the Riot area and presumably would have formed part of the secret organization, if organization there was. On my first visit, I heard nothing and did not want to question too closely. On my second, wanting to know what the women thought of a scheme for a small maternity home, I was told: 'We will ask Nwayinkwere, the spokeswoman of the women's meeting.' The suggestion came pat and further information was given with complete frankness, both by Mary, although this meeting was a purely pagan institution, and by Nwayinkwere herself. One of my most vivid recollections is that of the evening spent with Nwayinkwere in her house, watching the calm intelligent face as she bent over her cassava-scraping; listening to her voice, sometimes volubly explaining, sometimes slowing and tightening while she inwardly wondered how much it was wise to tell the white woman; appreciating the dramatic gift with which she described the women's call echoing from compound to compound, the clamour as the women poured out of their huts, the shrill cries: 'What is it? who wants us? which woman needs us?' and then the forward march to the war-song of which the lilt and the challenge and the impishness left one astounded. We parted good friends, after much mutual scrutiny, and she readily consented to call a meeting so that we might talk over a few things concerning women's interests.

Women

Two councils were held in my presence at Eziama and another one at a village I visited some forty miles north-east of Nneato (Mary constantly used the word 'meeting' but it is so often understood to mean meetings of Church members that I prefer to use the word 'council' as 'society' is too much tinged in West Africa with the idea of secret societies). All three times, the procedure was nearly the same and inquiries showed that this system was general in all that district.

The day before the council is to be held, the spokeswoman goes round the village beating two short sticks or a light wooden drum and calling out a short phrase in which she announces the time and place of the next council. At the appointed time, the married women assemble—all except pregnant women, mothers suckling their babies (this exclusion is only because the councils do not want to have any distractions or coming and going) and very old women who could take no useful part in the discussion.

In large village-groups, where the presence of all the married women would make the council too unwieldy, each compound nominates its own spokeswoman and she alone attends the meetings. These meetings either take place in the various spokeswomen's houses in turn, the hostess being expected to give refreshments to the members, or in an open space such as the market-place. The chief spokeswoman is apparently nominated by a consensus of public opinion. She has probably given good advice in some crisis and therefore the women turn to her in any fresh emergency and eventually she is regarded as their leader or, more correctly speaking perhaps, their representative, for she would be careful not to say anything in her official capacity unless she spoke in the presence of the rest of the council or had had the opportunity to consult with it. I was assured that neither seniority nor wealth played any part in the choice of these spokeswomen. They were chosen for their

106

'wisdom' and naught else. I was also assured that each council was a self-contained unit, with no affiliations of any sort, and under no central authority or even influence. The Nneato spokeswoman, for example, were she to travel to a neighbouring town, would be well received on account of her known social standing, but she would not be invited to take part in the local council, nor would the council of one town have power to give its members any sort of introduction or safe conduct to the members of the council of another town. Asked whether a member travelling from one town to another would be recommended by her council to the next council or be in any way befriended by the members of the latter, Nwayinkwere answered rather sharply that members had enough to do looking after their own towns without bothering about strangers. Apparently no 'official' affiliation with other councils nor means of communication between them exists, though of course in practice news is immediately carried by means of travelling traders and especially through the markets (see p. 88).

Although men are not allowed to attend the council meetings, these are not in any way secret; indeed the majority of men approve of them and wish them to keep their power. This may be partly due to the fact that they trust the integrity of the women in the matter of bribes more than their own. They also know that the women wish to preserve the peace of the town as it enables them to carry on their trading, and they seem also to think that the women have a greater sense of abstract justice. They would not be biased by personal prejudice and long-standing feuds as much as the men, and even when they decided to 'spoil' a man's or a woman's property as punishment for some offence, they would not do so in anger but in righteous indignation, a difference of motive the women often made.

The nature of the questions dealt with by the councils probably varies a good deal. However wide their scope

107

may have been in the past, in some parts it seems to have narrowed to purely religious matters. The council would decide upon sacrifices to be made to Ajala, the Earth-spirit, would consult a diviner as to the planting of women's crops upon certain pieces of land, would meet for ritual songs and dances. In other parts, the councils seem to have and especially to have had, a far greater share in the administration of justice than has yet been discovered. In all cases, the councils appeared to pass certain 'laws' relating to the protection of crops from theft or damage by live-stock and these laws were unquestioningly obeyed by the men, as if they recognized that it was both the right and the responsibility of the women to safeguard the fruits of the earth, i.e. of Ajala. But apart from these laws regarding crops, the councils, at least in Nneato, settled, sometimes alone, sometimes in conjunction with the senior male members of the families concerned, marital disputes, disputes between women, disputes between a widow and her husband's family, cases regarding extra-marital relations and pre-nuptial conception, for the women did not think family affairs should be taken to Court, not only because it was unseemly to wash dirty linen in public but because of the consequent wastage of time and money and chances of bribery.

Apart from these almost judicial functions, the councils seem also to have served in an advisory capacity. 'We are all for peace. If a widow quarrels with her stepson, we say: "Look, many of us are widows also and yet we manage better than you" and by quietly discussing the causes of the disputes, bring the parties to reason.' When asked whether these councils were not inclined to favour women to the detriment of men, the answer was firmly in the negative, with the added comment that the proof was in the fact that the men consulted the councils and wished them to continue.

This seems to be true but the difficulty immediately

arises: what is the status of these councils to-day and how can they enforce their rulings? In former times, the councils, within their own sphere, had both spiritual and temporal power in that their rulings were, so to speak, backed by Ajala, and could be enforced by means of what pidgin English picturesquely terms 'war', that is to say, the destruction of property or the infliction of corporal punishment, generally of a ridicule-making nature, by the women themselves and whether the offenders were male or female. Nowadays, fear of Ajala's anger has lessened and Government forbids the women to make 'war'. How can the councils maintain their prestige and uphold their authority? It is natural to say that the spread of properly constituted and supervised Native Courts does away with the need of these very local and limited institutions and that the day of the Women's Council is over. Nevertheless, when one has listened to one of their meetings, seen the order, the good sense, the knowledge of human nature displayed, looked at those strong faces and listened to those quiet voices, one cannot help feeling what a pity it is that not more use can be made of these women and this surprising organization.

It is true that if this form of feminine activity is doomed to disappear, another one is being created under the name of meetings of (Protestant) Church members. These are also called by a woman leader and are held regularly either in the church or at members' houses in rotation. After prayers and the singing of a hymn, Church matters are discussed and a collection taken towards the women's share of the local teacher or catechist's salary, repairs to the church, the entertainment of travelling members, gifts to a visiting pastor, etc. These meetings will certainly become more numerous and influential as time goes on but they are after all only attended by a section of the community, even if it is a growing one; they do not represent the full, ordinary life of the village and are, in the last resort, still under the authority of European pastors, representing an alien force.

Here in Nneato, there is so little antagonism between Christian and pagan that Christian women would be admitted as members of the Women's Councils but the former feel they cannot attend them as they might be asked to contribute towards some pagan feast or sacrifice or be asked to join some ritual singing or dancing that the *juju* had demanded. As far as business matters were concerned, there would be no objection as it is fully recognized that the council's decisions are moral, law-abiding, and for the greater good of the community, but the religious difficulty is insuperable.

VI

Primitive Woman—in Nneato

How far have the women been influenced by occasional Western contacts? What do the women feel about the old? what do they think about the new? Paganism and Christianity. Polygamy and monogamy.

The last two chapters have given a picture of the material side of woman's life in a nearly untouched agricultural community.

Now what of the woman herself as she moves hardy, busy, and important against the background of her simple surroundings? The only truthful answer is: 'I do not know'. Our common womanhood was a key to many of her thoughts and feelings: to her passionate desire for children, especially for sons to increase the consequence of her husband's family ('if a woman has only daughters, she cry plenty, yet she is glad to have a few', for will they not be more her own, her helpers and nearly her companions?), to her illogical shame when she bears no children and to the pathetic prayer, founded on the belief that it is the god of her husband's family who is angry with her and causes her sterility: 'God, love me, even if my husband does not.' It was the key to many small vanities and loyalties (such as the conduct of the woman who, against all the rules of hospitality, had not asked us into her hut 'because it was so poor she was ashamed and it would be letting down her husband to

111

let us see it'), even to the independent spirit of the girl who had left her husband to live with another man and proudly assured her parents they need not trouble to re-pay her dowry for she soon hoped to do so herself out of her immoral earnings. It was the key to her endurance, her philosophical acceptance of the chances and turns of life, her self-sacrifice where home and children were con-cerned. It was the key to all she was as a woman, girl, wife or mother, but not to what she was as an individual, possessing her own soul. Here one was baffled again and again, by her simplicity, her complexity, her intelli-gence, her stupidity, her conservatism, her modernity. Whether as the individual she was before the slightest Western influence had touched her, or the individual as she now is, in her process of transition, she is equally hard to grasp.

Let us take first her intelligence, judged by our own standards. No mental tests would have served any pur-pose even if I had wished to employ them; listening and watching were the only safe methods and even so, how much escaped one, how much one misinterpreted!

I should say the women of Nneato were intelligent—they *must* be intelligent with those mobile faces and quick movements, so unlike the heavy Yoruba peasants, amiable and slow. These, when living under similar conditions, struck me as being quite unawakened, and, shrewd as they were along their own lines, any general intelligence or power of thought had not yet come into being. It is not so with the Ibo. Apart from their natural gifts, their cleverness in trade, their quickness in calcu-lating where their interest lies, their memory, their easy grasp of some long, detailed story in the mazes of which the white man loses himself at once, they have intelli-gence as we understand it, the power of thought, and the power of reason. Yet their thought is still almost entirely self-centred, their intelligence very limited, flowing along the narrowest channel and mirroring only the slightest facts, their reason so unexercised that it cannot be counted upon. They are dangerous, in that they appear to be so much more advanced than they are.

The account already given of the Women's Councils shows how sensible the women can be, with what order and lucidity they can state their case, with what ease they put forward the essentials of a situation. Yet when questions of a slightly more general nature, with a rather wider bearing or deeper meaning, were put to them, these same women failed entirely to respond. They knew what they wanted at this very moment, to meet this present situation; they could ask for it clearly and sensibly; but of longer thought or drawn-out reasoning they were, as yet, incapable. They had no capacity of foresight: to questions that affect them deeply, such as the unemployment of their sons whom they had slaved to send to school, they could offer no solution. They repeated obstinately it was a good thing for boys to go to school and could see no further. Though conscious of the imminence of change, they did not think of how to prepare for it. Though realizing that vital customs such as the inheriting of widows were falling into disuse, they could not sufficiently visualize the situation and its consequences so as to be able to meet it.

It is no wonder and certainly no blame to them that it should be so. The only danger is, as I have already said, that we should ourselves be taken in and think their practical, day-to-day common sense stands for more than it does. This potential danger does not concern Government so much, but it does concern the Missions whose policy is to give more and more responsibility to their converts, men and women, with less and less supervision. There are of course exceptions. Mary, for example, possessed more than common sense; she could reason, even if there were strange gaps in her reasoning. She could discuss love and hate and immortality; from a stone engraved with the initials of the Nigerian Survey we found

113

on a distant headland she could make a picture of the
Empire, far flung, with King George sitting on his
throne in the middle of it; and above all, she could look
into the future, guessing at this and that and how it
would affect her people, wondering what this law would
become, how that custom would alter. But then her
natural aptitudes had been developed by long and close
personal contact with Europeans at the Mission—though
even she trembled at the thought of crossing bewitched
streams, walked quicker as we went through the 'bad
bush', and would not let me touch the 'bags of misfortune'[1] that hang upon its edge.

If the Ibo woman's intellect has just begun to open,
what of her emotions? If, by the word emotion used in
this context, I may mean such emotional experiences as
love, pity, remorse, sorrow, spiritual conflict, appreciation of beauty, then I should say her emotional lags
behind her intellectual development. Such a statement
may be unjust and is certainly impossible of proof. I can
only remember the number of times, in Nneato and
elsewhere, when, certain I was witnessing a genuine
emotion on what one could call a spiritual plane, I was
suddenly brought to earth with a shock at some sudden
revelation of the completely utilitarian, self-regarding
attitude of the speaker. The following two incidents,

[1] What Mary aptly termed 'bags of misfortune' are raffia bags in
which, by a *dibia's* command, a man who finds that he is constantly
losing some of his property such as money or crops or live-stock, puts
certain small articles, probably bits of chalk, camwood, etc., and, followed by the *dibia* singing a special song, goes to the 'bad bush' and,
having so to speak, put his misfortunes in the bag, throws it among
the branches of the nearest trees. Mary also showed me what she
tragically named 'pots of calamity', containing a hen for a woman or
a cock for a man, which are likewise thrown into the 'bad bush' by the
dibia's advice if his clients are being 'troubled' by a dead relative.
Another way of getting rid of calamities such as sudden death or the
relapse of a sick person is to tie a string loosely round the waist. It
falls to the ground, is lifted up by a *dibia* clear of the person's body
and thrown by him into the 'bad bush' with the proper 'incantations'.

unimportant in themselves, may serve as symbols: at a meeting of a Women's Council I had been struck by the passion underlying the request for a dispensary and touched by the anguish of the cry: 'Our children die and there is none to save them!' I thought to myself how unjust I had been in not recognizing sooner that there was at least one emotion which they were capable of experiencing in all its profundity and purity, that of mother-love. Later on we were discussing the general age of marriage. The women complained that girls got married much later now because it took the young men so long in these bad times to collect the necessary dowry. I asked them if it were not perhaps a good thing, the girls would be wiser and stronger and especially the mothers would have the joy of keeping their daughters longer beside them, to which came the reply: 'No. Our daughters might die before they could be married and then where would the dowry be?' Their voices were cold and harsh. I do not think it happens so very often that parents force a girl into a marriage utterly distasteful to her, unless, as is unfortunately sometimes the case, they are enmeshed in the tangle of the Ibo debt system, but it is evident that the adored child soon turns in its mother's eyes into little more than a dowry-bringer.

The second incident was this: after a long walk to a village to see some pottery, I was resting in the house of the native teacher attached to a small Roman Catholic Mission church. An elderly woman came in, of unusual distinction and gentleness of feature. When we left, she said she would accompany us a little way and walked with us to the cross-paths, chatting quietly with Mary. As we parted, she asked God's blessing upon us and looked me straight in the eyes. Not used to seeing just that look in Ibo women's eyes and having missed it very much, I went home elated. Even Mary said: 'I be sure that be good woman. She smile softly and ask nothing from us.' In my diary, I found I noted that evening: 'Met Elizabeth

—a lady.' Some months later, visiting the village again and knowing that Elizabeth was a Roman Catholic, knowing also that pictures were usually much appreciated, I took with me a carefully mounted picture of the Madonna and Child, coloured, which would make its value even greater. Elizabeth was sent for and the picture given. She thanked me but I felt she was somehow disappointed and wondered why she hung around. A few moments later, Mary came into my hut to say that she thought Elizabeth expected I would give her some tobacco. Obviously Elizabeth had not thought it worth while to come out again at the end of her day's work just for something which might be pretty, might even be holy, but had no practical use. Tobacco, on the other hand, she could either smoke herself or sell profitably in the market-place. These of course are only crude examples of what I mean when I say that every time I thought I stood on an emotional equality, I was disappointed. And I do not think it was because of our different outlooks. I had comparatively little difficulty in putting myself in their skins as regards customs and habits: polygamy was natural, twin murder reasonable, cannibalism understandable. Even when I could not understand, I could accept with respect the existence of another point of view, but I never ceased to be shocked at the general lack of sensibility.

This point is only important in that it brings up again the danger of over-estimating the present powers of the Ibo women to understand and inwardly digest religious or ethical teaching. We are trying to play tunes on a dumb piano and for all that the piano appears to be the right size and shape, with keys and pedals complete, no sound can come from it. Once more, it is no wonder, and certainly no blame to them, that it should be so and surely we are as unjust towards the native when we over-estimate his capacities as when we under-estimate them.

Let us now try to study the women's attitude in the

various emotional situations which belong to her ordinary life. The first one, fundamental as it is, eludes, more than any other, our comprehension; religion. Without going into details of which I am not sufficiently certain, the essentials of the Ibo religion as found in Nneato appear to consist in the worship of Ajala, the Earth and Fertility spirit, of minor spirits related to Ajala, of purely local spirits, and of the ancestors.

Although Ajala is a woman, she has no priestesses; yet it is thought by the men that women are closer to her and can obtain a quicker hearing 'being women together'. When in making sacrifice to her, or perhaps when swearing by her name—my informant was not clear—the elders beat the ground with their *ɔfɔ* sticks, the women make the same gesture with the sides of their hands. The only instance of women taking part in actual ritual at the same time as men of which I was able to hear was under the following circumstances: if a man has much trouble in his house (sickness or misfortune), four men and four women (four is the sacred number among the Ibo) go to the shrine of the *juju* who is supposed to have sent the trouble, take mouthfuls of palm-wine presented to them by the victim and spit it out, thus symbolically spitting out the evil that was in his house. Often Ajala through her priest calls the women alone to come and sacrifice to her; then she gives them her blessing and, said Mary, 'they go home happy as if they had been to Communion'.

I most unfortunately missed seeing a women's 'evening service' which took place in the grove a few yards from the Mission church where I was camping. As dark fell I heard singing and, calling Mary, went out to see, but the singing had just stopped and some twenty women were sitting round the foot of an immense tree eating a meal of pounded cassava. They had come over from a distant village to dance and sing in this particular shrine because it was the home of Ajala, who was the mother of

117

'all the Ajala in Eziama'. They ate their cassava, talking the while among themselves quietly but without solemnity. Yet one could not but be impressed: not only by the scene itself, the cleared grove patched with moonlight, dim outlines of war drum and the six painted figures of Ajala's daughters, upright in a row, the crouching women eating their communal meal, the giant trees blocking out the sky, but by that curious sense one so often had among Ibo women of private and independent lives, an existence of their own lived quite apart from home and husband and children. Here again no bond of sex could help me. We met as individuals with no common background. What were they doing and thinking, those women sitting in that dark place so quietly, so self-sufficiently? Would they walk back in the night the two miles to their homes, through the forest, across a stream, through a piece of 'bad bush', along the narrow stony path, 'happy as if they had been to Communion'?

Although there are no priestesses, there are women *dibia*. This word when applied to men appears to cover interpreters of the spirits (a priest has to call in a *dibia* to tell him the spirits' wishes in any matter), diviners, medicine men, native doctors. The *dibia* in any of these roles, and occasionally he combines them all, plays a very important part in Ibo society which needs to be more closely studied. When applied to a woman, I think it means primarily a native doctor and only very occasionally a diviner, that is to say, a woman who by means of various forms of divination, either by casting cowrie-shells, or beans or pieces of chalk and invoking the 'Agwu' or spirit of divination, is able to foretell the future, the outcome of a journey, the propitiousness or non-propitiousness of a season for undertaking a given task.

When I asked how a woman *dibia* was trained, I was told she would inherit the gift from her father, who would also have been a *dibia*; especially if the *dibia* had no son, the Agwu would order him to instruct his daughter so that when he, the father, came to die, 'the Agwu would have home'. These women *dibia* are consulted equally by men and by women, according to their skill. Their persons are not considered sacred in any way and they can be married by laymen.

The women doctors, employed chiefly as gynaecologists and midwives, are more numerous. A detailed account of one such doctor will be found in Chapter VIII.

I have never heard, either in Nneato or elsewhere, of a woman being an interpreter of the spirit's wishes or of one being called in to decide the cause of misfortune or deaths. Nor, curiously enough, are there any witches, though they abound in Onitsha and among the neighbouring Efik in Calabar Province.

It was interesting to learn that a woman could make rain, that is to say, if she belonged to a rainmaker's family. It must be noted that among the Ibo, rainmaking is not a kingly or priestly function as among so many other tribes. In Nneato, it is true, the senior rainmaker was regarded with high respect, but in Owerri, for example, rainmakers were looked on much as we would look on plumbers. Rainmaking was merely a profession. From conversation with the senior rainmaker of Nneato (who lived in Eziama), I learnt that the secret of rainmaking was jealously guarded in the same family for generations. The children learnt by watching their father and a daughter would learn too if she wanted to do so. Nevertheless, although it was recognized that she could learn the art and could possess the power of making rain, she would never be asked to do so, at any rate would never be paid for doing so, as the men were. But she could use her power for her own ends, for example, if she had a spite against another girl, she could send rain to spoil her new cloth or her wedding festivities. No girl would ever tell the secret to her husband nor would a rainmaker's daughter-in-law be allowed to

119

learn. No restrictions governed marriage into or out of a rainmaker's family.

What their religion means to the women, I could not tell. The inquirer is constantly up against this difficulty: the Christian is biased, the pagan is inarticulate. An educated agnostic is the surest informant, or an intelligent child. How far do love, trust, reverence come into their attitude? I once saw a woman kneeling alone in Ajala's grove—but the gesture with which the women throw a morsel of their food to the emblem of their *Ci* (a sort of guardian angel) is perfunctory. Emblems and figures are often shabby and dilapidated but then it must be clearly remembered that the Ibo does not bow down to wood and stone. He bows down to the indwelling spirit only and therefore troubles little about the outer husk. If you see a tree hung with strips of white calico, it is not the tree that is being honoured but the spirit that has chosen that tree for its home; should the spirit depart to another place, the tree would be again as other trees.

Most homes among the Ibo are untidy and it would hardly strike them that the spirit's home should be any tidier. Only once did I see a perfectly kept grove, as gay and peaceful as a wayside chapel, and in tune with it, on the other side of the path, stood the *juju* priest's house resembling nothing so much as the neat house of some village *curé*.

The women are superstitious, though where faith ends and superstition begins would be hard to tell. One feels instinctively there is a dividing line but one would be unable to define it. Yet it would be important to do so as it is probably just these superstitions which will be carried over into Christianity. (The people are quick enough to observe that we ourselves are not free from the practices we condemn so severely!) On the other hand, I cannot feel, as one is so often told, that their lives are obsessed by fear—or at any rate, not more than ours are. It is true that their world is full of spirits needing

120

constant propitiation, that sickness and death can never happen through natural causes but must be the work of angry spirits or human enemies; yet this same world holds also sun and rain, children, crops, good sauce rich with palm-oil and pungent with pepper, dance and song and the jokes that fly along the file of women as they go to market. If you listen in the twilight, you hear the comfortable sounds of a sleepy village; if you watch the faces in the morning, they are smooth, unstrained. Surely terror-ridden people do not walk so freely, talk so loud, are not so bright of eye and sleek of body. Yet I would not like to pretend that their lives are unshadowed nor that they are like Rousseau's conception of the simple virtuous savage living in childlike joy amidst idyllic scenes. The children are happy; but girls can be forced into marriages that do not please them, wives can be turned away because they are barren, old women can be neglected. There can be jealousy between co-wives, suspicion, underhand revenge. There is greed and anger and, cheerful though he is, the Ibo is hot-tempered and his matchet is quickly swung. All the same, here in Nneato at least, were one to put side by side a group of black men and women and a group of white, one look at their faces, one moment of comparison would destroy the illusion that it is they only who are the slaves and we who are the free.

If the comprehension of the pagan religious situation eludes us, perhaps that of the Christian one does even more so. Here in Nneato the converts all belong to the Methodist Mission and, though numerous in themselves, are few in comparison with the density of the population. There were services held every Sunday in the church school, led by a teacher or a catechist. The church was crowded, behaviour irreproachable. Men, in singlet and shorts, or in their loin-cloths, sat on one side, women and children on the other. The children slept against their mother's shoulders or sat upon the ground, playing silent

and absorbing games with stalks of grass. The leader of
the service stood, or sat upon a collapsible wooden chair
behind a small square table over which was thrown crookedly a torn piece of cloth. He read from the Bible in
Union Ibo and commented thereon; he gave an extemporary prayer; he led the singing, also in Union Ibo.

The service lasted an hour and a half or more and
finished up with a collection. What did the people make
of this act of worship? What did they bring to it? What
did they get from it? Even an onlooker as sympathetic as
myself hardly knows what to say. I had expected that
the very simplicity of the setting would have lent dignity, the very naïveness of the worshippers would have
brought some charm, the very fact that this handful of
Christians was ringed about by the cohorts of paganism
would have awed and inspired, would have given weight
and significance to every word and gesture. Instead, I
found it ugly, alien, *dull*. I think it was that that struck
one most. How could those people sit through that halt-
ing reading of which, even with the leader's comments,
they could hardly have understood a word (I remember
the last readings I heard were from Malachi and He-
brews), that ear-splitting singing of words which, set to
a Western tune, must have lost (Ibo being, as I have said,
a tone language) all their meaning? Religion, as expressed in the service, seemed neither to have grace nor
colour, neither mystery, nor joy, nor life. It seemed to
bring nothing into their lives except a new set of formu-
las, a new field for self-importance and—was this the
chief attraction?—a new financial interest. Watching
the service one almost felt it might be so. As I have said,
the behaviour of the congregation was exemplary. There
was no whispering nor fidgeting nor squabbling for a
seat on the narrow mud benches, the faces were immo-
bile, the eyes fixed brightly and intently on the leader.
They swallowed it all, hymns and psalms, prayers and
Malachi. But when the time came for the collection, it

was as if the wind of the Spirit had at last blown through the building. First an enormous enamel basin was handed round in which we put our halfpennies or our cowries, but this procedure did not satisfy everybody. Many preferred to come up the aisles themselves and personally place their offering on the table or on the ground near it. Soon there was a little mountain of cowries and immediately a couple of lads started counting them up, dividing them into little groups of six cowries each which were carefully ranged all over the mud floor. Late-comers to the table, impeded by sleepy babies, trod on these groups and all the work had to be done over again. . . . But the best was yet to come. Some, in a district which was not poor but short of actual cash, brought their offerings in kind: yams, cassava, peppers, native candles, and such like. These gifts were auctioned there and then to the members of the congregation. The excitement was intense, the bidding fast and furious. The finest lot I saw offered was a pair of white woollen baby's shoes crocheted by a schoolgirl home for the holidays. It was knocked down amid great enthusiasm to a stalwart man clad in a loincloth.

When the auction was over, there was still a roll call to be gone through and the church accounts to be made up. Not for a moment did the interest of men or women abate. All this they appreciated, it was part of the fabric of their lives, it was a reality they knew and understood. I do not suggest for a moment there was anything unseemly in the scene. It was only curious as representing what appears to be the culminating point of interest in an act of worship. Yet, if the Ibo's highest expression of himself is in finance, then it is no doubt good that he should sanctify it in this way.

As to how far Christianity affects the people's customs, it is hard to say. That it has a civilizing influence along certain lines, there can be no doubt. A Christian would not kill a man so readily as a pagan, would not try to put medicine upon him so often, would not throw out twins or deformed children in the bush—but neither must the civilizing influence of Government in such cases be forgotten. As to their ordinary lives, I was perhaps not in a position to know what change, if any, had taken place; nor, if there had been a change, whether it was due to an inward change of heart or to an outward conformation with the rules of this new society they had joined, membership of which, though sadly expensive, at least conferred upon them a certain prestige and some few advantages. What the women thought of it all, I could not make out. Mary's religious classes were well attended but she admitted herself that when there was not a sewing-class to follow, they were less well attended. And how could one be surprised? The women were content—what would urge them to seek a new faith? They were not yet sufficiently intellectually developed to doubt their old one, which after all fulfilled their greatest need in its reverence for fertility; and they were not yet sufficiently emotionally developed even to know what was meant by a God of love, from what sins a Saviour could redeem them, nor for what sorrows He could comfort them.

If the Ibo woman's comprehension of religion is impossible for us to gauge, what of her comprehension of love? Mary used the word and, exceptional again, divined much of its meaning. I do not think other women had as yet any conception of what it stood for. To the girls, marriage, arranged by the parents, was the natural goal. It involved a change of status, a new importance; above all, it meant the possibility of having children. So long as the man was not too old or too ugly, I doubt whether they considered the emotional relationship at all, or guessed even that it might exist. Once married, they took their husbands for granted and married life seemed on the whole to be an easy-going affair of give and take. Although I am convinced that the native does not regard

the payment of dowry as 'buying' a woman in any sense
of the word, any more than the French parents 'buy' a
son-in-law when they offer him their daughter's *dot*, yet
he probably does regard his wife as his possession, just as
the Englishman did till a short time ago; but on the
other hand, he knows he must treat her fairly well or she
will run back to her parents and if the case goes against
him, he will lose both wife and dowry. As to the wife,
though she will have to abandon her children to her
divorced husband even if he is the guilty party, no stig-
ma is attached to her (as there would have been in the
case of an English divorcee, even an innocent one) and
she is free to marry again as soon as a suitor presents
himself. That the wife resented being regarded in the
light of a possession I very much doubt. She knew that
in the last resort it was she who brought forth the children her husband craved for as much as she did; it was
she who (to a large extent) grew and cooked the food he
could not do without. But now her attitude may no
longer be so satisfied. She is being taught that Christian
marriage is based upon love, and though she does not
know what love is, she immediately feels dissatisfied
with pagan marriage. She is being told she is not a chattel, and immediately she feels conscious that she is being
treated like one. Here again it seems to me that missionaries and educators take too readily for granted that
primitive woman is capable of more feeling than she
really is and ascribe to her sentiments and sufferings
which she does not really feel. The woman, quite naturally, plays up to this conception of herself. Who can resist the temptation to have a grievance even if the nature
of the grievance be barely understood?

As to their attitude on the vexed questions of polygamy and monogamy, it varied with each informant. I
am inclined to think that the women who have no contact with Western opinion are satisfied with a polygamous order and can derive some vanity from it. The

125

more wives a man has, the more she feels she has
married somebody of importance, and if by her capacity
as a manager she can save enough money to pay the
dowry of yet another wife, she has the supreme satisfaction of hearing the latter say: 'This is the woman who
made it possible for my husband to pay my dowry, greatly will I honour her.'

But a woman of the younger generation will seek
satisfaction in another way: for her a monogamous marriage means partly that there will be no jealousies between co-wives, the bickering 'that's your work, not
mine', but especially that in the absence of other wives,
it would be on her alone that all her husband's money
would be spent. Of the ethical nature of the question, I
think they have no inkling. They are told polygamy is
sinful and they accept the statement as one more axiom
laid down by the white man, similar to his statement
that blood circulates, that mosquitoes breed in water,
that it is criminal to make counterfeit coins, that the
earth is round. They agree because it seems wisest and
quickest and politest to do so and the words hold so little
meaning for them that they do not even rouse a clash of
opposition.

Certainly there are advantages in monogamy for the
man as well as for the woman: less money to be collected
for dowries, possibly less nagging in the home, a certain
pride in being able to speak of 'my loving wife'—but
what of the moment when house and farm-work fall
heavy on the one woman and labour has to be hired and
paid for? What of the two and a half or three years during
which a mother suckles her child and even a Christian
husband hesitates so to scandalize public opinion as
to go near her? What of the girls who, owing to a
shortage of husbands, do not get married and, in the present economic situation, have only one way of gaining
money and independence? And both money and independence they will have. No more than the modern

Family Bonds

English girl is content to live at home arranging flowers in the drawing-room, will the Ibo girl be content to help her mother in home and farm indefinitely. In Nneato, the problem is not yet so urgent as it is in other less 'bush' parts, but it already exists and one wonders how it will be met. So far, I think the moral standard of the girls according either to native or European ideas is still high. Though in olden days, the punishments for adultery were heavy, I am not sure how strictly they were carried out nor how far they were an effectual check, but it is certain that prostitution was practically unknown. Not only was it punished with the utmost severity, but there was little room for it. Now, with changing conditions, opportunities and temptations are on the increase.

The emotional bond between parents and children has already been alluded to. What of that between children and parents? As far as I could see, the married daughter remained friendly with her mother, or rather, once the mother's anxiety as to the successful marriage of the daughter was allayed, there was a recrudescence of affection on the part of the mother. Though marriage in Nneato, and throughout Ibo-land, is patrilocal, the wife was free to visit her old home, and in any case the markets provided frequent meeting-places. As to the sons, the mother's affection never waned and on the whole I think this affection was reciprocated.

When asked out of ten husbands, how many would love their wives and out of ten sons how many would love their mothers, Mary, after profound reflection, answered: 'Three husbands would love their wives but seven sons would love their mothers,'[1] and I felt that not only was she right but that probably this mutual bond between mother and son represented the highest emotional development of which either were yet capable.

[1] This same proportion was spontaneously given me by other women in other places.

Women

And now let us take emotion in a wider, less personal aspect: love of one's fellow beings, pity, charity, love of beauty. As in other tribes, the Ibo possesses family loyalty to a marked degree and this not only towards members of his own immediate family but towards all members of his kindred, towards those whom he loosely terms 'brother'. But I do not think this feeling would extend beyond his family. If the dwellers in a town unrelated to his own, though Ibo-speaking like himself, were starving, I do not think it would even enter his mind that it could be his duty to help them. Only if he were in a distant country would he become conscious that ties of race in themselves demanded such and such actions on his part. For example, if an Ibo clerk died say, in Kano, all the other Ibo would attend, and probably contribute to his funeral irrespective of what town he came from or to whom he was related. The giving of hospitality to strangers and travellers is a thing apart, the laws of which I have not investigated except in so far as they came under my direct observation.

As for pity, I suppose the capacity for pity cannot exist without the capacity for love. Each family is under the obligation to care for its own sick and infirm, but this is a definite obligation laid down by law and custom, and were it only founded on sentiment would probably not be carried out.

Of charity in the way of almsgiving, the *sadaka* of the Mohammedans of the North, there appears to be no trace. Indeed one of my most vivid impressions was the difference in the way an act of mine was received. There was a leper at Ubaha, a pitiful sight, to whom I gave a blanket. It was the rainy season, he had only a grass shelter, and had never asked for anything. A number of villagers were present. A great shout of laughter rose up when they saw what I had done and men and women rocked with mirth. They were quite glad the leper should have the blanket and did not grudge it him, but

128

A WATER HOLE, NGURU

A BUSH TEACHER'S HOUSEHOLD

A SCHOOLGIRL

Aesthetic Appreciation

the idea of giving away a perfectly good blanket to a leper towards whom you were under no obligation appeared to them supremely comic. If the same thing had happened in the North, the onlookers would have said to each other: 'She is doing a good thing. She is giving alms. Thus is it written in the Book.' There would have been a stir of approval and some murmured '*Amin!*' Very likely it would have been but lip service but the fact that they recognized, even by empty gesture, the sacramental nature of almsgiving created a common ground on which to stand.

To be able to evaluate the Ibo appreciation of beauty is an almost impossible task. One is inclined to think that it cannot be deep or they would have tried to create more of it around them, in buildings, decorations, crafts. I do not think they see natural beauty nor the technical beauty of a well-hoed furrow, or a well-turned pot, or a well-made roof. But the women's natural sense of colour, before it is spoilt by attempts to copy Western clothing, is excellent. They can take three pieces of crudely patterned Manchester cloth, glaringly unmatchable, and somehow blend them harmoniously in kerchief and kirtle, but the 'educated' few will equally well wear in the heart of the bush a pink satin 'frock' with a crimson woollen tam o'shanter, brown stockings, and high-heeled black shoes. I do not think they see form but they certainly see movement, chiefly, of course, as expressed in dancing. One evening some girls and children came to dance. At first the children were shy and would take no part but soon the girls formed a half-circle and, softly clapping their hands to give the rhythm, called first one child and then the other to dance alone in the centre. I can remember nothing more lovely than the movements of those small bodies. Looking at the girls' faces, I saw they were as carried away as I was and our impulse to put our arms round those little things that had given us such delight was a common one.

129   E

Women

The outside influences under which the people of Nneato come are not many. At first sight, on the material side, the background of this self-sufficing agricultural community seems nearly unaltered. The farming methods remain the same; the buildings, except for the very occasional 'pan'-roofed houses of rich men, are unchanged. Few European utensils beyond a few bush-lamps, enamel bowls, spoons, have been introduced. Roads, owing to the amount of bridging and cutting that would have to be done, are lacking and therefore the lorry, swiftest of all transforming agencies, is lacking also. Emigration, seasonal or permanent, is unknown. Individual men go off to work in Fernando Po or try their luck at Onitsha, Enugu, Aba, Port Harcourt, but the number is still small. Laws are administered by the old village councils of elders. No forced labour, no work on European plantations, disturbs the normal cycle of their lives.

Yet when one looks closer, one finds numberless traces of infiltration. In the eyes of the Ibo, taxation is perhaps the greatest innovation they have had to accept and it looms extravagantly large in the native mind, considering that in Nneato the tax (in 1935) is only 3s. 6d. a year for each adult male,[1] old or infirm excepted. It is true that there is some difficulty in getting that amount in actual cash and one wonders sometimes whether the old system of short periods of so-called 'forced labour' was not after all the most equitable way of taxing people in primitive stages. Apart from taxation, one cannot see that the rule of the white man lies heavy upon them. Their liberty to kill their neighbours and to carry out some of the crueller practices of their religion is curtailed, but little else. On the other hand, they have much more security of person and property, and can move about more freely. This last facility leads to a certain widening

[1] Owing to better trade conditions, the tax was raised to four shillings in 1937.

of their horizon and an increase in contacts, with resultant diminution of customary authority.

As trade in the Nneato area is chiefly local, it has not much importance as an outside influence. Only the comparatively few men who carry the palm-oil to the European firms are directly affected by it; apart from them it has made practically no change in the ordinary life of the community. Nevertheless even the indirect knowledge that such and such things exist and can be bought, even the occasional sight of the white man's products, are creating new desires and these desires are being reinforced and, so to speak, legitimized by education and religion. The boy learns about the wonders of mechanical progress and immediately feels justified in wanting a bicycle; the girl is taught it is wicked to go naked and, delighted to find that vanity and righteousness go hand in hand, runs home and begs her mother to buy her a frock.

In the eyes of the investigator, it is the Mission that has wrought the greatest outward, if not always inward, changes. Yet it is hard to define them. There are naturally a number of obvious points; the cleavage, comparatively slight though it is, between pagans and Christians; the spread of literacy; of English; of clothing. But apart from these, there is an intangible something which has penetrated far beyond the actual range of church and school, all the more remarkable when one remembers the enormous population and the little direct influence the Mission can exert. After searching in vain for a definition of this minute alteration I found myself describing it as 'singlet-minded'. A singlet, the cheap white vest of English make one finds in every market where a few European goods are sold, is the Ibo's first step towards civilization. Schoolboys or lads or grown men, they 'go buy singlet'. But even those who have not got a singlet nor would even think of buying one, are yet psychologically on the way to wearing one.

131

This fact carries with it a willingness for change, a readiness to see old customs vanish, an acceptance of new values. It was general: even when talking to old men mumbling over their palm-wine, to *juju* priests, to farmers hacking down the undergrowth in some hidden corner of the bush, to diviners, to rainmakers, the reflection of the ghost of a singlet was in their eyes. Not till I got up into the hills, where there were walls of stone and the men carried spears upon their shoulders did the reflection vanish. Singlet-mindedness is naturally more marked the more Western contacts the people have, but it is all the more striking in Nneato just because these contacts were so few and that it existed even in those sections of the community one would have thought were the most conservative. It would probably be an exaggeration to say that this attitude of mind is entirely due to Mission influence, direct or indirect, or that the Mission is consciously aiming at such a result. Government, too, plays its part. Natural growth and development also. But the Mission means education and education means a miraculous ladder to fame and fortune, the renown of which has spread to the remotest parts. The people I have talked to, men and women, had little idea what education was in itself and none at all of the difficulties surrounding the giving of a good education. That teachers needed to be trained, that school books needed to be printed, that a sound curriculum needed to be thought out, all these necessities were brushed aside. 'Give us school,' was what they cried, indifferent as to whether the schools were good or bad, or rather incapable of appreciating that there could be a difference between them. This undiscriminating demand for schools is another danger: it is naturally hard for the Mission to resist the call as schools mean converts and new spheres of influence. Rather than forgo these and risk antagonizing the people by a refusal to meet their wishes, schools are opened which are inadequately

132

staffed, supervised, and equipped. The people themselves have to pay for these schools, good or bad, and in certain cases I am thinking of, I do not consider the people are getting their money's worth. In all good faith, they are being rather badly cheated. One is made all the more conscious of this when one compares the three shillings and sixpence they pay, with what heavy groans and expostulations, as annual tax to Government and for which they receive security, justice, roads, medical services, posts and telegraphs, etc., with the amounts they have to collect among themselves for·the monthly payment of the teacher,[1] often only an incompetent Standard IV lad, self-satisfied, lazy, indifferent, who neither by character nor training can impart anything worth having.

When I asked whether the relationship between parents and children altered when these children went to school, 'go learn book' as the saying is, various answers were given but on the whole there did not seem to be many complaints on the part of the parents that the children were less respectful or less helpful in the home. The chief disadvantage, and a great one, is that the boys do not regularly go with their parents to the farms, and thus do not unconsciously acquire both a love for the soil and the knowledge of how to make use of it. The same can be said of the girls but in Nneato the number of girls attending school is still very small. When I asked the mothers what form of education they wanted for their girls, they answered promptly they did not mind much about 'book' but they wanted their daughters to know how to manage their homes and how to care for their children.

One cannot help feeling that the present method of

[1] In this case, 'teacher' would only be a courtesy title as now no one can be a registered teacher who has not passed Standard VI, but vernacular schools or religious classes can employ non-registered men.

133

co-education, in all but the boarding-schools, is a mistake from many points of view.[1] I know it is largely a question of funds and of staff but also perhaps of inadequate thought given to a subject of which the importance is greater than male authorities might realize.

[1] This conclusion seems to have been reached by the Roman Catholic Mission, which is strenuously endeavouring to open girls' day-schools as well as boarding-schools.

VII

Sophisticated-Primitive Woman
—in Nguru

Reasons for choice of Nguru area. What a farming-trading community looks like. How one lives in it. What the women do in it. Mbari houses.

My reasons for going to Nguru were threefold. In the first place, though life was still lived under purely native and agricultural conditions, it was one degree more developed than that of Nneato in that it was in much more constant contact with the outer world and therefore provided an example of the next stage in transition. In the second place, it was in the midst of what had been the Riot area and some of the leading women who had taken part in the Riots were natives of Nguru. It would be interesting to know how much the Riots were still remembered and what shape that memory took. In the third place, it was the most thickly populated portion of the Owerri Division with a density said to be as much as a thousand to the square mile, and I was anxious to see what result such over-crowding and possible shortage of food would have upon the children.

Unfortunately, I had no guide and companion with me such as Mary Anderson had been. Salome, my present interpreter, quick-witted as she was, was too young to deal with the sometimes difficult situations that arose, nor had she any previous knowledge of the district. I had,

135

however, the help of an intelligent native trader whom
I will call B., who had a small store at Inyeogugu and a
depot for oil and kernels, which he bought from the local
farmers and sent in his own lorries to be sold in Aba and
Owerrinta. Also my known friendship with two white
woman doctors, one from the Roman Catholic Mission,
and one from the Church Missionary Society, who occasionally visited this neighbourhood, served as an introduction.

I was in Nguru in May and June, that is to say, just
after the beginning of the rainy season when crops were
already growing and in some cases weeding had already
begun.

The district is practically flat, covered with oil palms,
interspersed with a few rare forest trees, which generally
marked the site of an old shrine or a piece of 'bad bush'.
Though so monotonous, the scenery is curiously difficult
to describe. As one tops a small rise on the road which
comes from Owerri, the general aspect of the country
lying before one is that of a vast sea of palm forest. From
that distance it looks impenetrable, forbidding, lifeless.
Once one is in it, one sees that path after path winds
away between the palm trunks, plot succeeds plot planted
with coco-yam and fringed with maize, voices sound
from unseen huts, strings of natives appear from nowhere, cross one's road and disappear. Although the
ground beneath the palm-trees is clear except where a
patch of last year's undergrowth forms a green thicket,
the trees grow so close together that each path forms a
channel of brilliant light cutting through what seems by
contrast to be semi-darkness. At first, there is a certain
restfulness in finding one's horizon narrowed down to
these few yards but after a time the need for a distant
horizon becomes like a painful thirst.

So serious is the shortage of land that cultivation is
practically continuous, very little land being allowed to
lie fallow and then never for more than a year or two.

Communications and Long-Distance Trading

The sandy soil, both by nature and from being over-worked, is poor and the only manure available is that of the scanty ashes produced by the burning of weeds and light undergrowth at the beginning of the farming season.

Water, though the rainy season is longer and heavier than in Nneato, is scarce and, except for a very few streams, has to be collected in large holes by the side of the paths while the rains are on. These water-holes are strictly apportioned for drinking and washing purposes, but even they dry up shortly after the rainy season is over and then water must be fetched often from three or four miles away. With the help of Native Administration funds, efforts are now being made to sink wells wherever the need is greatest but they have to go very deep before reaching permanent water and will be costly, if valuable, improvements.

On the other hand, roads are good and comparatively numerous and even the bush paths are sometimes ten to fifteen feet wide and well cleared, though the bulk of them are of the usual Nigerian pattern, just wide enough for a single traveller.

Trade, as in Nneato, is of two kinds, but here the long-distance trade is of far greater importance than it is there, for we are now in the midst of the palm belt and the trade in palm-oil and kernels is intense. A small proportion of the oil is kept for household use.[1] The rest is sold in small quantities, perhaps a bowlful containing a pint or two at a time, by the farmer's wife in the local market. She sells it to the 'small' middlemen, i.e. young men who cycle round the bush markets collecting enough oil to fill the two or three kerosene-tins precariously balanced upon their bicycles and which they in turn sell to the 'big' native middlemen, or to the collecting-stations

[1] About two tablespoonfuls a day is used by an average household of two adults and three children, mixed in the sauce which is eaten with the mashed yam, coco-yam or cassava which forms the staple food.

of European firms along the main road, or to the firms themselves in the larger towns, the price obtained increasing by a penny or two the farther they carry their wares. Occasionally the farmer himself will wait till he has collected a kerosene-tinful and will carry it direct to the 'big' middlemen or to the European firm, but as the native gets more and more averse to carrying a load a long distance, the more he will make use of the travelling middlemen even if he gets a smaller price from them.

This trade all goes south to Owerrinta, to Aba, to Itu, to Port Harcourt. The oil or kernels is sold for cash which is often immediately reinvested in cloth or other European goods, for sale in the up-country markets. When I was in Nguru, the price of oil per four-gallon tin was about 3s. 6d. In the boom it had risen to 10s. and had dropped during the worst of the depression to 10d.

The local trade, carried out mainly by women, has the same relatively small economic importance and great social importance that it had in Nneato. Numbers of small markets are held in rotation in various localities, generally under immense branching trees at some spot where several paths meet or, in the case of the larger ones, where several roads meet. The biggest of all, perhaps even bigger than that of Eziama, and attended by an exceptional number of men, buyers of palm-oil, was that of Inyeogugu, held every eight days on a site close to the Native Court. It began about 9 a.m. and continued till 2 p.m. On one occasion, on one road alone, around 10 a.m., an average of a hundred persons going to the market passed every three minutes. As there were six roads leading to the market, the number of buyers and sellers can be imagined. The market itself contained the usual foodstuffs, yams, coco-yams, cassava, maize, ground-nuts (locally grown in small quantities), peppers and leaves for flavouring sauces, stock fish, palm-oil, meat. There were pots and mats brought down from Okigwi and native bags and baskets; also European

138

goods such as cotton cloth, soap, bush-lamps, enamel basins, cheap frocks, singlets, tobacco, tubes of vaseline and bottles of hair oil. There was also a little live-stock such as fowls, and a few goats and sheep. The meat on sale, if beef, was nearly always that of cattle driven down from the North by Hausa traders and sold and slaughtered just before a 'big' market-day. Although expensive, it was readily bought up, often in large quantities, which were carried away to be re-sold in remoter bush markets. The fact that meat was so plentiful in a non-cattle raising district (indeed, when Nguru is mentioned to almost any Ibo, he immediately says, 'They have plenty meat there') is a sure indication that the population cannot be as penniless, as it likes to make out.

One special feature of the market which gave it, in spite of its setting of gigantic trees and near-by *juju* shrine, a sophisticated appearance, was the number of bicycles offered for sale (as was indicated by a little piece of palm branch twisted round the handle-bars) or belonging to people attending it. I personally once counted sixty-nine for sale and a little later my cook counted a hundred and fifty. Cheap as they probably had been even when new (the second-hand ones were priced from £2 to £6), they represented in the aggregate an unexpected amount of wealth.

Housing seemed even poorer than it was in Nneato and was planned with even less uniformity. The compounds were generally smaller and were sometimes surrounded by a fence of closely woven palm leaves instead of a mud wall. Some of the huts were not enclosed at all. All of them were rectangular, some standing alone, some in a row, some in a three-sided square enclosing a small courtyard to which one gained access through another hut generally used as a stable for sheep and goats. They all had a curiously slum-area appearance which is rare in Nigeria, and though not the back-to-back tenements of the old East End of London, had just the same frowzy

139

and insanitary look. One expected to find women with cloth caps on their heads, arms akimbo, on discoloured doorsteps. Even the *ɔbi* which is such a distinctive feature in Ibo-land was sometimes lacking and none of the huts had a veranda. I saw no trace of decoration anywhere: there were none of the fine carved doors as seen in Okigwi and elsewhere and even the walls and couches were not well rubbed, though possibly the nature of the local mud with which they were built made this more difficult. It is also possible that the housing was especially poor in the immediate vicinity of Inyeogugu; when my walks took me five or six miles farther afield, there were better specimens, more rural and more home-like. It must also be remembered that I saw Nguru in the rainy season, a period when habitations would look at their worst. All the same, it seems strange that an area which must have collected such great wealth during the oil boom should not show any outward signs of it and should not, as far as one can see, have done anything to effect a permanent improvement in conditions of life.

As live-stock, there were a fair number of sheep and goats and plenty of fowls of a rather better type than seen—and eaten—elsewhere. This is perhaps due to the noticeable absence of hawks, whose presence in other parts, for ever circling above its head, renders the Nigerian fowl a mass of tight-strung nerves. There were hardly any cattle of the little white and black kind so familiar in Nneato, and on asking the reason I was told they were so frequently stolen that it was not worth while keeping them. 'Only those dedicated to the *juju* were safe.' Probably the lack of pasture and, with so much cultivated land, the risk of damage to crops, also accounts for their rarity.

With such a dense population and so many farms, there is no hunting worth speaking of; nor, with so few streams, any fishing.

The men are less stocky than those of Nneato but

roughly of the same type or rather diversity of types and colouring. The women are noticeably thinner. Most of the older men go naked save for the loin-cloth of a rather broader make than the Nneato ones. Of the younger men, about two-thirds wear some one article of European clothing, be it singlet or shorts, or cap or merely a pair of dark glasses. The older women have kept to their short kirtle but some of the younger ones, especially those who have come into contact with a Mission, wear either a European 'frock', a short-sleeved, loose garment belted at the waist and generally most unbecoming to the native figure, or a kirtle coming well below the knee with a short loose blouse (*buba*) on top such as the Yoruba women also wear. Head-ties were occasionally worn but I did not see as many elaborate styles of hairdressing as in Nneato.[1]

The only weapons I saw were a very occasional bow and arrow and the ever-popular matchet. Native utensils were poor and more European ones, such as enamel basins, spoons, knives, cooking-pots, were used than in Nneato. I once asked the native trader B., whom I have already mentioned, what the people felt about local industries being driven out by English products? It was true the question was only of academic importance as regards this immediate area, as local crafts were practically non-existent, but I instanced the case of the vast pottery trade of Ilorin which he knew well and which was entirely in the hands of women. He saw the implications,

[1] Though one hardly knows to what to attribute it, I noticed in Nguru for the first time a curious phenomenon with regard to nakedness. Although it would probably be true to say that the majority of the population still go unclothed, one had not that violent impression of naked humanity one had in Nneato, where, used as one was to the sight, one was constantly conscious of these masses of naked bodies. The splendid physique of these bodies may have been the cause that they obtruded themselves so startlingly upon one's notice. In Nguru, less striking because on the whole less well developed, they made no great impression and I had to make a conscious effort to notice who was clothed and who was not.

but was quite clear that if he lived in Ilorin, he would buy kerosene-tins or enamel basins in preference to breakable pots. 'Yes,' he agreed, 'it would vex the potters' and probably ruin them but 'it would not affect the rest of the population'. Kerosene-tins would win the day whatever one tried to do. The only way out was for Nigeria to produce its own kerosene-tins. This attitude was typical of that of most of the people I spoke to, either here or elsewhere. Nearly always, one met with the same indifference to the loss of their beliefs, their industries, or their old modes of living.

The whole of this area is practically in the hands of the Roman Catholic Mission. It has numerous large schools and churches, including some girls' day-schools supervised by the Sisters of the Convent of the Holy Rosary at Emekuku.

Nguru attends Abaja Native Court, situated at Inyeogugu. It will be remembered that the old Nguru Native Court was destroyed by the women during the Aba Riots and the site has never been used again.

I left Owerri on the 7th of May 1935 and went by lorry to Inyeogugu, a distance of fifteen miles. There I camped in the District Officer's rest-house next to the Native Court. These rest-houses are mere empty mud houses thatched with palm leaves, floored with earth, very dark and damp during the rains. Finding the proximity of the Native Court was a handicap as it made the people think I was connected with Government, I moved later on to the home of the friendly trader who offered me the semi-European house he had built for himself in his own village, some three miles into the bush from Inyeogugu. He himself moved to his store at Inyeogugu, leaving me the use of half of his house while his wife (being a Christian he was a monogamist) remained in the other half.

The house was simple, sensible, and well planned.

Making Contact

Cement floors, corrugated iron roof, whitewashed walls, green-painted doors and shutters, a little garden round it enclosed by a high mud wall, it should have given a sense of coolness and cleanliness: but as my notebook tersely puts it, it was 'just off-colour'. There were weeds and high grasses in the garden, the roof leaked, the green paint was dulled, the walls were streaked with finger-marks, what furniture there was was thick with dust, the flimsy curtains drooped crooked and forlorn. As was so often the case in the semi-Western houses all over the country, it was as if the letter of home-making had been guessed at but not the spirit.

Nevertheless this house made a better centre for investigation than Inyeogugu and, again thanks to some simple medical work, I got into touch with the women and was able to talk to them rather more freely. But I was never on the same terms with them as with the Nneato women, and though welcomed in a number of homes I never liked to ask too many questions, and therefore have gathered only a few notes concerning their customs and daily lives which I can consider reliable. It should be noted, however, that the attitude of the men differed from that of the women to a marked degree. Although I had taken no special steps to get into touch with them, they seemed to accept my presence with no feeling of suspicion, answered questions comparatively freely and seemed so sensible that I was all the more unprepared for the attitude of the women.

Division of labour seemed about the same as in Nneato except that here both men and women, in addition to their farm work, are engaged in the preparation of palm-oil to a far greater extent than in Nneato. Here also it is the men who gather the *banga* and the women, occasionally helped by the men, who pound the nuts to extract the oil. The oil is the property of the men, the kernels of the women. I gather fifteen average-sized *banga* yield a four-gallon tin of oil. Unfortunately I was

143

not able to find out accurately how long the process of extracting that amount of oil would take when done by hand. I do not remember seeing any oil-presses, though these are slowly finding their way into the other oil-palm districts, noticeably in the Onitsha Province. A movement is on foot, fostered by Government, for greater co-operation between palm-oil owners. Such co-operation would not only eliminate the middlemen to a certain extent but would enable communally owned oil-presses to be set up, thus improving both the quality and the quantity of the oil.

The daily life of the women, in so far as the outward happenings of cooking, wood- and water-fetching, farming and marketing are concerned, is much the same as that of the Nneato women but, owing to the uncertain attitude of the people, I had few opportunities for leisurely and unperceived observation. Even in friendly houses, they were continually watching me and thus creating an artificial atmosphere and altering the timing of speech and action. I saw life only in jerks and never had the feeling that I was caught up in the smooth rhythm of a peasant household as had so often been the case in Eziama. But, though, as already said, division of labour is in theory much the same as in Nneato, my impression was that in practice it was not so well balanced and that, on the whole, the women worked harder than the men all through the year. This may be partly due to the fact that cassava and coco-yams form the main food supply and as these are women's crops, more work falls on them than if the staple food were yams, which would necessitate more work on the part of the men. The natives themselves recognize that yams have a greater food value than other crops—when I asked a medicine woman what, in her opinion, was the best food for children, her contempt for my ignorance was obvious: 'All men know yams are best!'—but cassava and coco-yams grow more easily and require less space. Another factor which one must begin to take into consideration is that many more children go to school and though, in that immense population, even the numerous schools that exist only absorb a comparatively minute portion of the local youth, even so many houses are partially deprived of their normal number of young helpers, with the natural consequence that more work falls on the women.

Crafts there are none, except that of the weaving of fibre cloth,[1] which is practised mainly by the men. Only in one village did I find a girl weaving and she was a cripple. This fibre cloth is woven on small or large looms of practically the same pattern as those used for weaving native cotton cloth. The specimens I saw were only fair and no great pride seemed to be taken in the making of them. In former times, all loin-cloths and kirtles were made of this cloth—even now most of the older people wear it—but with the sudden prosperity of the oil boom years, there was a great influx of European cotton goods and the craft nearly died out. Since the depression and consequent lack of money to buy imported goods, some of the old looms have been brought out again.

Arts there are absolutely none, unless one mentions here that astonishing product of art, religion, journalism and obscenity known as the *mbari* house. These houses are only to be found within an area of about a twenty-mile radius round Owerri Town. They are, as a District Officer describes them, 'a primitive combination of a temple, an art gallery, and a wax-works',[2] and present, both in the method of their building and in their aim, a yet only partially solved psychological riddle. Neither from the mass of details that I have myself collected nor from comparison with other sources of information, can I offer any complete solution.

[1] The fibre is obtained from the *tumbo* (i.e. wine) palm (*raffia vinifera*).
[2] 'Mbari Houses' by G. I. Jones, *Nigerian Field*, April 1937. This article contains some excellent photographs.

Women

The word *mbari* means 'decorated' and is applied to any house with mural decorations but these particular 'decorated houses' are dedicated to a local spirit whose desire for such a house has been communicated to its priest. It would appear that these shrines were originally much simpler, but in time both the buildings themselves and the clay figures they shelter have become more and more elaborate, even to the point of occasionally being covered by a corrugated iron roof, source of much local pride and importance! Their erection is a long and costly affair and with the increasing number of Christian converts who are naturally not supposed to take any part, the burden both of labour and funds falls heavily upon the pagan community. It is therefore all the more remarkable to find how many of these *mbari* houses are still being built, even for example in such a supposedly impoverished area as that of Nguru. Once finished, these houses are never repaired, so rain, wind, and the encroaching bush obliterate nearly all trace of them in two to three years.

Leaving out the numerous and often conflicting details, variations due to locality, and the greater or lesser sophistication of the people, the procedure is as follows: about every seven years, in a certain village, a great deal of sickness will be noticed, or failure of crops, or barrenness among women, or fires or other accidents. The people will become anxious and will ask the priest of their particular spirit to consult a *dibia* as to the meaning of these signs. Or possibly the priest himself will have a dream in which he sees the spirit wandering round, crying out that it has no house, nor food, nor bed, while its priest has every comfort. The priest, much troubled, hurries to the *dibia* who says the spirit demands a home. The priest reports this to the senior men of the village who consult together and very likely decide that nothing can be done for the moment as the people are busy with the yam planting, or the harvesting, or the rains are on,

146

or any other excuse they can think of. Several months may elapse before the spirit manifests itself again, but this time so threateningly that priest and senior men understand the work can no longer be put off. A *dibia* who is able to 'bring out' the spirit, i.e. to interpret the spirit's wishes, gives the priest the names of the builders, possibly as many as a hundred, male and female in equal numbers, and both adults and children. The village waits in dread for the priest's return—although it is an honour to be chosen by the spirit, it is also a waste of time and a great expense—and that night he and the senior men go round the village marking with a smear of chalk those houses from which builders will be chosen. 'Early in the morning, the people come out and look anxiously to see whether their houses have been marked.' Eight days later, the priest and the senior men pass round again with singing. All doors are open to hear which names will be called as the priest cries out: 'The spirit says you are its son!' or 'The spirit says you are its daughter!' No one dares refuse to go, for the spirit might kill him or harm his relatives. Once chosen, the builders become, to a certain extent, a class apart, especially at certain periods. They do everything connected with the erection of the *mbari* house, clearing the site, which is always in the vicinity of the grove dedicated to the spirit who has asked for it, putting up the high and solid fence which hides the building from the view of passers-by and which is only removed when the work is entirely finished, bringing the mud for the walls and the special ant-heap earth for the figures, the palm-leaves and the bamboos for the roof, etc. When the male workers have put up the buildings, both men and women make the clay figures and paint the elaborate designs upon the walls. If the *mbari* house is to be a particularly fine affair, a man known to be a specialist in modelling and designing may be called in from a neighbouring town to teach the workers. He starts them in the right way, then goes on to teach another batch of workers somewhere else, and in time returns to inspect the first batch 'all same Superintendent of Education'.

The most common design for a *mbari* house is a central square-shaped shrine consisting of a square central 'cell' surrounded by an open 'veranda' and covered by a high, steeply-pitched roof supported by four thick pillars at the four corners of the veranda. In a half-circle round the back of this shrine lie what can best be called the 'cloisters', a low gallery roofed over. In the shrine itself is placed the figure of the spirit to whom the *mbari* house is dedicated, and also figures of other local spirits. In the cloisters are exhibited the 'wax-works', a strange medley of humans and animals, legendary monsters, native policemen, District Officers, *dibia* with their divining stones, tailors with their sewing-machines, curious reproductions of Madonnas and Crucifixions, motor-cycles and aeroplanes, women in childbirth, English and German soldiers firing at one another, schoolgirls with their satchels, goats with men's heads, and a variety of quite startling obscenities, especially those most strictly forbidden by Ibo custom.

The workers themselves, who for certain periods leave their homes and sleep in a large hut near the priest's house, are said to have what was described to me as 'goings-on'; yet I am not convinced that full sexual intercourse is permitted. The law of exogamy is so strict that it seems unlikely that men and women belonging to the same kindred should be allowed to have intercourse even under the most abnormal circumstances. On the other hand, a ceremony of purification, in some form or other, does certainly take place at the end of the building period and before the workers return to normal life. Another curious point is that, the moment the fence has been torn down, the workers themselves rush to look at the figures as if they had never seen them before and, with cries of amazement and horror, pretend that they are shocked to think that anyone could have produced such scandalous sights.

Whatever esoteric significance, if any, a *mbari* house may have, its ostensible *raisons d'être* may be given as (*a*) an act of worship and propitiation towards an angry spirit; (*b*) a channel of expression for an artistic instinct displayed with cunning and resource in the often remarkable figures, and with real beauty in the harmoniously coloured and wonderfully balanced patternings; (*c*) a representation of everything that, to the Ibo mind, has news value and which it is good for the spirit to know (when I asked why representations of, say, a *dibia* or Native Court members were included, since the spirit must surely be familiar with such ordinary sights, the answer was: 'It is like when the pupils give a concert in the Government School. They do the new school things but also native things so as to show that they know what goes on in their own town'); (*d*) as, possibly, a legitimatized discharge in objective form of the sexual repressions imposed upon the community by tribal law and custom.

This is not the place to describe the complicated rules which govern the lives of the workers during the building period, the ritual 'marriages' between the male and female workers, the special food they must eat, of the best quality so as to give them strength, the dress they must wear and the changes in that dress at moments which seem to correspond with more intensive work and closer retirement, the songs they alone can sing and which are taught to them by the spirit itself. Nor can the ruses be told by which workers seek to escape from their obligations nor the profit the priest can make out of this desire; nor can the sacrifice be described for which the priest himself must pay so as to ensure the personal safety of the workers (a version of the Employers' Liability Act?), nor the truce which exists, or should exist, in the village during the whole of the building time. But

149

mention cannot be omitted of one more instance of the Ibo's devotion to children, a devotion with which even the spirits are credited. Even quite tiny children will be 'called' to be *mbari* house builders for, though 'the spirit knows they cannot do any work for it, it likes to feel them round it and wants people to know they belong to it'. These children have their bodies rubbed with yellow or red 'paint' and wear black threads round their necks just like their elders but, delightful detail, the spirit allows someone else to hold the long wands they ought by right to carry, for fear that 'such small children might fall over them and hurt themselves'.

No one who has ever seen a *mbari* house can forget the impression of teeming, exuberant, one could almost say exultant, life that it conveys. Some Indian temples, even some corners of Gothic churches, might give the same feeling, but here it is a more concrete, more naked display, with no veil of allegory nor symbolism, more this-worldly than other-worldly. All that the community knows of life, all that it has seen of new things, all that it has heard of strange reports, is crammed together into this small patch of space. The material ousts the spiritual or rather the spiritual is so modernized that we do not recognize it. What of spirit can be found in a God of Thunder dressed in shorts and puttees, a sun-helmet upon his head? Yet there is a great variety in the 'feel' of these *mbari* houses. One I know, on the edge of a main road, seems frankly to have been built to attract tourist traffic, if such a thing were already known in Nigeria, and might easily bear the sign 'Ye Olde Mbari House', so shoddy and commonplace it is. Others show in every detail what care and pride have gone to their making. One I had the luck to find deep in the bush near Inyeogugu had only been finished the week before, and was really admirable both in architecture and in ornament. The priest was absent, but some of the older men took me round in the most friendly fashion and were obviously pleased that I appreciated the skill with which cubes and arcs had been combined and the accuracy with which the decorative designs were carried out on walls and pillars. It was interesting to remark that, though they let me gaze unmoved at figures and scenes which European standards would have labelled indecent, they carefully moved round so as to screen from me other scenes which they *themselves* felt to be improper. From the glimpses I was able to obtain, our opinions would have exactly coincided: the first were merely, and often humorously frank; the second were unpleasantly and perversely obscene. 'Nice' men would not like a 'nice' woman to see them. Once more I was made conscious of the underlying delicacy of mind which so facilitates the white woman's relation with the black man even in the most difficult situations. But perhaps the most uncanny memory I have was when, just before dark, in the midst of a tangled thicket, half covered with snake-like creepers, I discovered an almost full size model of a railway engine. Although far from any village, the site must have been that of a *mbari* house of which this was now the only remains. Built of mud and bamboo and kerosene-tins, with grass and ferns grotesquely pendant from roof and funnel, it loomed gigantic, incredible. And propped up in the cab, twisted round towards me, half disintegrated, was the clay figure of the white driver, so corpse-like, seen in the gloom, that his drunken leer appalled me.

Apart from the scientific interest of the question, the building of *mbari* houses has to-day a social importance as well, presenting as it does one more problem for the newly converted Christians to solve. The Missions absolutely forbid their taking any share in the work, yet a dutiful son or daughter, if called by the spirit in whom they still half believe, must needs hesitate to refuse for fear their parents may be made to suffer for their disobedience, even if they themselves do not.

151

VIII

Sophisticated-Primitive Woman— in Nguru

What the women say of dowries and of Christian marriages. Birth customs and a gynaecologist. Women's councils.

In the same way as I was handicapped in my efforts to learn what was the daily life of the women, so I was handicapped when it came to learning what were their customs and institutions.

Marriage customs appeared to be the same as in Nneato except here the payment of the dowry seemed to raise more difficulties and parents were more ready to allow their daughters to go to their husbands before the full amount had been paid. This led to endless complaints, as either the husband made no further effort to pay the remainder of the dowry or he was genuinely unable to do so. The girl might take this as an excuse to return to her parents: the husband would then sue the parents for the portion of the dowry that had been paid and the parents would sue the husband for the portion of the dowry that had not been paid.

The actual amount of dowry was a good deal higher than that which, since the depression, had been paid in Nneato, approximately £20 as against £5. One would judge such an amount to be beyond the means of the average farmer and the parents' insistence on such a large sum is yet another cause of domestic complications.

There is also a new factor in the situation on which the women laid great stress. Though it has not been brought up elsewhere, it is possible that it is already important and will of course become increasingly so. They state that many young men remain wifeless or marry late because their parents have expended on their education all the money they would normally have laid aside for their son's marriage. In some cases, the son might be earning enough to pay the dowry himself, but if he looked as in the past to his parents to pay it for him, they would be unable to do so. In consequence the girls remain on their mothers' hands and show a growing tendency to have irregular relations with men. This the parents on the whole condone, as, should their daughter have a child, it would belong to them and in any case the amount of dowry paid, were she to marry ultimately, would not be affected; on the contrary the future husband would be pleased to know that his bride was able to bear a child. I do not think the parents actually encourage the practice nor do they often know the father's name, but neither they nor the girl feel that any shame has befallen them. Similar statements were made by various independent informants but in how far they were true or only a variant of 'I'm sure I don't know what girls are coming to these days', it was impossible to say. The Roman Catholic Sisters, who had good opportunities for knowing the girls, speak well of them and maintain that they are moral; but, chameleon-like, the Ibo, as any other native, is incredibly clever at taking on the colour of the person to whom he is speaking. My own impression is that morals are more lax than, say, in Nneato, or rather public opinion which enforced these morals is more lax. When all—men, women, and girls—are out to get what they can, discipline and stability are not to be expected, and I certainly

153

heard more stories of desertions and unfaithfulness in Nguru than anywhere else.

Christian marriages are becoming more frequent but, as one woman ingeniously put it, parents prefer their daughter not to be converted *before* marriage as her betrothed, though ready to pay the customary dowry, might not think it necessary to give all the customary presents, pots of palm-wine, etc., which are usual in pagan marriages, and the parents would feel that they had been cheated of some of their perquisites. Should the girl become a Christian after marriage, that is her and her husband's affair.

A few instances of the ways in which Christian and native marriages are entangled may be of interest:

(*a.*) A had eight wives whom he had married by native law and custom. Only one, B, had borne him a child, a son. Yet another wife, C, was chosen for him by his family and sent to him, but by that time he was thinking of becoming a Christian and wished to marry her in church after having dismissed his other wives. The wife B, who had borne him a son, refused at first to go as she wanted to look after her son (A having paid dowry, the son belonged to him, whatever happened to the wife) but A refused to keep her as he preferred C and was set on marrying her as soon as she was baptized. However, to quiet B he gave her in marriage to his brother D, who had already three other wives, and who lived in the same village as himself, so that mother and son, though now belonging to different households, would be near each other. He then married C in church. Unfortunately she bore him no child and after several years, his family prevailed upon him to marry another wife, this time by native law and custom. This woman E did bear him a son but he died in infancy, and she also was given by A to his brother D. Since then A has resigned himself and, there being no prospect of his having a child by his 'church' wife C, has undertaken, much to C's annoyance, the education of one of his brother D's daughters, as also that of the son born to him by his pagan wife B.

From the above case it will be seen that possible hardship may be inflicted upon innocent parties, i.e. the pagan wives, who are dismissed in favour of the 'church' wife;[1] the intense conflict that must arise between a man's superimposed respect for the laws of the Church and his inborn respect for the wishes of his parents in the event of his 'church' wife proving barren; the difficulties in which the Church is placed when dealing with a sincere and upright man such as A, whom it is nevertheless bound to condemn when it is found out that he has contracted a native marriage with another woman subsequent to his church marriage; and, one might add, the great convenience of retaining a few pagan relations upon whom the Christian can foist superfluous wives.

(*b*.) A, whom I often visited, was an exceptionally good-looking young wife, Roman Catholic, married in church. She had conceived twice but had miscarried owing to her husband beating her. The penances imposed upon him were of no avail and he had beaten her again just as she had conceived for the third time. She (or her parents?) summoned him and he was sent to prison for three months. In the meantime she took refuge with her parents, where she had a child, who lived. The husband was shortly expected out of prison: 'When he sees the child his heart may be glad and all will be well.' Later on, she came to tell me he had come out of prison and had gone to his own town. He had not been to see her nor offered to pay for her keep during her confinement in her father's house as would be customary.

[1] The usual practice among decent people is for the husband either to send his wives back to their homes, where they will eventually remarry and he will not claim refund of dowry; or if they do not wish to do this, he will make some provision for their maintenance. All the same I have heard a Christian woman describing with bitter indignation how she saw a newly Christianized Ibo drive away his wives 'as if they were dogs' into the bush.

Women

A was much distressed. While her husband was in prison, he could not make any money so how would he pay her parents or keep her and her child if she did go back to him? Also there was the risk that he might poison her in revenge for having summoned him. She was still with her parents but they were getting impatient, wondering how they would get back the money for her keep. To crown all, the husband still owed them half the dowry he had agreed to pay for their daughter. Both A and her husband being Roman Catholics, they could not divorce. What was her future to be?

Here again, it will be seen that the law of the Church bears heavily. One would not wish the law altered but, till the people are capable of realizing the sacramental nature of marriage, of which they, except in a very few instances, have no inkling, even as they have no inkling of the love which makes that sacramental nature understandable, one could wish that some intermediate form of contract could be devised, more elastic and therefore less likely to be broken.

One sees also the disadvantages of short-term sentences in a society where the fact of having 'done time' brings no sense of shame at all, either in the culprit's own eyes or in those of his neighbours,[1] and where the fact of his having earned no money during that period is the only point of importance. The case also shows once more the constant preoccupation with money even under circumstances when one would expect nothing but parental pity for an ill-used child. And further, A's last words revealed again what one cannot help but call the innate graspingness, or superficiality, or self-centredness of the Nguru women. A had, or so it seemed, come to me with

[1] One hears delightful stories of ambitious fathers consulting the District Officer as to what crime their son had better commit so as to get enough time in prison to be able to benefit by the training there given. In remoter districts, the convict prison at Enugu is spoken of with respectful awe as in old days we would have spoken of our universities.

156

a real desire for help and sympathy. Her quiet bearing and graceful manner were in her favour. I was touched by her confidence and genuinely moved by her tale which I knew to be true, and could easily imagine in what distress of mind she must be. She may have been —but she seemed suddenly to forget the fact, and cut through my words of sympathy and advice with a bald and insistent request that I should give her a new cloth.

(*c.*) A girl of about fourteen came one day with her eldest brother to ask Salome whether she would take her with her to Owerri where she would live with Salome's mother in a position rather like that of a German '*Haustochter*'. As her parents had not had enough money to pay all the dowry required for their eldest son's prospective wife (both son and bride were Christians and were to be married in church), they affianced this girl to an elderly pagan, who paid an instalment of dowry amounting to five pounds which went towards the expenses of the son's Christian wedding. The girl, though not yet baptized, wished to be and wanted to come to Owerri to find a Christian husband who would eventually refund the five pounds paid by the pagan and set her free. This story is not, I fear, as pathetic as it sounds. The girl came to Owerri, was well treated by Salome's mother but repaid her by ungrateful conduct and then calmly declared she would go back to her parents, having apparently quite forgotten her antipathy to marrying a pagan; but it shows the accommodating mind of the parents who in order to get the money for marrying one child to a Christian were ready to marry the other to a heathen.

(*d.*) This case concerns native marriage only but gives a good idea of the latter's possible convolutions.

The story was given me by two elderly women who came to visit me and were comparatively friendly. The elder of the two said she had been busy nursing her

157

daughter A who had just given birth to a girl B. A's first
child had been a boy. He had died while still a baby and
her husband C had accused her of killing it. Indignant
at such an unnatural accusation, she had left him and
gone back to her parents. Since then, she had conceived
by another man, D, who presumably intended marrying
her but had not yet paid dowry. In any case C now refused to accept refund of his dowry and insisted on A
returning to him with the newly born B. Although he
was not the blood father of B, she legally belonged to
him as his dowry had not been repaid and therefore the
mother, A, was still his legal wife. On the other hand,
he had not paid, as was customary, the expense of A's
confinement. Should D eventually pay dowry and C
agree after all to accept repayment of his own original
dowry, B would then belong to D even though she was
born before the refund of dowry . . . and so the tale
went on and on, with endless permutations of children-
dowry and dowry-children.

   If a case such as the above is ultimately brought to the
Native Court, it can readily be understood what its un-
ravelment will cost the District or Assistant District Officer in time and patience. The natives themselves never
lose the thread of the story, however intricate, but the
chain of their thought is made of different links than
ours.

   Birth customs showed marked difference with those of
Nneato. A woman may deliver either in her hut or in
her courtyard. The courtyard is more usual 'because of
mess' but there is no taboo against her having the baby
in her hut if she prefers it. On the other hand, she must
not be wetted by rain and she might even die if she
swallowed any so she would in any case be brought into
her hut if it began to rain before she had delivered.
(I could not discover what made rain so dangerous.) In
olden days, the mother was not allowed to drink any
water for four days, though she could drink palm-wine

and some kind of drink made with 'medicine', but now
'a new law has been passed' by which a woman may
drink water even on the day of delivery providing some
'medicine' mixed with water has been passed over her
eyes. She can wash herself on the day of delivery and the
baby can be washed too. She can also feed her baby on
the same day; and can be visited by whom she likes.
This latter custom is again the opposite of what occurs in
Nneato. Expectant mothers are either looked after by a
female relative or by a native doctor. The naming day
is one lunar month after birth. The child receives six
names, two given by the father, two by its father's
mother, and two by its mother but it will only be called
by one of them, whichever most pleases the majority.
All the mother's relatives come to the naming ceremony and also those members of her age-grade (*ebiri*)
who are her friends;[1] the father's relations also come,
the members of his age-grade and the seniors of his
town. Goats are killed and a feast is made. In olden
days, 'sacrifices were made to the spirits but all that is
over now'.

It may be of interest to give here a description of a
medicine woman who came to see me shortly after my
arrival at Inyeogugu and whom I visited several times.
She was a striking and, compared to the misery-me's
with whom I was generally surrounded, an exhilarating
figure. A woman of about fifty, 'too old to go to a man',
she valiantly admitted, spare bodied, keen eyed except
when half-closed lids veiled untold secrets, her only garment an old discoloured cotton kirtle and on her head,
surprisingly, an old velour hat crammed down. Round
her ankles she wore the narrow strips of leather bound
in several places with brass wire which showed she had

[1] My informant said that neither in Nguru nor in Owerri Town
did the women's age-grades count for much once the members were
grown up: *ebiri* were little more than groups of children gathered
together for games and dances. The men's age-grades were of course
more important.

'made ɔzɔ title'[1] and which raised her rank in the medical world from that of 'a kind of chemist' to that of a fully qualified physician. Indeed Lɔlɔ could well be looked upon as a Harley Street consultant for she was known far and wide, especially for her skill as a gynaecologist. She had a medicine for menstruation pains (which are more frequent than one would think) and was adept at turning a baby who had got into a wrong position. The method was simple: she rubbed some hot 'medicine which burned like pepper' on the woman's body over the place where she could feel the baby's head. This caused discomfort to the baby, who tried to withdraw its head from the heat and in so doing twisted itself into its right position. If the woman was already in labour, then nothing could be done and the child, having been born in an abnormal way, i.e. feet foremost, was thrown into the 'bad bush'.

If a patient who lived at no great distance was near her time, her husband brought her to Lɔlɔ's hut and she was delivered in her courtyard. If the pains went on for a long time, she gave medicine and massage. Soon after delivery, the husband would come and take the mother and the child home again. If the child was a female, the husband gave Lɔlɔ a cock, cloth, yams, and money. When the mother was about to leave, Lɔlɔ in her turn cooked her a meal of yam and fish or, if she was too busy, gave the ingredients to the woman's husband to cook for her. When Lɔlɔ went later to the woman's house to 'follow up' the case, the mother-in-law would give her a present. If the woman lived some distance away, Lɔlɔ

[1] In spite of many efforts, I have not yet sufficient information to be able to explain accurately the meaning of 'making ɔzɔ title' in the case of women. The various accounts of the ceremonies entailed seldom tallied. The only fixed point was the fact that the taking of title was a costly affair—Lɔlɔ had paid £15 down in cash which was divided among the existing title holders—and that these holders of ɔzɔ title were given the name of 'Lɔlɔ', but it did not follow that all Lɔlɔs were medicine women.

160

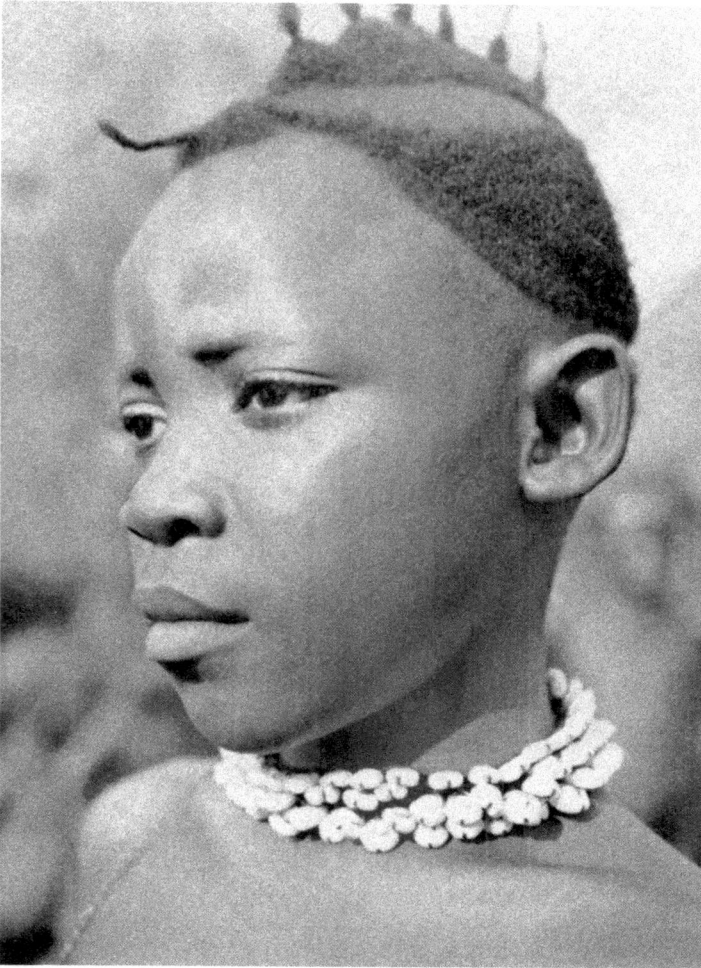

GIRLHOOD

OWERRI TYPES

attended her at her own home from the time the pains began.

For attending a delivery as much as £2 10s. could be charged, especially if it were a first one and therefore more difficult. Half the amount is paid before and half after the event but only if the results are satisfactory. (I know personally of a case where a husband took his wife to see a medicine man as she was suffering from painful periods. The husband put down 15s. in cash, the medicine man treated the woman by making a small incision on her body and, apparently, extracting therefrom a large worm and told the husband to come back with the balance of the fee, i.e. 15s., in a fortnight if his wife was cured. This was done.) Fees are, however, on a sliding scale and are presumably calculated on the wealth of the patient's family. For an average maternity case only 10s. would be charged, with the additional gift of the cloth the woman was wearing at the time her pains began. For a quite poor woman, Lɔlɔ said she would only ask 6d. and the woman's cloth. The biggest fees are obtained in cases where a husband brings his wife for treatment for sterility. These cases are the plums of the profession and a rich man will pay as much as £5 to the medicine man or woman who could enable his wife to become pregnant, even though it is recognized that children who are procured by medicine are delicate and often do not live long. I suppose the parents always hope they may be the lucky ones and will see their child survive but so well known is the fact that this is unlikely that a mother will exclaim irritably to a sickly child whom she fears may die: 'Are you so delicate because you imagine I bought you?'

Male medicine men are also consulted in cases of sterility and can command equally high fees. Lɔlɔ, at the time I knew her, was herself training her son-in-law, who, in a fit of temper, had abandoned his wife because she insisted on going to a distant market to which he had forbidden her to go, had bought second-hand a lorry which had promptly broken down, and finding himself unable to pay for it or for the repairs, had got some goods on credit from a firm in Port Harcourt, had sold them well but had spent his takings in 'foolishness' and, destitute, was on the point of fleeing to 'the land of the Hausa' when a friend found him and brought him to his mother-in-law's house. Lɔlɔ, although furious with the man for his treatment of her daughter, decided to make the best of the situation and, ever energetic and resourceful, offered to teach him her craft, an incongruous way of paying for the repairs to a derelict lorry but an eminently practical one.

From all I saw of this Lɔlɔ, I should judge she was good at her job although her surgery, which was also bed- and sitting-room, contained nothing but a few smoke-blackened gourds in which she kept dried leaves and roots and a few simple native-made instruments. But she had unlimited energy at the service of her conscientiousness, and distinct professional pride. It was with real dignity that she drew herself up in indignant denial when asked whether she would agree to procuring abortion, and there was all the contempt of the artist for the bungler when she described a maternity case to which she had been called in consultation, too late to save the victim of a colleague's mismanagement. Her manner was a perfect blend of importance and casualness, of airy frankness and weighty secrecy. It was delightful to recognize so many of one's own medical friends beneath that black skin and crushed velour hat.

As far as I could learn, a medicine man (*dibia*) would practise both curative medicine, 'medicine' in the sense of certain forms of spells, and divination. Medicine women, though also known as *dibia*,[1] practise only curative medicine and midwifery. It is true that I have heard

[1] Indeed once, while dressing ulcers beneath a tree, a passing medicine man hailed me cordially as a fellow *dibia*.

rumours of women diviners but have never met any nor could I find whether they ranked as high as male diviners.

No more than in Nneato, could I find in Nguru any trace of the systematic education of the children, no puberty rites or initiation ceremonies. Here also, all children are circumcised a few days after birth by a *dibia*. Lɔlɔ herself invited me to come and see the operation, but when it came to the point made varied excuses, perhaps because she knew the Missions did not approve of the circumcision of girls and was afraid I might try to stop her. I could hear of no 'cutting' ceremony like the one I had seen in Eziama (see p. 98).

Now what of the public life of the women of Nguru? The question which I especially wanted to study was that of the Women's councils so as to amplify the information obtained in Eziama. Unfortunately, as will be seen in the next chapter, the subject was one that could not be approached, so nervous and suspicious were the women. During the sitting of the Commission of Inquiry on the Aba Riots, there had been a good deal of indiscriminate questioning regarding these councils (or 'meetings' as they were termed) and this is possibly one of the reasons why information is now so difficult to obtain, any questions on these or kindred subjects being immediately related to the Riots and oneself put down as only one more inquirer acting on behalf of Government. It was only indirectly that I was able to learn that, as at Nneato, they had existed from time immemorial, had been abandoned after the Riots for fear Government should disapprove of them, but had within the last two years been brought to life again, though I do not think so completely as in Eziama and neighbouring districts nor did they deal with such a wide range of subjects.

Men were quite ready to speak of these councils and approved of them but their information regarding them seldom tallied. Some described them as being on the Nneato pattern; others said it was only the women of a single family (extended family?) who would meet; others that they only met together with men. I personally saw only one meeting, of about seventy women, held in a small empty market-place. It had just come to an end and from a member who was taking the same path as I was, I learnt a similar meeting had taken place a week before, and another would take place the following week. It passed 'laws' concerning the protection of crops, etc., and met thus three times in succession so as to make sure that all the members would know what the laws were. Other councils were held during the year but at long intervals. She spoke of them as well-known, important institutions, but quite local in their function. Unfortunately, this encounter took place only on the day after my arrival at Inyeogugu, before I had realized the difficulty of learning about these councils, or I would have profited more by this unusually frank informant.

The male informant who told me that the women of each family had their own council gave me an example of the kind of case they would try: a woman A sued a woman O for calling her a thief on the open road on the way to market. Both women belonged to the same kindred. A reported the matter to the women's council of that kindred. The council judged the case and ordered O, whom they knew to be a quarrelsome woman, to pay a fine of 5s. and seized from her a dog, value 5s. O appealed and the case was taken before the council of the elders (*amala*). The elders wisely said that if women were fined 10s. each time they were rude to each other, the wealth of the whole village-group would not suffice to pay the fines and dismissed the case altogether, holding the women's council had given a wrong decision.

The Christian women of Nguru, being nearly all Roman Catholics, have no meetings of church members similar to the Eziama ones.

Women's Status

That the women had a political sense and wished to exercise it, there could be no doubt. One woman who had played a conspicuous part in the Riots even went so far as to assure me that the Commission had promised that women should sit as judges in the Native Courts and asked why the promise had not been kept? Others claimed that they alone had kept the peace in their towns and spoke as if their authority were common knowledge. It is true that the men never admitted the power of the women but that is perhaps not conclusive.

IX

Sophisticated-Primitive Woman— in Nguru

How far have the women been influenced by more fre-quent Western contacts. Creation of desire through palm-oil trade. Arrestation of development through Aba Riots. Formation of anxiety state through over-population.

The foregoing chapters will have shown that it was likely to be difficult to get satisfactory answers to the three questions which, in going to Nguru, I had set myself to obtain.

The first one: 'In what way had increasing contact with the outer world influenced an agricultural commu-nity?' was perhaps the easiest. In the case of Nguru, con-tact with the outer world had primarily taken the form of trade in palm-oil. Palm-oil, much used in native cook-ing, had always been an asset to the district and an article of commerce but it was not till the advent of the white man that it had anything but a fairly local importance and it was not till during and after the War that that importance reached such huge proportions. The result of this contact can be summed up in one sweeping, simple statement: the creation of desire. It was as if the development of an economic crop, in contradistinction to that of a food crop, had disturbed the peasant's natural harmony of mind. Desire was on every side, in every form: desire for education, for jobs, for money; desire for

166

bicycles, for boots, for silk handkerchiefs; desire for power, importance, influence; desire for more food, more crops, more children; and above all, constant, vocal, universal, the desire to have what in their minds was the key to all else, better prices for palm-oil. Palm-oil domi-nated the situation, was the hub round which the whole economic and in consequence much of the social wheel revolved. Palm-oil, according as to whether its price rose or fell, made or marred; was a god showering blessings upon his people or a bogey stalking naked through the land: 'How can we pay tax if Government will not order the traders to pay us more for our oil? We have no money, we have no food. We die of hunger.' (The fact that tax for that area had been reduced to 1s. 6d. a year (in 1935) per valid adult male and that the price of oil was actually going up did not alter the refrain.) Ever since the boom which, from the psychological point of view was probably one of the greatest misfortunes that could have befallen the country, this preoccupation has influenced the whole outlook of the people. They had tasted the unknown joys of 'get rich quick' methods and have ever since lamented that golden epoch, either with bewilderment, or with anger, or with the unreasoning peevishness of a child. 'Why does Government not say that oil must be sold at the same price as kerosene (i.e. about nine shillings a tin)?' 'Why does not England send more money?' 'Write and tell the English people they must buy more of our oil.' They remain deaf to all com-parisons with the rise and fall of their own local market prices. Their minds are fixed on the miraculous solution: 'Government must distribute more money or increase the price of oil.' The fact, which one can occasionally make them admit, that they are not really hungry, nor cold, nor homeless, does not weigh with them. The boom brought with it an enormous influx of European wares of all kinds and at the same time vastly increased the native's purchasing power. His desires were awakened

167

and he had the means of satisfying them. His desires are still awake but the possibility of satisfying them no longer exists. He had seen himself on the highroad to material success (the only form which he, at present, recognizes), advancing with incredible ease and swiftness. Now he is back again on the old familiar path, toiling dully for food to live.

Whether the still constant contact with other centres such as Owerri, Aba, and Port Harcourt, has any good result in the broadening of the people's minds or whether it only makes the young men increasingly discontented with their normal farmer's lot, I could not decide. Although there was nothing like a serious exodus, nearly every household had a relative in one or other of these towns; their wives came back regularly for a spell of farm work; they themselves paid frequent visits and this coming and going, these 'week-ends', gave Nguru a curious atmosphere of suburbanism. Eziama had been the 'country' as much as if one had been in a Dorset valley; Nguru was not. Here one had the distinct though unexpected impression that, though one was living in what appeared to be a purely agricultural community, these people were urban rather than rural minded. The inhabitants of Nneato were akin to all the peasants one knew. Except that their manners were not so good and that they seldom had the distinction of those born on the soil, they were brothers to the Sussex labourer, to the Pyrenean peasant, to the Hausa farmer. There were whole expanses of their minds one could recognize because they reflected the universal things of the earth, rain and drought, sprouting leaves and green shoots. One moved easily beside their thoughts because they were common to all who work the soil and one could share without effort their pride, their anxiety, their satisfaction, their fear. But in Nguru this kinship seemed to be lacking. In some strange way, though these people lived by the soil, they seemed alien to it. The eyes of the men

168

who looked up for an instant from their task of tying up the yam tendrils reflected nothing familiar. The women planting the coco-yam seedlings, though they did it with care and patience knowing how much depended on it, had their thoughts elsewhere. How much this attitude is the actual result of contact with the outside world and consequent opening up of other means of livelihood and other methods of living, and how much it is inherent in the character of the Nguru population, I could not determine. It is possible that even the stoutest example of 'the born farmer' would lose heart and interest when faced with the problem of getting a reasonable crop out of such crowded and weary land.

As to the result of Western contact on things more intangible, such as the religious life of the community, its political institutions, the opinions and behaviour of the women, I feel I can only make very brief and tentative statements.

With regard to the religious situation, it has already been said that the Roman Catholic Mission holds practically the whole of this area. This Mission, having a far larger European staff than any other, is enabled to supervise its work effectively and to keep its members in direct touch with the Fathers who are constantly moving about. As is usual in Ibo-land, there is a real liking for going to church and the congregations are enormous. One Sunday, hearing a Father was coming to say Mass at Inyeogugu just after dawn, I went to the large mud-built school which served also as church. The building was filled to bursting with men, women, and children— there must have been at least 700 people there while a crowd equally large stood outside. All these people had walked in from the surrounding villages, starting long before daylight. Before the stars had faded, I had heard the padding of their feet along the sandy track that passed my rest-house. The service seemed to fit the congregation better than the one I had attended in the little Methodist church at Eziama. Though the altar was only a wooden table askew and the temporary chancel was unaccountably stacked with bottles and buckets and calabashes of water, though the heat, even at that early hour, was so great that we all streamed with sweat, though the crowd was so packed that once we were on our knees, we could not get to our feet again, yet the form of worship seemed somehow less alien, the Latin less out of place than a twisted Ibo or imperfect English. Though here also there was the sound of innumerable pennies clanking into the huge enamel basin that served in lieu of offertory-bag, yet to the outsider there seemed more of God and less of finance, more of spirit and less of matter.

The Father, a young, big-bearded, happy-faced German, came to lunch with me afterwards. He was newly out and was amazed at the eagerness of the people to receive instruction, so different from the uphill work he had expected. He realized that worldly considerations played their part but felt the Church could wait with patience for the spiritual to oust the material. Personally I should think that practically all the old people still firmly held to native customs and religious observances. There are numerous small shrines, and the existence of so many *mbari* houses, new as well as old (and, as has been seen, these *mbari* houses are costly affairs), testifies to the vitality of the old beliefs. In conversation with B, he affirmed that among the younger generation, they are dying fast. I would be more inclined to say that they are not actually dying, but leading a more or less recognized existence side by side with the new Christian customs and beliefs. These are spreading fast as conversion and semi-conversion is the easily accepted condition on which a child can attain to the school which will give him the learning which will give him the job. Many families contain both Christian and pagan members.

Justice in Nguru

They seem to live together in amity, so little does their creed matter to either side, or, it might be more charitable, and also more true to say, so tolerant are they of what their neighbour believes, so long as he shows himself a good fellow man.

As far as the political institutions are concerned, I had as usual little to do with them. Since the Riots, the much hated Warrant Chiefs had been abolished and efforts had been made to revive the old judicial system of councils of elders now represented by the reorganized Native Courts. With the District Officer's permission, I attended several sittings of the Native Court at Inyeogugu, chiefly to hear some matrimonial cases and incidentally to witness a spectacle to understand which one should read, in all seriousness, the trial scene in *Alice in Wonderland*.

The Court was held in a vast mud hut, earth floored, palm thatched. The fifty-three Court Members, that is to say the fifty-three Judges, hung up their battered hats and helmets and umbrellas on sticks cunningly lashed to the unsquared palm trunks that upheld the roof. Then they sat down, very slowly for they were very old, and their chairs were old too. The Court Clerk, almost the only literate man present, sat behind a table at one end, the Court Members ranged themselves in double lines on each side, the plaintiff and the defendant stood in the middle, the public sat or squatted in the body of the Court or overflowed into the bare compound outside. The force of the law was represented by a few Court Messengers, unarmed, in faded blue uniforms much worn about the seats through bicycling for miles along bush paths in search of elusive witnesses. Skilfully they prompted plaintiff and defendant alike, restrained upthrown arms ready for blows, or listened to tales of crime with the tolerant smile of men who have seen much. The oath was taken variously upon a Bible or upon an old Dane gun hung with bits of medicine swung four times round the swearer's head. One could not tell which

171

form was the most truth-compelling. The cases were intricate beyond the scope of any European imagination but the fifty-three kept the thread easily and even the old men who slumbered peacefully in their worn deck-chairs woke up with a start to voice some clear and instant decision. When the decision could not be come to in Court, all the Members trooped out to discourse more freely under the shadow of a tree. Even so, argument was swift and the younger men were already returning before creaking bones had been able to rise from creaking chairs and hobble out. Business proceeded in comparative silence except for occasional outbursts of fury when the lies of plaintiff or defendant became too obvious, or the roof echoed to the loud shouts of Rabelaisian mirth as, shamefaced or indignant, a husband unfolded the tale of matrimonial mishaps.

At one moment, seeing some curious beads upon a man's neck, I bent forward to ask the Court Clerk where the man came from. To my dismay, he translated the question in a loud voice. Immediately, the whole course of justice stood still. In wild turmoil, the Court surged towards me. All the fifty-three Judges had beads, all the fifty-three wanted them to be looked at. At last the Court Clerk rapped upon his table with a wooden ruler, a protesting prisoner was brought up, and the Court returned to their seats to hear the case of one Jemima, a bold middle-aged woman, very smart in gaudy cloths, with a broad band of *uri* painted across her eyes giving a vaguely Spanish mantilla effect. She was suing her son-in-law, a flashy Don Juan, albeit he knew 'book' and elected to swear on the Bible, for £7 as her share of her daughter's dowry. Much hard lying ended in the defendant, browbeaten by Jemima, lamely asking for a remand to collect another witness. The next case was that of an elderly man who demanded the return of his wife, whom he had inherited from his deceased brother and who apparently had had a child by another man while on a visit

to her father's house. This the Court considered a good
joke and shook with mirth. Judgment, as in several other
cases, was given then and there, with no questions asked
and no proofs sought for, but the Court Members naturally know all their neighbours' family histories and can
usually grasp the situation at once. My diary ends the
day's doings with the remark: 'Strange show, but probably as good as anything else', a conclusion endorsed by
later experience. Much depends upon the Court Clerk,
whose integrity is not always above suspicion. The Court
Members are also open to bribery and are influenced by
intrigue but it probably balances out in the long run and
any too glaring injustices are picked out by the District
or the Assistant District Officer, who go through the records of the cases kept by the Court Clerk every month
or so. There is also of course a right of appeal and the
remedy to what miscarriages of justice there are lies
chiefly in the hands of the natives themselves: public
opinion and individual honesty can do away with corruption[1] and a less litigious spirit can lessen the number
of cases brought to the Courts.

As far as the women are concerned, increasing contact
with the outer world had resulted in their participation
to the same degree as the men in the sudden exacerba-
tion of desire caused by the influx of money during the
oil boom and in the ensuing phases of resentment, disappointment and bewilderment. As to any visible results
of this contact, whether direct or indirect, with Western
ideas actually showing in their daily lives, one hardly
knows what to say. Outwardly, only the younger ones
show any signs of having been influenced, at least to the
extent of possessing a rosary, of wearing a trifle more
clothing, of boiling the water they give to their babies.
Lack of money restricts whatever ambition they might

---

[1] It is satisfactory to note that I have never heard even the most
anti-Government native in Nigeria suggest that any white man would
take a bribe.

have had to live under better or more European conditions so one could not gauge satisfactorily how strong these ambitions were nor what shape they would take if they could be indulged in. The Sisters at Emekuku affirmed there was a marked difference in the homes of the young wives who had been under them as schoolgirls. My own impression of the few Christian homes I saw did not confirm this, but it is very likely that, seeing so few, I just happened to stumble upon those that were not a credit to their mistresses.

Comparing them with the Nneato women, one is inclined to say that they are more awake, more developed, but not so sensible. This seems an absurd contrast to make, yet, in thinking back, the words that invariably attach themselves to my memory of the Nneato women are: independent, purposeful, secret; while the Nguru women immediately call up such terms as: unreasonable, fantastic, excitable. The Nguru women were independent —the Aba Riots sufficiently proved that—but not in the quiet way of the Nneato women; they were purposeful too, but as a buzzing fly is purposeful, tenaciously trying to pierce a glass window pane. Wherein lies this difference? what has caused it? It would almost seem as if some powerful outside factor had disturbed or arrested their normal development, for on the whole they have more in their favour: more churches, more schools, more roads, more dispensaries, more contacts with travelled and at any rate partially educated people. Why have they not surpassed the mental stature or rather the personality of their Nneato sisters, remote beside their streams and high-banked, fern-hung paths?

It will be remembered that the second reason for my stay in Nguru was to find out how much the Riots were still remembered and what shape that memory took. I believe that as palm-oil dominates the economic-social situation, so do the Aba Riots still dominate the psychological situation. This assertion can hardly be proved, yet

174

Psychological Effects of the Aba Riots

as Peter Fleming's *Brazilian Adventure* bravely maintains: 'This book is all truth and no facts', so do I also claim that this chapter contains few provable facts and yet embodies the truth. Try as I may to give a more plausible, sensible, and practical picture of the women of Nguru, each time my memory goes back to them I invariably find myself caught up in the unreal, super-sensitive, egocentric atmosphere of a vast concourse of neurasthenics, I invariably hear the illogical arguments, the exaggerated reiterations and see the tense faces, the thin bodies and slightly glaring eyes. It is true there were whole days when I saw only the other, the more normal side: children coming for their dressings, a gift of an orange in a grubby hand; mothers smiling as they held out their babies; greetings called from doorways as the family sat round the evening meal; a dance of children at the cross-paths, lit by stars. And yet all this seemed by the way: the real texture of their lives, the stuff of their thoughts, was made up of suspicion and fear, self-pity and self-justification, a sense of frustration and a sense of guilt. They were so keyed up that whatever happened to them struck a note higher than was normal: they were never hungry, they were always 'starving', they were never ill, they were always 'dying', they never died, they were always 'killed'. Their voices were shrill with anxiety, their bodies ready poised to dive off the deep end. They continuously expected the worst and would have scorned to hope for the best. They begged for help and then refused it; asked for advice and then, thin-lipped and bitter, turned away from it. They were both servile and truculent. And their cupidity knew no bounds.

In all my experience of Nigerian women, I had never met this type before nor indeed had I ever looked upon them as potential or actual 'nerve cases' until I was face to face with this mass neurosis. Even now, I wonder whether I exaggerate or had preconceived ideas or even

175

projected on them a neurosis of my own; but continually
in my notes I find I compare them to patients I knew at a
certain clinic for psychological cases where I used to
work, and look for psychological causes for their present attitude. And these are perhaps not far to seek, for
the Riots are ever present in the women's minds and
the memory of them is compounded of fear and anger
and a sense of guilt, balanced by a sense of power and
victory. As far as one could see, there were two strains:
anger that Government should ever have thought of
perpetrating such monstrous injustice as that of taxing
women,[1] fear, real or pretended, lest the danger might
still exist, a sense of guilt when they remembered the
excesses to which their zeal had led them—and on the
other hand, a sly delight in having worsted the white
man, in having, they poor feeble women, overcome the
might of Government, shown it what women at bay
could do, and forced it to rescind its orders and admit
its defeat. I think they still firmly believe it was neither
magnanimity nor wisdom which made Government recall the imaginary order to tax women, but sheer fright,
and even though they were punished and their villages
fined, yet they had gained their ultimate end. But here
again their minds were divided: as much as any other
women, the Ibo want to eat their cake and have it.
While they unconsciously displayed their pride in themselves as rebels, they consciously sought to prove what
loyal subjects they were, what assistance they had given
to Government in bringing back peace to the country,
what protectors they had been of Government servants
and Government property. And as a natural sequence,
came the demand: 'Why has Government not given my
son a post as messenger?' 'Why did Government not
agree to make my brother a road-gang foreman?'

If the Riots were only a memory, however vivid, they

[1] As has already been shown (p. 55), there was never the slightest
intention of so doing.

would not be of such great importance, but being bound up with the idea of taxation, an ever-present, ever-discussed, ever-resented subject, the two together form a complex round which their thoughts dangerously and endlessly revolve. The very sight of a white face sets this train of thought in motion and fear and suspicion immediately spring into life. After I had been only a few days at Inyeogugu, a group of women came to see me, led by Lɔlɔ, the medicine woman. There was more curiosity than welcome in their attitude but nothing definitely hostile. After some desultory conversation, I asked, not realizing the dangerous ground I was treading on, whether the women of this neighbourhood held councils such as I had seen in Okigwi. My interpreter unfortunately used the English word 'meeting', the word that was so much in evidence in the Report of the Aba Commission. The effect was electrical. The women, lounging on a low mud wall, sprang to their feet, tense with excitement. Why did I speak of meetings? was there trouble anywhere? what new thing had occurred? I changed the subject directly but suspicion was not allayed. The shock was as great to them as it was to me, for though I guessed these people would have to be handled carefully, I never thought the reaction would be so violent and so immediate.

As one can imagine, this attitude created an atmosphere in which it was wellnigh impossible to get reliable information. Not one single subject would be touched on which would not be made to refer to tax or riots, whether it was interest in a baby's age or the colour of a woman's goats or the origin of a patient's toothache. Either I was secretly searching for the real leaders of the Riots or I was 'writing a report to give to my husband who would then come and tax the women'. How far this fear was sincere and how far it was put on out of love for the dramatic, out of the already-mentioned tendency to see the worst side of everything, out of the desire to feel

177

injured so that there should be an added reason for self-
pity, out of a child's trembling enjoyment of his self-in-
duced terrors, was impossible to tell. They probably did
not know themselves and their intelligence was still so
limited that no one could help them to disentangle their
motives. The very neutrality of my position was a stum-
bling-block: neither missionary nor trader, I *must* be
Government. When crossing a crowded market-place, a
woman rose up and shouted: 'Tell the white woman
nothing. She has only come to harm us!' Again, walking
back one evening with a band of women returning from
their farms, chatting peaceably about crops and prices,
one, evidently the *esprit fort* of the group, strode up
beside me: 'You who are Government, tell us why the
price of oil has fallen?' I explained once more I was not
Government but it was no use. 'Tell us why Government does not give us money. Tell us why we are taxed.
Tell us why Government starves us.' Voices got shrill.
Excitement grew. 'Our children die. We ourselves die.'
The women stopped in a serried group, with hostile looks
and murmurs. 'Government kill me! See how thin I
am!' and the speaker, momentary madness in her eyes,
by some trick of posture turned herself into a living
skeleton and threw herself into a wild war dance, two
feet in front of me. Fortunately I was thin too, and by
the time we had compared bones and knuckles, the
women were laughing and the difficult moment was
over. I would have thought they had just been trying it
on, partly as a joke or to see whether they could get anything out of me but that glint of madness was real and I
can only repeat the remark made in my diary: 'Queer
creatures. All right when you have only a few of them,
but thousands as in the Riots. . . .'

Up to a point, one can sympathize with them. Apart
from the, to a certain extent, artificial anxiety about
palm-oil prices, there does exist the very natural anxiety
about actual food supplies and here it seems to be the

woman who has to bear the heaviest responsibility. In theory, a man is expected to provide food for wives and children but in practice it is the woman who by her wise management ensures that the supply is constant. And again, though only the man is taxed, yet so interwoven is male and female labour, that the woman feels she shares with him the burden of taxation. In how far climate and the monotony of that endless flat palm forest contribute to a pessimistic disposition is impossible to say but one seldom had that cheerful 'feel' which was so noticeable in clearer, hillier Eziama. And apart from these tangible causes, there were others equally potent but of a more psychological nature which one could only dimly guess at. Concerning the Riots, they still felt uncomfortable: although they considered their cause was just, they knew they had gone too far, had shown themselves lawless and destructive and had openly, again and again, defied the white man and scorned his agents. Retribution had come, but was it over and done with? White men moved slowly: the thing they called 'justice' especially so, and who knew what they might still have up their sleeves? Indeed, how could they be sure that what they were told was 'trade depression' was not Government's secret form of punishment? They had been well on the road to prosperity and now where were they? They had a subtle conviction that they had gone back in the social scale, had been, perhaps, pushed back. And joined to this was the memory that they had had money in their hands, the wherewithal to buy cloths and head-ties and necklaces, and they wanted them again, with obstinacy and with passion, not only as finery but as a woman's most personal form of wealth. Once more like neurotic patients, they would go over the same ground again and again, holding tight to their grievances, their fears, their regrets, apparently incapable of getting free from the strangle-hold of the past, or of constructing a plan for a more stable future.

179

Women

The third task I had set myself in going to Nguru was to examine as far as I could whether over-crowding and possible under-feeding was having any effect upon the children. On the whole, I was surprised to find how little these two factors apparently told on them. I saw Nguru at its poorest time when last season's yams were finished and only a few of the new season (women's) yams were ready to be dug. The population depended on cassava and coco-yam and a small amount of very poor corn (maize) for its daily food. The over-farmed land produced smaller and smaller crops; there had been some disease among the yams and the dry weather of the last year had still further diminished the yield and yet, although rations had presumably been short for most of the year, the evil effects on the physique of the people were hardly noticeable. It was true that the old people were very thin but so they were in well-fed places like Eziama or Owerri Town. The men were of good physique. The women were thinner, too thin sometimes, but no consistently underfed mothers could possibly have given birth to such beautiful babies. And these babies were quite exceptionally fine. Even Salome, very jealous for the reputation of her home town, remarked that they were finer than Owerri children. After roughly five years of age, they tended to get a little weedy but not to any marked degree. I did not see one case of yaws, so prevalent in other districts, though doubtless I would have found some in the houses; malaria, scabies, sores, ulcers, worms, were present, but to a superficial observer like myself, in no greater quantity than elsewhere. On the other hand, there was a great deal of guinea-worm, common in the North but not seen before among the Ibo. As to infant mortality, no direct information could be obtained but casual inquiries did not indicate an abnormally high rate. Amid much good-natured laughter I was told about a woman who had actually had twelve children, all of whom had lived! This was admittedly an

180

exceptional case but families of four to six children (by one wife) were frequently met with. One intelligent woman volunteered the information that more boys were born than girls but could not or would not say whether more boys died in infancy than girls.

If food shortage had not affected to any marked degree the physique of the children, had overcrowding diminished their worth in their parents' eyes or altered their status of spoilt darlings? There again the answer seems to be in the negative. In the maze of changing values, in the collapse of ethical standards, in the general mental muddle, the children alone remain inviolate, they alone retain their unassailable position, they alone stand out as a steady and unchanging feature. Whatever the sins of their fathers and mothers, their meanness or cruelty or graspingness, the children are safe, at least from the material point of view. They may be separated from their mothers, thrown from one family to another, but wherever they are, they are well looked after, fed, housed, and well treated. When I remarked to B that, considering the poverty of the soil and that we were in the most difficult season when food was shortest, the children looked remarkably well fed, he said without hesitation that everyone would go without food rather than let children suffer.

But though it might be a profound satisfaction to find that the children were safe, yet their very safety was, one might almost say, a cause for alarm. How can the population afford to increase? how can the land carry any more lives? and if it cannot, where can the people go? It is true that there are still vast tracts of Nigeria which are sparsely inhabited but the Ibo farmer does not move easily. He has his set ways, his special crops, his own methods; above all he has the links forged by ancestor worship which bind him tightly to his own home. Here and there, young men could very likely be induced to seek their fortunes elsewhere but those who would do so would wish (as indeed they do already) to find that fortune lying on an office desk, not in the fields or forests of a foreign land (and to them, once out of earshot of their own village-group, they are in a 'foreign' land). Nor would it be enough to settle even a considerable number of young men elsewhere: their wives must go with them, the unmarried ones must be encouraged to choose brides from their old homes or the whole social fabric goes awry. The future of this particular section of Ibo-land, more than any other, is in special need of a wise and prudent planning.

How can one resume the self-contradictions of this chapter? how sum up the tangible and intangible factors that create the uneasy situation described? how convey the curious anomaly of a townsman's mind in a country-man's skin? how find the words in which to crystallize one's impression of a social fabric, not yet destroyed by any means, but waiting to be destroyed, almost one might say, wanting to be destroyed? The only ones that invariably come to my mind are those of the clumsy paradox which gives its name to this section: sophisti-cated-primitive. Sophisticated in that the outlook of the women has widened beyond its old limits, in that they are no longer satisfied with their old conditions of life; primitive in that their outlook has only widened on the material surface with no corresponding mental growth, and in that conditions of life are actually almost more rudimentary than in the veriest 'bush'. Again and again one is struck by the contrast between the extravagant ambitions of the women and the poverty of their surroundings, and by poverty in this case I mean poverty of resource, of ingenuity, of any effort after greater comfort or convenience, quite apart from the improvements or luxuries that money could buy. No slum family suddenly transported to a desert island could look so uncomfortable and so unadapted, nor could it be more vocal against

182

A New Orientation

Government for not supplying it with a town hall, a picture palace, free education, and water laid on.

This contrast between ambition and realization probably accounts, at least in part, for the impression one receives of instability and stress, of the sudden break in continuity, of the little hold custom and tradition now have.

I revert to the symbol I have already used, that of the singlet. I said that in Nneato there was the ghost of a singlet in everybody's eyes. Here in Nguru, it is the singlet itself, tangible, quite close, immensely desired. There it had been a thought, crossing a sleepy brain, here it was a reality, only just beyond the reach of hungry hands; there it had merely tinged life with a certain colour; here it was a blinding light drawing dazed moths round it. And if in Nneato singlet-mindedness was just beginning to temper daily habits, outlook, and customs, it almost seemed as if in Nguru it had already given them a new orientation.

X

Woman in Transition—in Owerri Town

Reasons for choice of Owerri Town. What an urban-farming community looks like. How one lives in it. What the women do in it.

My reasons for going to Owerri Town had not, in the first instance, been very carefully thought out. It happened that it was a convenient centre from which to radiate; it was a good meeting-place for my colleague and myself; the constant kindness of the Government officials made it seem almost home. But apart from these aspects, I had looked upon Owerri Town as a semi-official agglomeration, of no possible interest. It was some weeks before I realized that, on the contrary, it was a precious example of a native community in a transition stage, more advanced than Nguru and yet still an entity with some roots in the past. The population was urban and agricultural at one and the same time; it was in constant touch with the outside world by means of a network of lorry-covered roads; it was in direct and continuous contact with Government, represented by one or more white officials always in and out of the station; and with the machinery of Government as represented by the District Officers' office, the local treasury, the post office, prison, school, native hospital, etc. Yet, unlike Aba, which I had first thought

184

of choosing as a place of study, it had a life of its own, it was more 'itself' than Aba, now so full of strangers and passers-by that it would be almost impossible to rediscover its original nature or to picture what changes it might have been through. I was there at various times throughout the year, sometimes for a few days, sometimes for a few weeks, so I was never quite out of touch with the life of the town.

Owerri Town is the headquarters of the Owerri Division of the Owerri Province. The Division has an area of 1,085 square miles and an approximate population of 455,261, which represents a density of 419·5 per square mile. The population comprises 223,214 males and 232,947 females. Owerri Town has officially (1934) a population of 2,061 (I would put it at nearer 3,000), excluding a population of strangers, i.e., Hausa, Yoruba, etc., amounting to 142. There are no Syrians nor Indians as at Port Harcourt and a few other towns.

The town lies in a shallow basin in the middle of the palm belt, though actually round Owerri neither oil nor wine palms are as plentiful as elsewhere. The surrounding country is flat or gently undulating, watered by a few shallow streams. The roads cut through mile upon mile of forest in which palms predominate. This forest is intersected by paths in every direction and farms and bush merge into each other almost imperceptibly.

Although five roads lead out of it, Owerri Town is not primarily a trading-centre such as Aba or Onitsha. The daily market is for local produce only; the larger eight-day one displays some European goods as well as native pots, mats and foodstuffs brought in from villages situated roughly in a fifteen-mile radius, but there is no large-scale trading in oil or kernels. In appearance, it has little character. Some fine trees and a few corrugated-iron roofs rise above the huddle of mud walls and palm-thatch roofs. One single broad road lined with small

185

booths belonging to tailors, carpenters, bicycle repairers, or to women who sell little bits of soap and handfuls of cigarettes, leads to the market. What is striking about the town is that, wide-spread as it is, it is much more compact than most Ibo agglomerations. Even in an English sense, one can speak of the 'town' of Owerri, although there is a considerable area of more or less waste land between some of the quarters.

Broadly speaking, the town is divided into five quarters (*nci*), each one surrounded by a continuous mud wall and a wide sweep of sandy track bordered by trees. The division into quarters is of course a common one, but seldom are they so clearly defined by an encircling wall as at Owerri. Each quarter is inhabited by a group of extended families owning a common ancestor. Each of the extended families has its own 'gate' or 'gates' by which it goes in and out of the quarter. One of the quarters, Umuonyeche, houses not only a group of extended families but also some Aro families who settled here some time ago[1] and have adopted Owerri customs and dialect, identifying themselves even to the point of accepting Ibo sons for their daughters (an Aro man would marry an Ibo girl but an Aro girl would ordinarily despise an Ibo as a potential husband), although the members of the Umuonyeche quarter feel that they themselves live too closely together with the Aro to be able to intermarry with them. This quarter is an exception in that it consists of *two* walled units in close proximity, one lived in by those of Owerri stock, the other by those of Aro stock.

The rule of exogamy is strictly applied, as all groups claim to be descended from one common ancestor. The only exception is in favour of the Umuoyima quarter, whose inhabitants are recent immigrants from the neighbouring village of Nekede.

[1] There are Aro settlements throughout Ibo-land whose history and present relationship to the surrounding populations deserve particular study.

Habitations in Owerri Town

Near each quarter is the compound of the *Osu* (cult slaves) belonging to that quarter. These cult slaves, though they form an integral part of the population, are, to a certain degree, not socially considered as belonging to it.[1]

Housing is adequate but without any features of interest. The casual passer-by looking in at a 'gate' sees only what appears to be a patternless array of huts, kitchens and stores. There are no individual houses except a few belonging to such people as rich traders, retired constables, or senior clerks, which have sprung up quite recently, are built in semi-European style and stand in their own grounds, generally a square enclosure, with the house in the centre, a slight attempt at a flower-bed or a row of ornamental bushes in front and an untidy yard all round. There are few of the improvements one might have expected in a comparatively advanced town such as Owerri. The semi-European houses referred to above are built, with little skill or style, of cement blocks or, more usually, of mud blocks washed over with cement and are roofed with 'pan', i.e. corrugated-iron, but seldom does a purely native dwelling show any effort to rise above its ordinary rather squalid type. That this can be done, with the expenditure of a little trouble and a very few shillings, was shown by the three-roomed house I visited, belonging to a teacher living under ordinary conditions in his father's compound. With better planning and higher walls, with slightly larger windows and a thicker thatch, whitewash and a flowering shrub, he had made a gay and comfortable home for himself and his, alas, rather dull and indifferent wife. It would almost seem as if the home-making instincts were more developed in the Ibo man than in the woman.

The European station is half a mile from the town and consists of the District Officer's bungalow, a hot and gloomy horror of wood and corrugated-iron, three

[1] For a description of the Osu system, see *Africa*, April 1937.

semi-bush houses (that is to say houses built of mud and thatched with grass or palm but with cement floors, colour-washed walls and larger rooms) for the Assistant District Officers and the Medical Officer, and a couple of rest-houses for people passing through. There is generally one white official in the station with one or two on a tour. The Medical Officer resides permanently in the station but is out visiting dispensaries (of which there are now six and one in course of erection) nearly every day. The present Medical Officer is a well-qualified African, trained in Edinburgh.

There is a native hospital (82 beds and 6 cots), a Government school (252 boys and 58 girls in 1934; 270 boys and 60 girls in 1935; 270 boys and 51 girls in 1936); and a bush prison.

The Government school is inspected by a white Superintendent of Education about every three months; every month or six weeks an officer of the Agricultural Department pays a short visit to the various experimental plots in Owerri and the neighbourhood. The Resident in charge of the Province, whose headquarters are at Port Harcourt, stays a few days several times a year. A travelling Judge and a Magistrate hold courts every month. The local Native Courts meet six to ten days every month.

In the town there are schools and churches belonging to the Roman Catholic Mission, the Church Missionary Society and the African Church; and the Faith Tabernacle has a church. The Salvation Army has also a station here. The Church Missionary Society church and school are seldom visited by a white missionary but the Fathers come in more frequently from their headquarters at Emekuku, about six miles from Owerri. The African Church and the Faith Tabernacle are entirely African.[1]

---

[1] I have just heard (May, 1937) that the subversive Watch Tower Movement from the United States has also begun its activities in Owerri Town but so far without much success.

Girls' Training Homes

The Salvation Army has little following and the native officer in charge is away touring a good deal.

There is a fine Roman Catholic Mission station, including a boys' and a girls' school and a hospital at Emekuku; and an old-established Church Missionary Society station including a Central School, a girls' training-home and a small maternity home at Ebu, three and a half miles from Owerri.

As these girls' training-homes, as opposed to girls' schools, will be referred to again and play an important part in the general scheme of girls' education, it will be worth while to give a short description of a typical one such as the Ebu-Owerri 'Girls' Training Institution', although this one, being so long established, under fairly constant European supervision, and in good buildings, is rather ahead of the others.

The Church Missionary Society had already founded a station and school at Ebu-Owerri in 1906. Faced with the difficulty of providing Christian wives for their young catechists and teachers, it was decided to open a home for brides where they would be prepared for baptism, taught to read and write in the vernacular, and would be trained in the elements of house-craft. The home consisted of huts built in the native style, every girl had her own little kitchen and store, fetched wood and water, etc., exactly as she would have done at home but with more care and method. The home was popular and the young men themselves asked that their brides should be taken in, paying the small fees and providing the girls with sufficient food. At the same time, housed in a separate building, older women who were still pagan though wives of teachers and catechists, were equally being prepared for baptism and taught to read, an essential condition for baptism except in cases of age or infirmity. These women came for varying periods of from three to twelve months, bringing their babies or smaller children with them.

189

Women

As the reputation of the home grew, girls other than those affianced to Mission workers were admitted and paid for by their fiancés, traders or clerks or the more progressive farmers. Occasionally, parents themselves would send their daughters, hoping to get better husbands for them, out of whom they could recoup their expenses, but chiefly the girls were sent and paid for by their young men. The scholastic education given was limited, in some of the smaller homes opened at a later date it was almost negligible, but the domestic training and the general civilizing effect were good, though one sometimes felt that, even if run on exactly the same nearly-native lines, the details of the scheme might have been a little better carried out. But once more lack of sufficient European staff, either for individual direction or general supervision, is the cause that full advantage is not taken of potential educational opportunities, using the word educational in its broadest sense. Nor must it be forgotten that, in the climate of, say, Owerri Province, living under quite possible but far from inspiring conditions, it is no easy matter for a European woman to cope continuously, creatively, and vigorously with thirty to forty bouncing Ibo girls, good tempered and well behaved though they generally are, but completely lacking in any will to perfection.

One could have wished that more of these homes, under careful supervision, had been opened in the early days instead of the much more advanced girls' boarding-schools or co-education day schools. They would have cost much less and so could have been more numerous, and are better suited, in my opinion, to the needs of the country. At the moment when I was most in touch with Nigerian education, Government was quite ready to favour them but the Missions seemed to have lost interest and it is only quite recently that attention is once more being paid to them. Ebu has suffered least as European direction has been fairly constant, and now that an exceptionally well-qualified Lady Supervisor has been appointed to visit all the Church Missionary Society homes in the Onitsha and Owerri Provinces, one hopes that their value will be increased. Though they are perhaps not so essentially valuable now as they might have been in the past, yet they can still play a big part in the transition stage between the illiterate bush girl and the up-to-date product of the girls' schools, and men often prefer to marry girls who have had a 'home' training rather than a 'school' one.

The European station at Owerri is healthy in so far as there is little sickness among the white officials but the continuous damp heat is very trying. The atmosphere during February, March, and April is, at times, almost unbearable. When the rains begin, towards the end of June, it becomes pleasanter, but later on, towards October, it heats up again and though there are a few days of Harmattan, the cold, dry, sand-laden wind from the North, about Christmas time, they only serve to emphasize the ensuing heat.

The amount of sickness in the town is hard to gauge. There is no striking evidence either of poverty, hunger, or disease. In fact mortality is probably high though the few chance statistics I have seen, too incomplete and over too short a period of time to be of any real value, do not give such a gloomy picture as one would expect. The town is fairly clean; incinerators are installed and some public latrines; the houses and the yards within the quarters are often untidy and unkempt but do not smell. In an otherwise rather waterless area, Owerri is lucky in having a clear stream always running from which water for all purposes is obtained.

Naturally a much larger proportion of the population is clothed, or more fully clothed, than in the bush, either native fashion with cotton cloth or European fashion. Hardly ever do the women and girls, if dressed in European fashion, show the least particle of taste either as

191

regards colour or form, and the habit of wearing ill-fitting shoes spoils the Ibo woman's greatest asset, her smooth flowing walk. It is particularly among church members that one finds an insistence on 'frock' and shoes. Indeed, few would have the courage to go to the 'smarter' churches with bare or sandalled feet. Whether this comes from a sincere, if misguided, feeling that to appear with bare feet would show a want of respect for the house of God, or is merely a form of snobbery, I could not judge.

At a very rough guess, Owerri Town must be about 300 years old. Old men will go back eight or ten generations to the supposed founder and common ancestor, Ekwem Arugo. The site of his grave is known but no special respect is paid to it and nothing seems to be remembered of the man himself. With no architecture and no literature, neither written nor oral, historical landmarks are practically non-existent.

The European station dates from 1901, year of the Aro Expedition against the Long Juju of Aro Chuku. It appears to have been chosen purely because it was a convenient camp for the troops and on account of the good water supply. Later, when the troops withdrew, the administration stayed on and so the station grew up on its present site, more by chance than by any fixed design. The town has never been of any great importance, nor does the Oratta clan[1] which inhabits this area present any very distinctive features.

Only one character stands out, that of the old Chief Njemanze, dead in 1920, and the tales of him, told me by his grandchild, an attractive girl of seventeen, captured the imagination. They are not strictly relevant to my subject but nevertheless seem worth recording as evidence of a golden age, local and short-lived though it was, and of a man who even amongst the ultra-democratic Ibo had succeeded in imposing himself. It is true his title of Chief given to him by the white man had no real meaning,

[1] Dr. Meek calls it the Oratta sub-tribe.

but he had obviously been a leader, holding incontestable authority. 'No one made peace or war without consulting him. His permission was asked before anything could be done.'

I often visited the quarter to which he had belonged, that of Ama Awom. It was a huge rabbit warren of little huts and courtyards divided by mud or palm-branch walls. It was still fairly full of people coming and going, women preparing food or cooking it over small wood fires, men talking in the *obi* near the gate, children playing, young girls coming in with firewood or water from the near-by stream, but one felt the absence of the master spirit, one saw evidences of slackness and decay, the light of glory no longer shone upon its walls. It was only while I listened to Salome as she sat, wide eyed, looking back into her own babyhood, mixing her own slight memories with all that she had heard of her grandfather's life, that I was able to reconstruct this golden age which had flourished for a few years and then died down, all the more remarkable because so few people or facts ever stand out clearly from the apparently colourless maze of the Ibo past.

Chief Njemanze was a rich man for, beside his fifty wives, he had about two hundred servants. 'He loved children too much' and had built for them, inside his compound, rest-houses (slight shelters of mud and palm) to which all might come. 'In the middle was the "big" rest-house, which must have had a hundred poles, some carved, some covered from top to bottom with the skulls of all the cows and the sheep and the goats he had eaten. From the roof hung the corn cobs which the servants had brought in from the farms, in big baskets, on their heads. Some of the corn cobs would be given to the children. Then wood would be brought and as many as twenty fires would be lit before which the children roasted their cobs with play and laughing'; or they would race to see who could climb fastest up the poles, clasping the carved

G

monkeys and the parrots, and when the boys came back from school, they would have games of touch-wood between the poles. Salome sat still, seeing again the golden cobs hanging from the smoke-darkened roof, hearing again the laughter of the chasing children. Then she went on: 'In his *ɔba*, he had at least twenty rows of stored yams. Any poor person could go and help himself. Often there would be two or three rows of men and women in the compound, each with a basket of yams. Njemanze, my grandfather, would come out, walk up and down the lines and say: 'That is right, my people. I see what you have taken. It is all right.' Again she came back to his love of children: 'If he heard a woman beating her child, he would tell her never to do such a thing again. He would take the child to his own hut and give it something to eat or a little present, whispering to it not to tell its mother. On big market day, he would give a shilling to all his children to buy fairings with. He would also buy pieces of cloth and give a yard to all the girls about to be married; he would also provide food for all his people on the feast of Oru Owerri.' Every morning, Salome, who was his son's first-born, went to salute him. She could just remember him. He was tall and stout, and very fine. He wore coral beads round his neck and a necklet of black medicine which he had inherited from his father and which showed he had taken his father's place. He would say to her: 'Come here, my child!' The remembered softness in the intonation as imitated by Salome all these years after was remarkable. He would give her a yam which she would carry back to her mother, strutting, the big yam clasped to her stomach. 'While he was eating, there was silence in all the compound, no one would dare so much as to pick up a twig. Two or three of his wives would sit by him while he ate. Children would bring their bowls and he would give them little bits off his own plate. . . . There was always peace in his time. . . .'

Departed Glory

Doubtless Salome exaggerated but probably the picture of plenty was true, the wives bending over the
cooking-pots, the servants coming in from the farms
laden with baskets, the poor people going off rejoicing,
the big rest-house hung with the glowing corn cobs,
skulls, and medicines, and the children running, shouting, between the high carved poles. And clearest of
all, one sees Njemanze, rich, strong, and generous,
flinging round his shillings or striding between the
huts, a child upon his shoulder, undermining maternal
discipline.

Now all that is left of the old rest-house are the stumps
of a few poles and some of the poles themselves, cunningly carved, lying rotting on the ground. 'No one
bothers to take care of the old things.' Njemanze's own
meeting-house still stands but is hardly used. It is nearly
square with steeply pitched roof and remarkably well-
built bamboo frame to which is lashed the palm-leaf
thatch. The walls have wooden pegs driven into them on
which are stuck old bottles and drinking-horns.[1] In one
corner stood a large wooden box which might have been
meant for a coffin. There were two old drums and, hanging from the roof, various baskets and odd-shaped round
bundles which might have been human skulls, but 'no
one knows now what they mean'. Yet, though all other
glory has departed, one marvel remains. Njemanze was a
pagan but his children became Christians. When their
father died, he was buried according to custom in the
courtyard outside his own hut, but over his grave rises a
life-size marble angel, finger pointing heavenward, a
look of mild surprise upon its face. The marble coping,
spattered with the blood of sacrificial fowls, bears the
name of a monumental mason in Kensal Green.

For a long while, the angel was such a thing of wonder

[1] I was interested to observe that in the immaculate Buffet de la
Gare at Vallorbes on the Paris–Lausanne route, milk bottles were
stored in the same way.

that people came, a hundred at a time, from far and near to gaze upon it. So new and splendid did it seem that expert modellers, engaged upon a nearby *mbari* house, came to look at it and forthwith rushed back to copy it, in clay and coloured chalks, for the adornment of the shrine of Ɔlogba. The angel's whiteness was a 'mystery'. At night, people hardly dared pass by it, fearing it might be the spirit of Njemanze himself, and when they wanted to relieve themselves, they would go ten at a time to the latrine, running past it very quickly. It is still known as 'the monument' and strangers are taken to see it and to read the inscription, in English, to 'the greatest chief Owerri ever had'.

If he were alive to-day, in spite of a number of non-native elements such as lorries, bicycles, corrugated-iron roofs, signposts, concrete sheds in the markets, he would not find much contrast in his town between old and new. The change has been too gradual to be dramatic and so easily absorbed that there is no visible sign of conflict. The very formlessness of Ibo life to which reference has already been made allowed changes to take place without any notice being taken of them: one Mission came and then another; one native path was broadened into an earth track, and then hardened into a road; one boy went to school instead of following his father to the farm, then two, then two hundred. A few of them went away to work elsewhere but not enough to make the faintest impression on the masses left behind. The Christian clerk has three wives: the priest of Ɔlogba has a son in Standard VI. The rich Aro puts up a signboard to say he is a civil engineer and licensed surveyor and in his large pan-roofed, crucifix-adorned house, lodges the Salvation Army officer.

Very roughly one could say that 82 per cent of the population are still either partially or predominantly farmers; 3 per cent are catechists, teachers, clerks, small artisans; 10 per cent are unemployed educated or semi-educated

young men.[1] Of the women, 97 per cent are farmer-
traders, 3 per cent are slightly educated wives of teachers,
etc., or ex-schoolgirls waiting to be married. One should
note though that the term 'farmer' is misleading if one
takes it in the ordinary English meaning of the word.
Indeed, one often wonders what appellation to give to
the Ibo, and more especially to the Owerri farmer. His
work is so seasonal—very heavy during periods such as
that of the clearing of the land before planting the new
crops, practically non-existent during other periods when
the work is in the hands of the women—that one cannot
regard him as a farmer in our own whole-time sense of
the word, especially as his live-stock, which would require
the English farmer's daily care even when the actual
agricultural work was slack, is never given a moment's
attention. Yet, even in Owerri Town, everybody 'owns'
land and readily says he is a farmer. In fact, in contra-
diction to the peasants of Nguru, who, though living in a
much more purely agricultural environment than the
Owerri people, struck me as being so urban-minded, here
one is surprised to find how rural-minded these town-
dwellers are. In conversation, men and women of all
classes make constant reference to their farms, what
needs doing, what they themselves must see to, what
labour they can hire. Indeed, 'the weather and the
crops' is a much more popular subject of conversation in
the heart of Owerri Town than it was among the cassava
stalks and the oil palms of Nguru. The older women
especially have, I think, a kind of passion for their farms.
Bent old hags sally forth every morning with hoe and
basket, driven not so much by necessity as by the longing
to see what sun or rain may have brought forth since the
day before. I once met Salome's mother, gaunt with
fever, staggering along the road that led to her little bit
of land. In answer to my remonstrances, Salome said:

[1] This proportion is doubtless smaller now than it was during the
period of trade depression which coincided with my stay in Owerri.

197

Women

'My mother love her farm too much. Were she dying, she would go there.'

On the whole, it struck me that Salome was right when she maintained that the women do more farm work than the men, even in connection with the yam crops. In my frequent walks through the farmlands around the town, I always met more women than men and the clearing of the bush at the beginning of the farming season was more often done by labourers[1] hired from another district than by the Owerri men themselves. The three weedings of the yam plants, customary in Owerri, are done by the women.

Yam, cassava, and coco-yam form the staple diet, yam being the favourite food. Dried corn, though apparently much used in the past, is seldom seen. Fresh corn is eaten in large quantities but its season is short though it comes at a very useful moment, just when the yam stores are almost empty and the new yams are not yet ready.

As land is still plentiful, the ground is allowed to lie fallow for four or five years and reverts to fairly heavy bush, though in the immediate vicinity of the town there are now stretches of land where few trees or palms are left standing. The usual system of clearing the land by hacking down the bush and burning it is followed. When harvested, the yams are stored in ɔba, which are not built contiguous to the owner's own dwelling as in Nneato, but are distributed round the town, between the last dwellings and the first farms. Each quarter possesses its own group of ɔba neatly fenced in and containing row upon row of light bamboo-and-pole staging to which the yams are carefully tied, graded according to size and kind.

With such a comparatively large number of children going to school I was anxious to know what training they

[1] These labourers, if strong adults, would be paid from 4d. to 6d. a day without food, or 2½d. to 3d. a day plus their food, but many of them were children and young girls and would be paid less, 1d. to 2d. a day with food. I am told (1937) that the rates of pay are now higher.

got in farming. As usual, it depended on the individual. In many households, school children are expected to help on their parents' land during the holidays. The boys especially are required to do so, not only to learn farming but to get to know the boundaries of their fathers' land. This is important as, so indistinct are these boundaries to the inexperienced eye, that it must take much practice to enable one to pick them out. In other cases, 'parents pet their children and let them laze about,' and I fear they are only too ready to do so, thus creating a section, still small, but rapidly growing, of literates and semi-literates for whom there seems no room in any sphere at present.

Even less than elsewhere is there a sharp division of labour. Farming and trading are divided about equally between men and women; but men alone are employed in the Government offices, as lorry drivers and small artisans; women alone look after the house and prepare the food.

Meal-times, and the nature of these meals vary as much as elsewhere. They alter according to seasonal occupations and other factors, but, as in Nneato, three meals a day seemed to be the rule. A farmer would have a small 'breakfast' before leaving for his work; about 11 a.m. a wife would carry another meal out to him; about 7.30 p.m. he would eat the evening meal at home. There are no rules against men and women eating together.[1] If a man has only one wife, they usually take their meals together if no strangers are present. (Husband and wife may even drink out of the same cup.) If a man has four wives, each will cook for him for four days and he will sleep with her on those four nights (this differs from the Eziama custom, see p. 88). If, however, he has a number of wives of whom 'he is not quite sure'

[1] Although food is usually put into the mouth with the right hand, a left-handed man may use his left: 'it only shows his mother has not trained him properly'.

as my informant delicately put it, he will choose the one he loves best and she will do all his cooking, 'not forgetting to lock up her kitchen when she goes out. . . .' All the same, the husband will be careful to give as good presents to the other ones as to the favourite one, partiality on his part in this matter being hotly resented. The wives whose turn it is not to cook for their husband, cook for themselves and their children.

Sleeping arrangements are as in Nneato: small children sleep together or with their mother, growing boys when eight or nine go to sleep in a hut of their own or in a portion of their father's hut if he has a room. It is a recognized taunt for boys to say to each other: 'What, you are still sleeping with your mother!' Schoolboys may choose to sleep together in a special hut, 'so that they may study during the night', a slightly senior boy to coach them, a rickety table to write on, and a dim bush-lamp to see by. The 'prep' system at its worst.

There are no crafts in Owerri Town. Neither grass-cloth, nor mats nor pots are made. As in Nguru, the only artistic outlet for men or women lies in the building and decoration of the *mbari* houses.

XI

Woman in Transition—in Owerri Town

What the men and women say of marriage with educated girls. Birth and burial and second burials. New dance clubs and old ceremonies.

Marriage customs in Owerri are as fluid as elsewhere and are further influenced by a number of outside factors: as already mentioned the rule of exogamy is very strictly applied; many of the young men reside temporarily in Aba or Port Harcourt so their courtship cannot follow quite the usual steps; some of the girls are educated with resultant changes in the amount of dowry expected for them. There is also a larger number of Christian marriages,[1] involving much in the way of bridal veils and high-heeled shoes yet not altogether exempt from the pagan touch. Was not the wedding-feast of a Roman Catholic couple spoiled by the meanness of the bridegroom who had not sent a fee to the rainmaker to keep off the rain and was he not so shamed by his guests whose best clothes were getting spoiled that he sent a messenger post-haste to the rainmaker with apologies and a half-crown?

As to the amounts and methods of payment of dowry,

[1] Official statistics give the number of marriage licences issued in 1932 as 398; in 1933 as 450; in 1934 as 477; in 1935 as 364; in 1936 as 975.

the more intelligent one's informant, the less hard and
fast are the rules he can give one. One and all stress the
fact that the human factor counts for much and constantly I heard phrases such as: 'a kind father would not
mind if the young man could not pay full dowry'—'if
the girl does not like the man who offers the bigger
dowry, her parents would not force her'—'if I had a
daughter, I would send her to school, no matter if her
husband could not pay me back the fees'—or, on the
other hand: 'there are some parents who only give education to their daughters so that they should get more
money for them'—'some parents are so proud that they
refuse all the poor men and then cannot find a rich
one. . . .' These variations in attitude with consequent
wide fluctuations in the amounts expected and given are
understandable, though it is all the more unfortunate
from the investigator's point of view as dowry is naturally one of the central features in the Ibo social system
and one which should be described coherently and
authoritatively.

From one woman informant, I gathered that no
more dowry was expected in the case of the daughter of
a 'rich' house than in that of a poor one. Equally, a
father would be ashamed 'to ask for a higher dowry just
because his daughter was pretty or clever or well born'.
It would be regarded as 'selling' his daughter if he bar-
gained as to how much more or less she was worth. I also
understand that the girl herself does not want the dowry
to be too high as, should she not get on with her husband, it would be difficult for her parents to find the
money wherewith to refund it and in the meantime she
would perhaps have to put up with a husband who was
cruel to her and 'would die before it was her time to die'.
All the same, the degree of schooling a girl has received
does often affect the amount of dowry paid or rather,
though the actual dowry may remain the same, the
parents will demand that the young man should bear

some of the educational expenses incurred on behalf of their daughter.

From another equally reliable informant, a man this time, I got the following account which seems worth reproducing in full and in his own words, especially as it gives a sidelight on the attitude of an educated man towards the educated girl viewed as a potential wife. As the informant in question is a teacher himself, of the best type, it is likely that his criticism is aimed at the type of education given in girls' schools rather than at women's education in general. He first refers to the foregoing paragraph and says: 'To say that no more dowry is expected for the daughter of a "rich" house than of a poor one is only true in so far as a sum above the customary maximum bride-price may not be demanded. But the rich father nearly always argues that, in giving his daughter away to her husband, he would give her many more yams, goats, fowls, ornaments and such other house property than a poor man could afford to give. Under the circumstances, the rich father certainly expects more dowry than a poor one would, and the husband who also would expect many things in return would not hesitate to pay the higher price. It is a shameful thing for a father to take a high price without giving in return such property to his daughter as would be deemed reasonable for the dowry paid.

'According to custom, yams are given to young wives by their mothers, who also demand a certain sum from the husband for giving these yams. This is usually not included in the dowry paid to the father. The mother who gives forty sticks of yams takes about £3, one who gives sixty or eighty, takes £5 or £7. Here again a rich mother demands a higher sum just because she would give more than a poor one.

'Yes, the girl herself does not wish the dowry to be too high lest she might be perpetually tied down to a cruel husband. But as no dowry is refunded in respect of a dead wife, the preservation of the wife's life is the first consideration of all sensible husbands. The higher the price paid the greater the loss in case of death, and the greater the care usually taken of the wife's well-being. Marriage means more than a contract between one man and one woman to live as husband and wife. Each single marriage is as it were one link in the chain of mutual relationship between one village and another or between one town and another. If a man deliberately becomes cruel to his wife and she runs away, the husband can scarcely hope to recover the dowry paid on her behalf, except of course if she re-marries. Even near relations of a cruel husband would hold no brief for him and should his wife run away from him as a result of cruel treatment they could refuse to help him to recover her.'

He then goes on to say: 'You have asked for more information about the amount of dowry paid in Owerri Town nowadays. The original custom has lost so much ground that there is now no royal road. The amount demanded from suitors varies with their social status and ranges from £10 to £30. The dowry question seems much more easily settled among the non-Christians and uneducated native farmers. Among this class, payments under £10 are sometimes accepted and where the suitor is unable to pay in a lump sum, payment may be spaced over a number of years.

'It has become the rule rather than the exception to demand a higher dowry on a girl who has been to school. The amount usually demanded sometimes frightens prospective suitors away, and what is more dreadful about it is that in many cases what one receives in exchange for the higher dowry is a delicate and over-indulged sort of wife, rather more expensive to maintain but less able to perform those duties which circumstances impose upon African womanhood. Please excuse me if I have not treated the case of the educated girl with sufficient indulgence.

Dowries and the Educated Girl

'In order to make my points more clear, I shall attempt to give an account of certain marriages I have heard of lately: A well-known man was engaged to a girl from a Christian home since eight years. Immediately after performing the engagement ceremonies, the father resigned all the care of the girl to the young would-be husband. During these eight years, the young man had to pay, not only for the girl's educations, first in a day-school, and then in a boarding-school, but he also had to buy her dresses and all necessary toilets. As far as I know the father of the girl has scarcely made her a Christmas present, much less thinking of buying her a book. Every pin the girl needed had to be supplied by her intended husband, who, in addition, paid a dowry of £29 in one sum to the father and £7 to the mother. When the young man was going to marry the girl in church, the father objected to the marriage on the ground that not enough dowry had been paid. He wired the reverend gentleman in charge of the District asking that the marriage be not solemnized. The reverend gentleman advised the husband-to-be to go and set things right with his future father-in-law before anything else. The young man travelled a long distance to see his father-in-law and tried in vain for two days to persuade him to forgo the additional dowry, but he would not even accept a promissory note that payment would be made after the wedding. The young man returned home in disgust and despair and, but for the encouragement of friends, nearly decided to break the engagement. Although the girl was very much against her father's unpleasant action, yet she could not do anything as, according to custom, a woman should not discuss matters pertaining to her own dowry. The young man was obliged to get the additional sum of £5 somehow and paid it to his father-in-law before the marriage could take place. This is only one instance of several similar cases that occur nowadays.

'Now look at another case of marriage which occurred

in the same village nearly at the same time. The girl and the one referred to above are of the same age, but the former did not go to school and was not married in church. The betrothal was made early last year. After the preliminary ceremonies, the young man paid £6 10s. as dowry and promised to make it up to £10 or £15 within six months. The parents accepted this sum though of course with a little reluctance. By the end of June the young girl was some three months under pregnancy. According to native custom, a woman's dowry ought not to be discussed when she is pregnant. It could be before or after but not during her pregnancy.[1] The girl has now given birth to a female child and it is very unlikely that the husband will redeem his promise before another year, if ever he does so at all. The girl is reputed to be a very industrious young lady, good at farm work, can carry a big basket of yams or bunches of palm-nuts,[2] go to trade at a distant market, and know how to look after a large family. All that goes to the man for £6 10s. Fairly cheap, is it not? One cannot help thinking that in such a locality where human beings are all the machines available for the necessary daily work, strong muscles would be preferred to clever brains!

'From the foregoing instances, it would seem as though I had given you the two extremes of the question. It is all because there are in Owerri to-day two kinds of girls: the educated Christian girl and the uneducated heathen girl. In the case of the former the minimum dowry is £25. It might be higher according to the standard of education reached. As a rule, in these

[1] I think that in some parts this rule extends even to the discussion of another woman's dowry or even dowry in general. In the Okigwi Division I was trying to get some facts about dowry from a small group of men and women when my interpreter Mary turned the conversation, giving me a significant glance and I noticed a pregnant woman was sitting near me.

[2] This phrase might give the impression that the value of an Ibo wife lies solely in her capacity to act as a beast of burden. This would of course not be admitted either by the men or by the women.

206

cases, the dowry is paid in a lump sum, and where a period of time is allowed in which to make full payment, that period extends up to, but never beyond the time of the actual wedding in church.[1]

'With the heathen girls the amount of dowry hardly exceeds £15. It might be anything between £5 and £10 for a first payment and could be paid by easy instalments (nowadays always in cash) up to such an amount as it might be believed the husband could afford. But as cheaply married girls are sometimes a sort of threatening [i.e., are apt] to walk out of the husband's house, men do not scruple even to pawn their persons[2] in order to bring the dowry up to £10 or £15.'

It will be seen from the above notes that the parents of the bride do not make so much profit out of the dowry paid as one would think. Quite a fair proportion goes back into the trousseau of the young wife. It will also be seen that both public opinion and expediency are against cruel treatment of the wife; but it is interesting to note that the girl wants a low dowry so that she may more easily get away from her husband and the husband wants a high one so that he may more easily keep her.

Other informants gave further particulars regarding the payment of dowry in the case of educated girls, which I will add as the subject is of immediate importance. Three methods seem to be followed:

(*a*.) The young man is betrothed to an uneducated girl and arranges to give, say, £20 as dowry, but he wants her to have some training before he marries her, so he sends her, at his own expense, to a training-home such as the one already described at Ebu-Owerri, and

[1] In spite of many inquiries, I have not been able to find out whether the rule of not permitting a Christian marriage to take place until the full dowry has been paid is a general one. I am inclined to think that it is not but varies with the mission and locality in question.

[2] That is to say, the man volunteers to work for a given time for a temporary master who, in return, advances him a lump sum of money.

keeps her there for a year or two. The expenses he incurs will not be deducted from the promised dowry of £20, but on the other hand, should he die or his wife leave him at some later date and wish to marry again, her second husband would have to refund to her late husband's family both the dowry and the amount of the expenses incurred by him on her training.

(*b.*) The young man is betrothed to a girl who is still at school. The dowry is again settled at, say, £20, but the parents demand that the young man should pay in addition at least half if not the whole[1] of her school fees and any expenses incurred in buying her books, uniforms, etc. The complicated accounting this leads to can be imagined. As in the first case (*a*), should the dowry have to be refunded for any reason, these sums would be added to it.

(*c.*) The young man is betrothed to a girl who has already left school. This time the parents, in fixing the amount of dowry they will be willing to accept, take into account the expenses they have had in educating their daughter and raise the amount accordingly. Nevertheless, I have heard of illiterate girls for whom as much dowry was paid as for literate ones, either because the girl was more popular, or because the men were afraid of embarking upon matrimony with such an unknown and expensive quantity as a 'school-girl'.

Many contradictory opinions were expressed concerning the actual financial value of virginity. Apparently some sections of society were more particular than others. The amount of dowry paid does not seem to be affected and if a girl has got a child by another man, the husband, though it belongs by rights to the girl's parents, may be quite ready to take it and bring it up as his own, glad to

[1] My first informant affirms that cases where the parents continue to bear even part of the schooling expenses of their daughter once she is betrothed are the exception rather than the rule. Practically always, from the time the parents of the girl agree to a proposal of marriage, all such expenses as school fees, cost of books, uniforms and dresses, are passed over to the prospective husband.

think he has already got the beginnings of a family, so to speak, ready made. On the other hand, the custom exists, even if it is not always carried out, of making a gift of money and palm-wine to the bride's mother, should the husband find that she is a virgin. This gift is a compliment to the mother 'for the care she take for her daughter's belly', so it shows that in theory, at any rate, the bride's virginity is prized.

Birth customs resemble those of Nguru rather than those of Nneato. The mother has her baby in hut or yard, relatives and friends can visit her at any time. Occasionally, after delivery, she goes and stays in her mother-in-law's hut, and it is the latter who prepares her food until the child's naming-day; in other cases, she stays in her own hut and female relatives or friends do her cooking. Naming-day takes place after twenty-four days (i.e. six Ibo weeks of four days), amid great rejoicing.

A child whose mother dies at birth will be occasionally suckled by the dead mother's co-wife, if she has weaned her own child.[1] Under no circumstances will a woman suckle two children at a time, 'it would be too much like having twins', which, it will be remembered, is an abomination. More often, the motherless baby is taken to a Mission station or hospital, where the baby is kept long enough to show the accompanying relatives how to feed it on tinned milk—one sees touching pictures of fathers or elder brothers patiently pouring teaspoons of milk down baby throats—but the mortality is high where there is no easily available help.

[1] Again and again, one hears accounts of old women, past child-bearing (or even women who have never conceived), being able to give milk after their breasts have been 'washed' with a medicine prepared by a *dibia*. Several times, when I have asked who looks after the baby while its mother is in the market, I have been told that, if the mother is unable to return in time to feed it, its grandmother will do so. Is it possible that, as the normal suckling period is so long—two years or more—a more constant supply of milk is induced? The doctors I have questioned have also heard of similar cases but had never actually seen one.

Women

A woman who dies in child-birth will have no funeral ceremony, no singing, no wailing. As my interpreter graphically described it, she will die 'all same like fowl'. Before burying her, her husband will send to a neighbouring village for a man, a stranger, to remove the child from the womb, otherwise the infant in whom the woman will eventually be reincarnated will be born 'with big belly'. The stranger who is thus called in will bring his own dish or bowl and drinking-cup, so as not to contaminate anyone else's, and though he will be given food, no one will eat with him. Towards evening, the body is carried to the edge of the 'bad bush' and when the child has been removed, both bodies will be thrown into the bush. Any articles used by the woman during her last days, such as her cloth or her mat, would be thrown away too. Her cooking-pots might be used by her own daughters, but by no other woman. When money was more plentiful, the stranger would have been paid 10s. to 15s. for his services, now he would not receive more than 5s. As some time must necessarily elapse between the woman's death and his arrival to begin his gruesome work, he richly deserves his fee.

As elsewhere, burials take place in the compound, except in the case of Christians who might be buried in a cemetery. A married man is buried in his own backyard; an unmarried lad might also be buried in his father's backyard, 'although to save the man the pain of seeing his son's grave at every moment' he would be more likely buried in his own yard, supposing he already had a hut of his own. A young girl is buried in any part of the waste space within the compound, while a baby would be buried outside. A married woman is generally buried by her own people in her old home. Should her children wish especially to keep her body, they must pay the woman's relatives for the privilege. This occurs chiefly if the woman herself has asked to be buried in her husband's compound. Nevertheless, even if she has not done

210

so, she will always be reluctant to leave her children, especially if they are still young. I was given a dramatic description of how a dead woman will struggle to stay with them, causing the bearers of her coffin[1] to sway and stumble, her spirit forcing them to turn right round and carry her back to her husband's house, or, if she cannot prevail upon them to do so, then obliging them to stop first at this neighbour's house and then at that one, so as to put off as long as possible the dreaded moment of leaving her children for ever. The neighbours are naturally only too anxious to get rid of such an unwelcome visitor but are afraid of showing it, and say soothingly: 'But why do you stop here? Why do you keep looking round? Surely you are glad to be going back to your parents?'

Occasionally, if there has been some long-standing feud between the two families, the dead woman's relatives will refuse to fetch her, the husband and children will fear to bury her in case such action should bring bad luck, and the impasse thus created might last for weeks.

I was unable to get any very reliable accounts of women's funerals and was never able myself to witness the whole ceremony. Here is one account: 'When a woman dies, all her "sisters" come to cry and sing and men also. If she dies in her husband's house in the morning, messengers would be sent to her parents' house and they would arrive in the evening. They would sing all night in their son-in-law's house, then go home, notify all friends and relations of the dead woman and again return to their son-in-law's house to fetch the body.' At some stage during the burial ceremonies, a woman of the deceased's own family is sent for to cook a meal for the dead woman in her old kitchen. The food thus cooked is thrown away. A 'smart' woman is chosen for this ceremony, who knows how to cook well and quickly so that

[1] Bodies are either rolled in a certain kind of mat and tied down, or placed in a rough plank coffin of European shape.

the deceased will be equally 'smart' in her next reincarnation.[1] I have often noticed that the Ibo have a strong dislike of slow women who dawdle over their work, and as a rule the women are exceptionally quick movers and workers.

The question of Christians attending second burials or performing second burial rites for their pagan father or mother is a vexed one. Missions do not approve and even forbid their adherents to attend any such ceremonies. The Ibo, genuinely distressed at not being able to pay these last respects to the deceased, uncomfortably conscious of disapproving native public opinion and probably a little fearful of what ill luck may befall him if he breaks away from tradition, often compromises by giving the necessary funds for the second burial, but does not take part in it himself. In families where all the members are Christians, more or less elaborate memorial services are held, instead of the second burial ceremonies.

These second burials appear to vary in significance according to the area under consideration, and are more or less frequently carried out. The clearest accounts come from the Onitsha area, where it is believed that when an individual dies, his spirit leaves the body and wanders about, restless and homeless, until the second burial is performed, after which it is able to go back to Chuku, the creator spirit with whom it finds rest and peace, and in whom, according to some informants, it is absorbed. (The co-existence of this belief with the equally strongly held belief in reincarnation seems to offer no difficulty to the Ibo, but is baffling to the European.) If no second burial takes place, the spirit remains at large, ready to take revenge upon the living whenever possible. Should the second burial be long delayed, probably through lack of sufficient money—for the ceremony, with

[1] Cf. the ceremony of the 'killing of the dog' for a dead man (Meek, *Law and Authority in a Nigerian Tribe*, p. 305), of which I was also given an account.

its dancing, feasting, killing of cows, letting off of guns, is a costly one—then the anger of the deceased spirit will make itself felt, first through small mishaps to members of the family, then through serious disasters.

In Owerri, the religious aspect, so to speak, seemed more nebulous and the second burials were more like social events carried out in honour of the deceased, but also as a proof of the riches and importance of the survivors. They were, therefore, less frequent and had a less obligatory character, though all the best people would seek to hold them and in some cases were forced into holding them by the vindictiveness of their dead relatives as interpreted by the *dibia*.

Second burials are accorded to women in Owerri Town and in its neighbourhood, just as they are to men, although less frequently. Unfortunately, I did not think of making inquiries on this subject either in Nneato or in Nguru. These second burials may take place several months or even several years after the person's actual death and as a rule would only be accorded to older women and only 'if she had good children'. If she had no children and only a husband survived her, he would not make a second burial for her as her co-wives 'would think it a waste of money'. The second burial always takes place in the deceased's husband's house. 'The co-wives of the deceased put on their best clothes and jewellery and go round the market on "big market" day, singing and clapping. Every one looks at them and if they are very much admired, the onlookers give them a few pennies or cowries. Then they all go home, guns are fired and a feast eaten, as for a man's second burial.' From my own observation, I should say that not very many women were given second burial unless their spirits had made a nuisance of themselves to their late household, and in searching for the explanation of illness, money losses, or crop failures, the *dibia* had declared the cause to be the anger of the deceased at not

213

having any posthumous honours paid to her. Much human nature was contained in the phrase supposed to have been said by a *dibia* interpreting a dead wife's feelings: 'While I was alive, everyone told me all day long what a rich woman I was. Now that I am dead, why does no one make music for me?' In any case, this particular woman was getting her own back. The second burial ceremonies had already lasted a fortnight and had still ten days to run (the usual Ibo six weeks of four days). The special dancer, the best of his kind I have seen, and an excellent band with remarkable bell-noted drums, had been obtained from a distant village. Their fees must have been considerable, and they, as well as a number of relatives, had to be lodged and fed during the whole period of their stay. (This was at Emi, which had different customs to Owerri, six miles away.)

Although there were various meetings of women church members, I was not able to trace anything resembling the Women's Councils of Nneato and elsewhere. My closest inquiries brought forth nothing more cogent than accounts of social gatherings known as *oru* or *otu*, though usually now termed 'meetings'. Originally, each quarter formed its own *oru*, composed of young men and girls and children with a few older married men as seniors. These members met to rehearse dances which were performed at 'Christmas and Easter' (as the *oru* date from pre-European days, these dates must have roughly coincided with some native festivals, but I could not pin them down). Visitors were entertained with the money collected regularly from the members, and were themselves expected to give presents to the dancers. In later years, the *oru* in Owerri Town became more and more social gatherings run on European lines, with presidents, treasurers (whose accounts were controlled by all the members, a typically Ibo procedure!), masters of ceremonies, European dances and, in the case of one quarter at least, a brass band. Good discipline was kept:

members who quarrelled or were rude were judged by their fellow members and fined. The standard of dancing was high: specially gifted members were sent to other towns to learn new steps or an expert dancer was invited to come and give an exhibition. But when the elders objected to the impropriety of Western styles of dancing, these meetings were abandoned and instead the *oru* held occasional picnics at which, after a good repast, they dance in European fashion. In the bush around Owerri the *oru* still retain their more primitive form. Even if the native dance is modified by the introduction of dumb-bell drill or physical exercises learnt by the children at school, the sexes dance separately to the music of a native band. At Nguru, in the month of June, various parties of children were busy rehearsing their dances, eager to outdo each other. When they had got beyond the initial stages, they practised behind high screens of palm-branches, presumably so that others should not copy their best 'steps'. After the day's work was done, under the stern leadership of an older boy and girl, they spent hours going through one set of steps after another. There was no talk or laughter: the little bodies swayed and swerved in obedience to the sharp commands; the little feet lifted and stamped to the difficult rhythms; the little faces were set in a rapt and happy concentration. Only when they wore some article of Western clothing did they become alien, unbeautiful.

There are two annual festivals, that of *Oru Owerri* and that of *Mgbu Mgbu Uzo* which are peculiar to Owerri, but owing to the opposition of the Missions and to the general lessening of respect for traditional customs, they are fast dying out. I tried to get exact information concerning them and also to witness them, but although I obtained several accounts from different informants, they neither agreed among themselves nor did the accounts given tally with the fragments of ceremonies that I was able to watch.

Women

I think many observers would agree that, to the European at least, few Ibo ceremonies seem to have either beginning or end and that the people themselves are so casual about them that it is wellnigh impossible to grasp what is the essential part of them. I witnessed a ceremonial cooking of corn (maize), a part of the *Mgbu Mgbu Uzo* festival, in an old woman's hut. No one objected to my presence in the slightest. When the time came, a portion was handed me to eat as a matter of course, but looking at the way the women drifted in and out, or squatted down, gossiping or playing with the children while the old woman (Salome's grandmother) meandered round, absent-mindedly dropping portions of oil bean, pounded pepper, palm-oil, salt, into the pot of cooked corn, it was impossible to guess whether the ceremony had still a profound significance or whether it had become merely a funny old custom, which one kept up if one happened to remember it.

This was all the more disappointing as in this particular case the explanation of the rites, given me some weeks before, had been fairly clear and concise and I had thought that, for once, I would be able to follow intelligently an interesting women's ceremony. The account had been as follows: 'The ceremony of *Mgbu Mgbu Uzo* is the women's festival [before the eating of the new yams] as *Oru Owerri* is that of the men, and takes place after the latter. By this time [i.e. end of July] the corn the people will have been eating has become a little hard and over-ripe. On a certain day, the women, helped by their children, gather a quantity of corn cobs, strip them and boil the corn that same evening, in large cooking-pots. Only married women [that is to say, non-Owerrians, Owerri being exogamous] are allowed to cook the corn. When the cooking is nearly finished, unmarried girls and married Owerri women who have come on a visit [that is to say all 'daughters' of Owerri] stand by the kitchen door and beg for some of the corn. They are

216

given small portions and the ones who get it first and find it well cooked run out into the yards, their spoons in their hands, calling: "Mine is done! Mine is good!" Although it often happens that it rains on that evening [July is well in the middle of the rains] they run round all the same. Next morning the married women mix the corn with oil, etc., and the day is spent feasting on this corn, men and women together, but the men will have been invited by the women, in the same way that on *Oru Owerri* the women were invited by the men. A special dish of corn will be passed round among the Christians as they will not want to give a portion of it as a sacrifice [I think, to the ancestors], as the others do. On the next morning, the married women take a little of this same cooked corn in small earthen pots, and go out to their farms where they throw small portions of it over their yam crops, saying to the yams: "We have been eating corn all this time and it has done us no harm. Now we come to present you with some of it and may you not hurt us when we eat you any more than the corn has done." They then dig up three or four yams and carry them home. They could eat them at once but it is preferable to wait a month or so as they are rather moist and nasty when first dug up. On the day the corn is being mixed and eaten, no one must draw water from, nor go near, the stream sacred to the female spirit Nworie, as she would not like it, and also all the snakes that live in or near the stream are out having a holiday. It does not matter about prisoners fetching water, as that piece of the stream has been given to Government [i.e. it has, so to speak, been secularized and so no sacrilege would be committed in approaching it].'

A minor ceremony, that of the driving out of the old year and the bringing in of the new year (*ichi afɔ*), I was able to watch from beginning to end, but even that was performed by only a portion of the women and was probably shorn of a good deal of its original ritual,

217

although the rule still holds good that men are forbidden to witness it. It is considered that the old year is always a bad one and misfortune would befall any man who saw it being driven away. Consequently the ceremony takes place very early in the morning 'before the first cock-crow'.

Knowing the elasticity of the term 'very early' in the Ibo mind, I chose to sleep in a friendly compound so as to be on the spot. Just before dawn, the women came out of their huts, each carrying a lighted brand. Softly, for fear of waking the men, they ran through the compound gate and down the sandy track that led to the market. Other women joined them. The night was full of low cries and points of fire. Calling to the old year to take away all its sorrows, begging the new year to bring peace and prosperity, they ran past the market to a piece of 'bad bush' which stood beyond it. There they stopped. Faintly visible in the swift-coming dawn, they raised their arms. With one last vigorous curse, they flung the burning brands into the midst of the bush and turned back towards the market-place. Running, swaying, singing, they came to an open space, stopped and formed a circle. Four senior women went into the circle and danced. The song changed and four other women took their place. This happened four times over. Then, with one of their strange clanging shouts, the circle broke. The women, with a last laughing 'May the new year be good to us!' hurried to their homes. The old year lay buried with the burnt-out brands.

On the evening before *ichi afɔ* the whole compound must be carefully swept and any left-over food is thrown away so as to start the new year with, so to speak, a clean sheet. Men as far as I could find out, took no part whatever in the ceremony nor did they have a corresponding one of their own. Probably women, in their role of house-wives, were considered the most suitable persons to deal with the past year's rubbish of troubles and misfortunes.

XII

Woman in Transition—in Owerri Town

How far have the women been influenced by frequent Western contacts. Modern morality. Harlotry, polygamy and monogamy. Marriage as partnership. Yams and babies.

Instead of becoming easier to sum up as they rise in the scale of civilization, the Ibo women become more difficult. Their cleverness develops but not their intelligence, if one may draw so fine a distinction, and their characters cannot yet bear the onslaught of new ideas and new desires. They vacillate, become purposeless, lose their personality. The stiff clay of which their mothers were moulded has returned to a soft paste, awaiting the hands of a new potter. The older women and the more backward of the young ones live in the old way, though even they are in touch with the outside world through husbands or sons or brothers who live in the big towns, but the 'bright young things' of Owerri, whether literate or illiterate, have a touch of irresponsibility, of fecklessness, of 'let's have a good time at all costs', which augurs badly for their future. Facts are hard to come by and the older generation enjoys painting the present with the blackest colours, but it does seem as if the morality of the younger generation had become increasingly lax within the last few years. I was told, for example, that out of a sewing-class started the year before of twenty girls, all belonging to the most respectable families, only one had kept straight, and to my own knowledge even that one had lapsed from virtue before the end of my stay.

Much as they cried about their poverty, I do not think that it was ever real necessity that drove the girls to immoral ways. It was more a glad throwing off of all restraint and a blind grab after money, new clothes and tasteless finery. The mothers shrugged their shoulders, said they could do nothing with their daughters, and let them go their own way. One educated and broad-minded man seriously deplored the introduction of European dancing that gave so many dangerous opportunities; on the other hand, the Missions objected to native dancing. Christian marriage was becoming more common, with the result that, if a man could have only one 'church wife', he had to have concubines or at least temporary relations with prostitutes. These were easy to find: the girls had got lazier, they did not want to toil in farm and market like their mothers, and here was a simple, effortless road to fortune. With so many changing customs, who could tell what was right and what was wrong? And in any case, had it so great an importance? So Owerri girlhood smirked and giggled and gladly 'got belly' by all and sundry, so long as they had new clothes by it or a present of a few pounds.

Of course, there were some happy exceptions and when the novelty of misdemeanour has worn off, there will be a swing back to the innate good sense and industry of the Ibo woman. Indeed, when I got to Port Harcourt a few months later, I was told there were already signs that such a reaction was taking place. But admittedly circumstances often make strict virtue difficult. Talking one day with a young girl, she said that an educated Christian girl might stick out some time for a Christian monogamous marriage, but if no suitor presented

himself, she would accept a Christian polygamous one.
Rather surprised at this juxtaposition of terms, I
asked her whether she meant the girl would accept a
member of the 'African Church' which, while following
the lines of the Church Missionary Society from which it
seceded, yet admits polygamy, but my informant said
'No', there were many regular church Christians who
were polygamous and yet attended church services assi-
duously and though they could neither take Communion
nor preach, nevertheless they were members for, she
added conclusively, 'they take part in all money things.
. . .' Whether the church they attended was of the same
opinion, I do not know, but the native himself was convinced that the taking part in 'all money things' was
sufficient to prove him a true and worthy son of whatever denomination he had adopted and the Christian
bride-to-be would have no misgivings on the subject of
her future husband's orthodoxy.

On the other hand, and quite apart from these cases,
the lot of the Christian couple which does sincerely
accept the principle of monogamy and wishes to hold to
it is sometimes a hard one. Should the wife prove childless, though the husband himself may be ready to make
the best of the situation, his parents will force him to take
another 'wife' by native law and custom, so great is their
desire for their sons to have children. This they wish
from all points of view, partly economic but chiefly
psychological, including a subtle feeling of shame that
their son should not have proved himself capable of
making a child. With the possibility in view that the
woman might be barren, it follows that many Christians
prefer to marry according to native law and custom
rather than in church, so that either a divorce could be
more easily obtained or a second wife could be legiti-
mately added to the household. The Churches of course
disapprove of this compromise but, given the circumstances, it is a very natural one. And the Ibo has a

genius for compromise, as witness the following authentic tale:

Pius Anoku had several wives. A year ago, he had a change of heart, sent his wives back to their homes, and renounced their dowries even if they were to marry again. One of these wives was pregnant by him. Then, his conscience being clear, and his house empty, he married a new wife, with all due ceremony, in the Roman Catholic Church.

Some months later, Pius's mother, standing in her doorway near the Owerri market, saw one of her son's ex-wives carrying on her hips two beautiful twin[1] boys. They were albinos, with skins as white as milk. Struck by their appearance, the mother called the woman to her and together they went to show the twins to Pius. Pius, proud as a peacock, rented a little shelter near the market and exhibited the twins to all and sundry, thereby raking in a few coins and cowries. (Pius had the right to keep the twins if he wanted to as dowry had not been repaid, and even though he had voluntarily renounced it.) His ex-wife is still in Owerri in her mother-in-law's house and it will probably end in her and her twins staying there altogether and being treated as one of the family, although she is no longer counted as Pius's wife. When I asked what the 'church' wife thought of it all, the answer, with a discreet smile, was: 'She doesn't say.'

With regard to polygamy in general, I once more tried to find out what were the women's feelings in a rather more advanced community such as Owerri. I should think opinions were equally divided. One informant went so far as to say she was sure the average woman preferred polygamy, but quickly added the proviso, 'so long as she was the first wife and bore the first son and the

[1] Although in remoter parts, twins are still looked on as 'abominations', the feeling against them is no longer so general. Curiously enough, such distinct abnormalities as albinos have never been considered 'abominable'.

first daughter', which, of course, would give her importance in her husband's eyes and a superiority over the
other women.

What a man thinks of certain aspects of polygamy is
shown in the following account written for me by a
young man of Owerri. I transcribe the whole of it, as it
is a résumé and a confirmation of much that I have
stated in the foregoing chapters of this section and, given
the slightly bookish flavour of the style and the obvious
desire to please the white man, it is of value as showing
on what the native himself lays special emphasis. He
entitles his account 'Life in a Native Family' and says:

'Before considering the mode of living in a native
family, one must first of all know what the occupation is
of the people who make up the family. The chief occupation of the inhabitants of Owerri is farming and so the
occupants of any native family will be farmers. As
farmers, let us think for some moments how their business is carried on. The native's method of farming compared with the white man's will be seen to be too primitive and backward. The poor natives have been helped by
nature by allowing them a good expansion of land
scattered in five definite sections. This year he farms in
this section and does not plant there again until after five
years' time, during which period he has gone round the
other sections. Totally ignorant of the rotation of crops,
he keeps on moving from one bush [i.e. fallow ground] to
the other. The native is the chief overseer of his business. If he finds the work too much for the people of his
house, he hires labourers from the interior villages. In
this way he sees that all work in his farm is done.

'No set of children who are not trained grow to
answer [to the name of] good men in the world. Like the
white man, the poor native has different ways of training
his children. The first thing the native would make his
children know is to tell them his friends and enemies.
When a child is about fifteen or seventeen years of age,

223

the parents take him to their different farms to show him the boundary of their farms and other peoples'. Any child who does not know such boundaries in the farms is said to be foolish.[1]

'The native, of course, trains his child to know about farming but in some cases some don't ask their children to do farming business. When they have their children put to school, they won't worry this boy again to do farming business. If a boy likes to farm, he goes to help them say on Saturdays, when he likes.

'No special time is taken to teach the children about the manners and customs of the people. Like the white man too, he trains his children to be kind, honest and gentle. There are no laid down principles as regards the training of children but he [the father] in most cases trains his children unconsciously. There are certain signs the children are trained to know. If a child is sitting with the father and someone enters, the father makes a certain sign unknown to the visitors and this sign means that the child should go out. If the parents think that their child has not behaved well, they scold him or flog him and the highest punishment is perhaps to refuse him food. In such a case, the boy takes refuge in a neighbour's house. After a day or two the neighbour goes to the child's father or mother and asks for the boy's forgiveness. For the sake of the neighbour, the parents will receive him again.

'In the case when the wife finds she has not been well treated by the husband or when she fights with the husband, she escapes to her village. After some days according to custom the husband will go to her village with a jar of palm-wine. When he reaches, he makes an apology

[1] The writer whom I quote is distinctly of the young man-about-town type, dressed in European fashion and hoping for a post in Government service, and yet he immediately states that his fellow citizens are predominantly farmers and shows what an important matter the land is to them. This supports my contention that the Owerri townsfolk have remained definitely rural-minded.

to the wife if he feels he is in the wrong and the wife follows him home again. In the case of the wife not running away, she summons the husband before the elders living near them. These elders will go into the matter and give decision accordingly. Anyone found guilty is asked to give something to the other. In the case where the husband is found guilty, he is asked to buy a loincloth for his wife. But if the wife is guilty, she is asked to prepare a very sweet soup for the husband, using fish [dried fish is a great delicacy] costing up to any sum of money they may fix.

'The native has many ways by which he can maintain himself and family. Yam being the chief industry, the native tries as much as he can to get it in good numbers. These yams are tied to sticks in rows and when he feels like it, he can sell some of his yams. From this stock of yams, the family is maintained. The native who is good at climbing goes out into the bush and cuts the oil-palm nuts. He reduces them to oil and sells it. With this money he is able to buy things to make soup. He goes out into the bush with his gun, and when fortunate sometimes kills animals, takes them to the market and sells them, or if he likes he uses them himself for his food. In this way the native is able to upkeep his family. The wife, if she has a little money, puts it into trade and with the profits she makes buys such things as fish, salt, etc. If the native has a child working for Government or a mercantile firm, this child sends money to the parents and with the money the family is also supported. So we see that from the united efforts of the wife and husband the native finds not much difficulty in maintaining his family.

'In families where the husband is a polygamist, life really is not worth living. In this case the maintenance of the family both in food supplies and peace presents much difficulty.[1] As many wives look to him for help, he has

[1] In practice, the food supply is mainly the responsibility of the wives. The keeping of the peace is another matter.

H

got much to do. We will now consider how the husband gets himself just a little bit released from the troubles and worries of so many wives. The husband, finding that he will not be able to do all the work, sees that some of his wives are supplied with domestic servants, whom they still refer to as slaves. Here comes in another striking information: how are these so-called slaves got? Now for instance, a man has got a son. He, the father, is in danger of being imprisoned by a creditor. To free himself, he takes his son to any person he thinks he can get money from. If he receives say, the sum of £5 from the man, he leaves his son with him to work for him. This son will remain with this person until the father is able to repay the borrowed sum. The question of the amount of money to be repaid depends upon the agreement made. So the native in this way gets servants who help his wives in their work, which releases him from some worries.

'In a household where there are many wives, there are necessarily many children. When the father gives something to one child, the other wives ask that the same should be given to their children. The first male born in a family is looked upon with more respect. He gets a bigger share of everything than the others. In the case where the first male born is only by a few months or years older than the next one, there is always great confusion in that family. This kind of thing has been causing so much trouble that some sensible parents at the point of death will with their last breath share all things between their children.[1] So we see that the native always has much to do in the case where the family comprises so many persons.

'In all spheres of life, peace is required. So we shall consider for a time what steps the native takes to make peace in the family.

'The native in order to keep the people in his house at

[1] The making of wills is practically unknown except among a small section of the educated community.

peace has made certain rules. If any two people in the family happen to fight, certain things belonging to the two parties will be seized from them. After some days, the people in the family will meet together and try the case. If anyone is proved guilty, that person's thing is forfeited, or he is made to pay a certain amount of money instead. Certain family matters are not allowed to be tried by the public, but in the case where the matter looks serious, the important men in the compound are summoned up to try it. There are also rules that on such and such days any people fighting, quarrelling, or crying will give a fowl [as an indemnity]. It is ordered that if anyone goes against these rules, the "medicines" he has in the house will be offended. The person who offends the said "medicine" is asked to buy a fowl which is used to restore the "medicine" to activity. This helps to check the people of the family from fighting or doing anything of that nature. The head of the family also uses another thing, called *afolaja*, to maintain the peace of the family. By this he goes to a native doctor and inquires what he will do in order to make peace in the family. The doctor will give him certain instructions. He believes that if he carries them out, his family will behave well. He makes a kind of medicine called *onye adumara kwe*. This is a medicine which adds certain powers to the voice of any person in charge of a family. By the power of this medicine, it is believed that all in the family will listen to his word.

'So in conclusion, we see that the native has many ways in which he can create or maintain the peace of the family.'

On the other hand, from time to time, curious little sidelights are thrown upon monogamy and its disadvantages: a monogamous wife has a poor time if her husband dies and her relations-in-law do not like her, and they are not slow to take it out of her whenever they can. For example, the usual fee for her head-shaving, which is customary on her becoming a widow, would be one shilling. If there had been, say, five wives, the husband's female relatives who always undertake this shaving would thus have received five shillings. This they point out to her and spitefully add: 'It was you who wanted to be alone. It was you who prevented your husband from marrying other wives. Now you can pay us five shillings instead of only one shilling!' And again, 'they might force her to go alone into her dead husband's room to wash the body and they might lock her in so that she fear too much and she would sit and cry: "If ever I marry again, I will choose a husband who has other wives!"'

I have already stated (see p. 197) that the bulk of the Owerri adult women are engaged in farm work. This was confirmed by an intelligent man, who added the following remarks emphasizing the independent character of the Ibo woman and the novelty of her outlook upon marriage: 'It would be a reproach to a woman not to contribute anything to the household. Other women would say of her she was stealing from her husband, was no better than a thief, taking all he had and giving nothing in return.' (It is noticeable how often this point of view crops up. Apparently the fact that the woman cooks, looks after the house, etc. does not count as a compensation.) 'Even the wife of a quite rich man, a Government schoolteacher, for example, would farm and trade, so as not to hang round her husband's neck.' The wife herself prefers to take part in farm labour as then she need not be asking her husband for money all the time, for though she may not sell anything without her husband's consent—neither his nor her yams, her goats nor fowls—yet the small profits she can make on her trading can be kept by her to do with what she likes, provided she has first bought all that is required for the household. And again, if she does not farm 'other women suspect her of getting money by a bad life rather than by honest means.'

Women's Property in Owerri

I noticed that the informant with whom I had the above conversation, though a Christian and a church member of long standing and having an excellent command of the English language, yet referred to a wife as a 'possession' and, once the dowry paid, considered that the husband in possessing the woman possessed all that she had—that was why she had to seek his consent even for the sale of the goats or the seed yams she had brought with her as a bride from her parents' house. This may be exact: the question of the holding of property by a woman is, as has already been mentioned (see p. 102) a nebulous one, but I am inclined to think that once more information received from a man tends, quite unconsciously, to belittle the status of the woman and to give a restricted picture of her rights. Certainly, I heard much less of the necessity of obtaining 'the husband's consent' in conversing with women than I did in conversing with men. For example, both Mary and Salome, and other women elsewhere, maintained that what a woman brings with her as a bride is hers absolutely. If for any special purpose of her own, probably to buy some commodity for trading purposes, she wanted some extra money, she would go to her husband and ask him either to advance her the money or, if he preferred, to buy, say, her goat from her. If the husband wished to do neither, she would sell the goat herself and keep the money. I suggested that as the goat had probably been originally bought with a portion of the dowry given by the husband the goat might be said to belong to him, but to this Salome at least would not agree.

From chance conversations, it struck me it was customary for a number of financial transactions, founded on strictly business lines, to take place between husband and wife. For example, if a husband objected to his wife sitting every day in the public market, he might advance her five pounds to set up a stall in her own house with a stock of soap, cigarettes, etc., which would be considered a more

229

'refined' form of trading. Later on, he would expect her to refund him the capital and only a 'loving' husband would allow her to keep the profits. Similarly, he might buy her a sewing-machine and repay himself out of her earnings. But in all these transactions, again and again, the worldly-wise Ibo makes it clear that no hard and fast rules exist, that the human factor predominates in all situations. The 'loving' husband would do this, the 'angry' husband would do that, the 'smart' wife would do the other. There is no general pronouncement: thus would men do; thus would women do.

At the risk of repetition, one cannot emphasize too strongly these business aspects of the marital relation. Whether in bush or town they are there, though circumstances naturally modify their expressions, and no accurate view of Ibo society can be obtained until one has realized that here is a situation quite different from what one might consider the traditional ones. Here one has a relationship which is neither that of master and slave, of owner and chattel, nor yet that of defender and weakling, of the strong male protecting the helpless female; but one much more original and modern, that of business partners in a common enterprise, an enterprise which ranges in scope from the mere maintenance of the family to the making of money for its own sake. Husbands and wives are partners, though it is possible that the woman is the working partner to a greater degree than the man.

One often hears it said that the Ibo man 'lets the woman do all the work'. This is more true of some areas than others but even when cases of what appears to be manifest injustice arise, one must be careful to inquire, before passing judgment, into all the circumstances. One may have happened upon the one period of the year when farm labour falls heaviest upon the women or one may not realize that the work she is doing is for her own personal profit and that she chooses to do it. One also hears it said that the Ibo man 'does not respect women'. He does: he even respects her in a way again so original and so modern that Europeans have only just begun to think of it. He respects her desire to be herself. In conversation one day with an educated man whom I knew well, a man who was both proud of his own customs and appreciative of Western ones, I purposely emphasized the old-fashioned aspect of English marriage, in which the man was the active breadwinner and the woman the passive housewife, and showed him how different was our conception of the man as the protector and sole supporter of the family. At the thought of the man as the breadwinner, he laughed, but when I went on to say that many men would be ashamed to let their wives go out and work for money, his remark was startling in its psychological insight: 'But if she has gifts . . . ?' By gifts, he did not mean as we might, artistic or intellectual gifts, but qualities of initiative, industry, shrewdness, alertness. These are all qualities desirable in trade and money-making, but they are also just the gifts the Ibo woman herself would be most proud of and desire most to use. In expecting his wife to carry a heavy load to market and sit there all day in the dust and heat, the Ibo man is not driving a helpless slave to perform a cruel task but is giving his wife the opportunity fully to express her personality. If the woman succeeds and profits accrue, he is the first to praise her. 'See my wife she buy lorry with her own money.' When the rarely heard word 'love' is used, it is often in the case of the man who 'loves' his wife because she has rented a cement stall in the market or has embarked upon a kernel trade with Oguta. And often the word 'respect' follows the word 'love'.

That there is even perhaps more intellectual partnership than one thinks I am occasionally led to believe. Intellectual is of course too big a word but there are certainly occasions when the husband consults his wife, lays his plans before her, whether they affect himself or his children, and listens to her advice. He would not do this until he had carefully tested her discretion and her wisdom and he would probably be more ready to pour forth his own troubles than to listen to hers, but all the same he allows her to share his thoughts and to a certain extent to guide his actions, though, were his parents still alive, her opportunities would be less and her opinion would not carry weight against theirs.

I do not think husbands and wives ever 'do things together' or enjoy each other's society as such, for the pleasure of the give and take of ideas—that presupposes a more delicate comprehension of the art of living than they have yet attained—but one often sees men and women talking together, the women obviously holding their own. Mary Anderson, for example, would answer back with complete assurance and her jokes and repartees would often bring down the house. In Owerri, it struck me the women had rather less personality. I did not meet any striking individuals such as Nwayinkwere of Eziama, Lɔlɔ or Ekeomo of Nguru, or the Amazons of Oguta, but it may have been that no outward circumstance nor emotional reaction brought out the vitality of their real natures. Though I remember two elderly women who corrected the statements of a well-known and senior man and did not hesitate to give their own views in his presence, they belonged to the older generation which, as already remarked, seems to have more individuality and stamina than the present one. When I asked them which time was best, the past or the present, they tactfully and truthfully replied: 'We liked our time, the young like this time.' Here again they show a modern capacity for appreciating the attitude of the rising generation. These women, for example, frankly said they thought modern times bad because the old customs were going and forbidden things were practised, but they knew that life could not stand still and

Old and Young

that the young would have a different outlook. They
accepted the fact with perhaps a tinge of regret but no
resentment and, rather to my surprise, did not even vent
their prejudice in querulous complaints that children
who went to school were less respectful to their parents
or that they were less well behaved. Whether their
emotional resistance to the new had spent itself and the
attitude I took for tolerance was in reality an acquiescence born of fatigue and a sense of defeat, was impossible to guess.

On the whole, looking back at Owerri, a town I knew
so well, I am surprised to find how little I remember it,
how faint is the impression that has remained upon my
mind. Reading my notes recalls of course special incidents, certain individuals; hints of gossip give transi-
tory life to otherwise dull records; memory holds a few
touches of humour, beauty, or humanity but the general
impression is one of a commonplace town, inhabited by a
mass of undistinguished people, whose future is bounded
by the walls of materialism. One cannot even say that the
transition period in which we now find it holds anything
that is striking, inspiring, or unexpected. There is no
depth to the picture. It is like an under-exposed negative, thin and grey, and by mistake the negative has
been exposed twice so that we see the new superimposed
upon the old, confused but unmingled.

The women were perfectly friendly but in a detached,
non-committal way. I never felt I had got near them as
individuals. They took no more interest in me than I did
in them. I neither liked them as the Nneato women nor
disliked them as the Nguru ones. Our mutual indifference was complete and it was only through chance conversations and unsought encounters that we occasionally
caught a glimpse of each other as human beings. But as
usual the land was a firm bond between us. There was a
walk I took with Salome one morning to find a very old
woman, who we knew was going to cut her yams, a

process I wanted to see. It was peaceful and green in the little paths among the yam-vines. At first there seemed to be no one there. Then, quite suddenly, behind the green walls of maize-stalks and staked vines, voices sounded from every side. We found the old woman at last, intent upon her delicate task of separating the new tubers. She had tucked up her underskirt tight round her and was greatly enjoying herself. Near her, working on another plot, was a woman from the same compound, fat and comfortable, bending low over the yam heaps. Two little baskets lay between them, containing their midday meal. They were two knowledgeable, free, independent women out for the day, able to take care of themselves, expert at their job, enjoying each other's company. Together we scratched up the earth with our fingers so as to lay bare the tubers and were as familiar to each other as though neither colour nor language differed between us. But close as we were, I still could only guess at what I firmly believe to be the one mystical trait in the Ibo women, the connection between the fertility of the soil and the fertility of their bodies.[1] A good yam crop, quite apart from the fact that it represents their material wealth, stirs profound depths in them.

[1] There is a belief in Owerri Town and perhaps elsewhere, showing a strange sort of relationship between the parents' child and the parents' crop: if a woman or a man steals a yam (a heinous offence in itself), the child of the owners of the stolen yam will fall sick and will probably die if he or she eats of it. If the child eats of a yam stolen from anyone else, it is not affected. As a rule, mothers do not like their children to eat in another woman's house 'for fear they might taste even a morsel of a yam stolen from their parents'.

The yam takes precedence over any other kind of food and is endowed with what one might almost call supernatural qualities. It is believed that yams are alive and that they have speech—people are afraid to go alone to the big *ɔba* outside Owerri Town after dark for fear they should hear the yams talking. If they are obliged to go, they cough loudly so as to drown the uncanny sounds. Yet it is said that 'yams do not know their owner for, should an enemy take a piece of yam from your *ɔba* and carry it to a *dibia*, the *dibia* can put medicine upon it and all your yams will turn against you and kill you when you eat of them'.

Yams and Babies

Their yearning that both the earth and their bodies should be fertile is perhaps the purest form of spiritual hunger to which they can yet attain; and their joy when their wish is granted is the nearest approach to spiritual satisfaction of which they are yet capable.

One wonders how soon education will give the girls something as important, as satisfying, as pervasive, as the land gave to their mothers.

XIII

Sophisticated Woman—in Port Harcourt

Reasons for choice of Port Harcourt. What a purely urban community looks like. How one lives in it. What the women do in it.

My reasons for going to Port Harcourt were two-fold: in the first place, the Ibo I would find there would be in the last of the transitional stages which I had purposed to study. He would have become entirely urban, divorced from all his natural environment, living under artificial conditions created in the first place solely by, and for, European needs, separated from tribal associations and unable to follow except in a limited degree his tribal customs; and not only would he be living under new conditions and following new occupations but he would be continually rubbing shoulders with new neighbours. His women-folk, if they had followed him, would find themselves in an equally new sphere and though the care of the home remains a constant factor in a woman's life, even that factor would be influenced by altered circumstances, not to speak of the enormous difference made in her life by the increase in leisure due to the absence of farm and garden work. In the second place, knowing personally the home backgrounds of some of the Ibo I would meet there, young men and women chiefly from Owerri and Inyeogugu, I would be able to judge

236

Port Harcourt

how far they had wandered from these backgrounds and had taken on the colour of their new surroundings.

I would also find there Mrs. Grainger, a woman missionary to whose friendship I owe many happy hours and whose understanding of the Ibo women made her an invaluable guide. She let me attend her classes and her sewing-meetings, took me to schools and churches, introduced me to the leading Africans, and by her charm and humour broke down those barriers of racial self-consciousness that so often hinder mutual sincerity. Up to this year, she had known only the women of the bush. She was having her first experience of the semi-educated, semi-sophisticated women of the towns. Her impressions would be fresh and illuminating.

I was in Port Harcourt during part of August and September 1935; I therefore saw the town during a period when both the gloom of the rainy season and the gloom of the trade depression combined to depress the onlooker. On my second visit, of a few days only, in December 1936, I was conscious of much more activity and buoyancy.

Port Harcourt is the headquarters of the Owerri Province. It lies on the eastern bank of the Bonny River, some forty miles up from Bonny Bar. It is built upon what is practically reclaimed land and is nearly surrounded, except on the north, by mangrove swamps. One wonders how such a dreary site could have been chosen until one remembers that Bonny Bar can be crossed, at any rate at high tide, by ocean-going steamers and that Bonny River is navigable by them right up to the wharves of Port Harcourt. At the same time the site is the only one where a railway could be brought down to tidal water over relatively firm ground. This is the Eastern Railway, which links up the coast east of the Niger Delta with Kano and beyond, via the great Benue Bridge at Makurdi in the Northern Provinces. Although the bulk of the ground-nut trade passes down from the

North by the Western Railway to be shipped at Lagos, the Eastern Railway carries the tin from the Bauchi mines, large quantities of palm-oil and a certain amount of coal from the Udi mines near Enugu.

Port Harcourt has a population of about 20,000, of whom (in 1937) 125 are Europeans, 40 are Syrians, and 11 are Indians. The Europeans live in a well-kept but unattractive reservation separated from the native town by a stretch of dismal no-man's-land. The township is even more depressing though it has nothing like the slum quarter which existed in Lagos until a few years ago. Roads are broad but unshaded, houses are according to official specifications but have not one single feature of comfort or of beauty, stand-pipes and latrines and incinerators are installed but only emphasize the unkempt, inhospitable look. The township has not the squalor of poverty so much as the squalor of alien ugliness. The streets are thronged with men in ragged singlets, dirty shorts and shapeless felt hats, going to their work among the freight wagons or the cargo boats, the lorries or the casks of palm-oil. Women loll at the windows, the overcrowded schools spill their pupils out on to the pavement, the church bells of fourteen different sects beat thinly on the hot, moisture-laden air. All round lie the swamps, black mud and sucking water, walled by the stilt-like roots of the mangroves.

I do not know how much it has cost to found and develop Port Harcourt. Doubtless it is a great feat of engineering skill, doubtless it serves its purpose, but if someone had said, first to Nature and then to Man: 'Do your worst', one cannot help thinking the result would have been: Port Harcourt.

Yet there are obviously some excuses: the town is still new—it was not begun till 1914, after it had become clear that another harbour would be wanted east of the Niger and that the Udi coal and up-country oil needed an outlet to the sea. Choice of sites was limited by the difficulty of finding suitable ones along this low-lying coast. Numbers of foreign natives were attracted by the hope of work and though some settled down, they more often formed a moving population with no stake in the country. What very little indigenous population there was in that area, was backward. The more advanced Ibo from other parts came to make money and went away again. Though the boom years after the War brought great prosperity, the depression that followed was correspondingly acute and Port Harcourt shares that specially desolate air which seems to surround any place of which the growth has been suddenly arrested.

The population is mixed and shifting. Even to this day, the admixture of foreigners, Yoruba, Efik, Gold Coast, Sierra Leone, is great and till recently the Ibo element tended to be almost submerged by these often richer and more educated immigrants; but now the Ibo in Port Harcourt are coming to the fore and though they started late in the race it will not be long before they outdistance the Lagos lawyer, the Sierra Leone pastor, the Gold Coast clerk, whose places they are already beginning to take as the former retire or are superannuated.[1]

In addition to the foreign Africans, Syrian traders have brought their families to Port Harcourt and do considerable business. They are looked upon as good citizens and do not seem to arouse the jealousy of the native traders as they did in some places west of the Niger. None settle here for good, nor do they spend much money in the country. There are also several Indian firms, selling silks, trinkets, and knick-knacks.

Here in Port Harcourt, the compound system has been abandoned. Individual houses, of more or less European type, are the rule. They are normally lived in by

[1] The same movement is taking place in Onitsha, which, in its character of long-established trading-station, had a large population of Yoruba and Gold Coast clerks.

husband, wife or wives, and children, but shelter also lodgers, poor relations, and boys and girls, not necessarily related but who have been entrusted to the master of the house for training and who fetch and carry, accompany the women to market or run errands for the master in return for board and lodging and, in some cases, their school fees. These children may have to work pretty hard but Mrs. Grainger confirms my opinion that so ingrained is the love of children that one never sees nor hears of any case of ill treatment and in any case the children are quite wide awake enough to be able to defend their own interests and to demand an immediate return to their parents if that is what they wish.

As many single men come to Port Harcourt in search of work—in the total population the men outnumber the women—lodgers are numerous and provide an added source of income for the householders on whom the initial building costs or the monthly rent in cases where the house is not their own property would otherwise fall heavily. Besides these single men, married men also often prefer to come alone, leaving their women-folk to look after their farms and returning to them at intervals by the ever-popular lorries, on which fares are low even if discomfort is acute and which now run, more or less frequently, upon practically every road in the eastern provinces.

Women also come down regularly from such places as Onitsha, Owerri, Aba, either to buy or to take on credit their provision of cloth for re-sale in the up-country markets. When the cost of the lorry fare is added to the cost of the cloth, profits are small but the turnover is quick, they are clever buyers so that stock is seldom left on their hands, and they apparently know no greater bliss than to sit, tight-wedged between their bales, choking with dust and heat, in an over-crowded lorry lurching over the pot-holes on its six- or seven-hour journey up from the coast. Men come also, but in smaller numbers and more often to buy crockery and enamel-ware than cloth.

The one form of long-distance trading consists in the export of poultry to Fernando Po, where there has been a serious disease among the fowls and where imported chickens, bought by the exporters in the bush markets for 6d. or less, fetched in (1935) 2s. 6d. in the market of Santa Isabel, while eggs could be sold for 2d. each. A Yoruba, to illustrate the sharpness of the Ibo, explained that the exporters took good care to send only cockerels to the island so that the inhabitants should not be able to re-start breeding for themselves!

The cost of living in Port Harcourt is not unduly high. In 1935 a labourer with wife and two children could live on 2s. to 2s. 6d. a week. Food is plentiful though naturally more expensive than up-country. Only stockfish is cheaper. Hardly any European tinned food is eaten except perhaps by Sierra Leoneans, but bread and hard unsweetened biscuit of the old ship's-biscuit variety, are popular. Tins of sardines, salmon and bully beef are also seen in the market but only in small quantities.

A few of the women rent plots of waste land from the township at a nominal rent of 1s. per annum. On these they make small farms or rather what they term 'gardens', consisting of a little cassava, maize, beans, peppers, etc., for their own consumption, but there is nothing like the daily exodus to the farms as at Owerri. On the other hand, as will be seen later, nearly all the wives return, say, twice a year to their husband's home to see to the planting and the harvesting of his land.

The cost of building-material fluctuates a good deal but (in 1937) the usual type of cement-washed mud-block and pan-roofed house would cost between £80 and £100 to erect. If it is a 'story house', i.e., a house of two floors, it would naturally be more. To the cost of erection must be added the ground rent collected by the township and which varies from £1 to £20 a year within the township, while a European firm would have to pay about £80 for a plot in the special area where they have their sites. There are also some Government-built quarters reserved for Government clerks. A good three-roomed house can be rented for 18s. a month by a clerk earning a salary of, say, £120 a year, and a two-roomed one for less by those earning smaller amounts.

Together with my missionary friend, I visited a number of Port Harcourt homes: they ranged from the spacious flat above a Syrian shop in the main road of the township to the corrugated-iron shanty in a back street. Some showed a real effort towards a higher standard of living but as is so often the case, the effort was never quite sufficient. The flat had a cool green carpet and softly coloured chintzes but the flowers in the vases were faded; the catechist's home had mats and curtains and framed photographs on the walls but dust lay heavy in the corners. There was never any evidence of African taste nor African experimentation in the decorative arts.[1] What there was was purely imitative of European, or of what was thought to be, European fashions. The green-carpeted flat was reminiscent of Mayfair, the far more typical catechist's house of West Kensington or Bloomsbury. Indeed, I think one could safely say that nine-tenths of the educated homes of Nigeria are laid upon a foundation of plush tablecloths and antimacassars.

As far as clothing is concerned, the fashions are as mixed as the races and one can see every style from the nearly naked countrywoman coming in with her basket of yams on her head to the voluminously enfolded

[1] Such experimentation is occasionally found in other places. In Ilorin, the rich native houses had plates and small mirrors let into the mud walls, forming a not unattractive decoration. At Oguta, there were some interesting experiments at frescoes of geometrical patterns and some highly successful bamboo ceilings painted over with bright enamel paints of various colours.

The Town and Schools

Yoruba, her wide scarf thrown over one shoulder, or the one and only really smart—in the European sense—Sierra Leonean, trim, neat, and well-poised as any Frenchwoman.

One European firm boasts plate-glass windows behind which are shown attractive summer dresses, but no matter how well the African woman or girl holds herself nor how beautiful are the tints of her luminous skin, specifically English cut and colouring seldom suits her. I well remember a nightmare morning spent trying to choose a dress suitable for a woman catechist, which would be bright enough to satisfy her eye for colour, demure enough to suit her rank, and ample enough to conceal her noble proportions!

The township affairs are administered by an Advisory Board on which sit Europeans and five Africans. A member of this Board told me there was very little serious drunkenness in the town and, as far as one knew, no evidence of drug-taking. There is probably a good deal of immorality but neither privately nor officially 'organized'. Indeed, after a month's stay in the town, I found that its life was less sordid than its appearance. Even when walking alone, nobody stared nor begged nor pestered; if I lost my way, guides were quickly forthcoming, friendly and cheerful in spite of their scoundrelly looks. It is true that no service was rendered for nothing but that is true of most of Ibo-land.

There are schools of every denomination, including a newly opened Roman Catholic day school for girls and a privately owned, mixed High School whose Principal is a Sierra Leonean. It is worth noting here that, in spite of the comparatively large population of Port Harcourt and its more modern standards of living, it does not yet possess schools of outstanding importance. These were founded farther up-country, before Port Harcourt was thought of, in the healthier climate and among the more ambitious and virile Ibo of the hinterland. The mixed

High School[1] mentioned above is an interesting venture as being one of the few private schools in Nigeria. When I was there, sixteen girls attended it and about ninety boys. Though the girls wore school blazers and looked the part of the High School girl to perfection, a friend who had volunteered to teach them sewing and games remarked wistfully: 'They have no team spirit. . . .'

Port Harcourt also possesses a cinema, proudly termed the Palladium, run by Africans. Seats cost from 1s. to 6d. and the most popular films are, curiously enough, Wild West ones, closely followed by Charlie Chaplin, religious films, and 'Tarzan of the Apes'. As I believe this is still the only cinema in Ibo-land, one cannot yet gauge what will be their future influence.

Wireless sets are owned by a very few of the well-to-do Africans but, judging from my own limited experience, reception in Port Harcourt is of the kind that was 'quite wonderful' yesterday and will be 'first-rate' tomorrow but is invariably a mere roar of atmospherics to-day.

The bulk of the male population, except for some few independent traders, are wage-earners, ranging from senior clerks in Government offices at a maximum salary of some £400 a year, to casual labourers at 6d. a day. In a wage-earning community such as this, the division of labour is once more clearly defined. The men go off to their daily work in office, workshop or shed and the women look after their homes, cook and trade. This is a typical woman's day in Port Harcourt as described to me

[1] The prospectus of this school states: 'The —— High School provides Secondary Education both for boys and girls. Pupils are prepared for Overseas and other Examinations including Oxford and Cambridge Locals, College of Preceptors, etc. There is a competent and qualified staff of Trained Teachers. A very high percentage of passes were obtained last year at the Cambridge Local Examination. A limited number of Boarders can also be accommodated at an inclusive fee of £3 10s. per term. This provides each pupil with Lodging, Boarding, Tuition, Library, Electric Light, Laundry, Games, Teacher's supervision in his studies, etc.'

244

A Woman's Day in Port Harcourt

by an Ibo-speaking pastor's wife who was an exceptionally good informant: she gets up as soon as she hears the
six o'clock siren, goes to the factory to buy cloth or soap
or stockfish or oil or salt, carries her goods to the market,
where she arranges her stall and then runs quickly home
(leaving the stall in charge of one of the boys or girls
whom she is training) to prepare her husband's breakfast. When that is done, she hurries back to the market,
where she stays, buying and selling, until about eleven-
thirty when she once more comes back to cook her husband's meal (the time of which would vary according to
the nature of his work). As soon as it is over, she runs
again to the market and there spends the rest of the day
till she packs up her goods about five-thirty and comes
home. Women who live alone, i.e. who are widows or
have been abandoned by their husbands, spend all the
day in the market, taking a little food with them. 'All
these women are petty-petty traders, not big traders like
the women of Oguta.'[1]

It will be seen that the average woman does not have
much time for looking after her house nor for caring for
her younger children, although, while she is actually
suckling a child, she would not spend so much time away
from home. Later on, she can leave it in the care of an
older child, the ubiquitous nursemaid or nurseboy whose
conscientious attention to their charges has already been
described, and in Port Harcourt, as everywhere else, it is
the accepted thing for the married woman to contribute
to the common exchequer, nor would she willingly forgo the pleasure of meeting friend or foe in the market-
place.

A few women who have had a domestic training while
at school take up dressmaking as a trade. In addition to
their charges for making up their clients' materials which
vary from 2s. 6d. to 7s. 6d., these dressmakers also

[1] The women of Oguta are famous throughout Ibo-land for their
wealth and power.

receive fees from the apprentices they undertake to teach, thus the profession is a lucrative one, although a little capital is needed to begin with, as sewing-machines must be provided, hand-sewing being at a discount.

XIV

Sophisticated Woman—in Port Harcourt

Reaction of women to urban conditions. Relations between white and black. Women's Church Meetings.

Port Harcourt is not, as might be expected, a melting pot where races and speeches, customs and characters will fuse and mingle and out of which a new and stable people will emerge, but rather a railway platform with people coming and going, each family party holding closely together, contemptuous and suspicious of the others, and where nothing of importance to the real life of the family is allowed to happen. No one takes root in Port Harcourt, no one visualizes his future in Port Harcourt, no one hopes to die in Port Harcourt. Men come to make money and have no thought of settling there for good. If they build houses it is only to save rent and to make more money by letting out rooms. The house of their ambition will be built in their own town, within full view of their envious relations.

In such an impermanent atmosphere, there seemed nothing new to be learnt about Ibo customs. Each family brought its own customs with it, be it from Owerri, or Aba, or Okigwi, or Onitsha. There was nothing which was in itself peculiar to Port Harcourt because Port Harcourt did not exist as a social entity. It was a place people merely passed through, bringing, so to speak, their own spiritual luggage with them. That that luggage might be considerably lighter when they left than when they arrived was to be expected: life in a town, no matter how temporary and no matter how deeply one's real interests lay elsewhere, could not help but be disintegrating. It is unfortunately true, in regard to what we term 'primitive religions' at least, that 'the deep and abiding traditions of religion belong to the countryside. For it is there that man earns his daily bread by submitting to superhuman forces whose behaviour he can only partially control. . . . He is obviously part of a scheme that is greater than himself, subject to elements that transcend his understanding. The city is an acid that dissolves this piety. How different it is from an ancient vineyard where a man cultivates what his father has planted. In a modern city it is not easy to maintain 'that reverent attachment to the sources of his being and the steadying of life by that attachment'.[1]

The absence of this 'steadying of life' is increasingly noticeable: nevertheless, the Owerri man who is temporarily living in Port Harcourt has at least one very strong link both with his compatriots and with his own home-village and consequently is not yet altogether emancipated from the beneficial influence of this 'reverent attachment to the sources of his being', being constantly reminded of his duties and his privileges as a member of a society comprising both the living and the dead. This link is provided by the very active 'Owerri Union' which binds together all the twenty-three 'towns' of Owerri Province. There is a General Secretary and twenty-three sub-secretaries representing these towns. Meetings are held about every month. Apart from the regular subscriptions, extra collections are made 'for sending a corpse back to its home town' (there is naturally a great desire to be buried in the ancestral home and though lorry passengers do not seem to mind travelling

[1] *A Preface to Morals* by Walter Lipmann.

with a dying man, they object to a dead one, thus necessitating the expense of chartering a special lorry); or, if they are sure of the innocence of one of their members, for engaging a lawyer to defend him in court; or, if a member wants a loan, for lending him the money at a lower rate than would an outsider. The Union also settles minor disputes between members (thus to a certain degree taking the place of the village *amala*) and serves in many ways to remind them of their tribal obligations. I asked whether the Union would make grants to necessitous widows, the fate of a widow among strangers being an uncertain one, but was told 'no': there would be too many of them and if the other wives who had been left up-country heard of it, they would come hurrying down to see whether they could not make a little out of the Union too!

Thanks also to this Union, and to the strong family feeling which still persists, there is no real destitution in Port Harcourt among the Ibo, although when I was there at the end of 1935 there was a good deal of poverty due to unemployment and the general trade depression. The Local Authority could only remember three cases of destitution, men who had come looking for employment and had failed to find it, had been supported for a long time by their compatriots, had perhaps got into trouble, and were eventually brought to him to be repatriated to their homes, through their District Officer. This speaks well for tribal solidarity, for at that time no class could have had much money to spare. This is all the more true as the salaried worker is of course expected to send money home constantly, not only to his immediate family but to any of his numerous 'brothers' and 'sisters' who think they have a claim upon him. A railway official told me he had numerous applications for transfers to a more remote station, merely for the reason that the men either wanted to get away from their wives, or from relations pestering them for money.

Women

How much of tribal life and customs actually persists
is hard to determine. Native dances, almost exclusively
attended by young men, are still held in open spaces in
the town; but the more educated men have forgotten
how to dance them and instead attend 'balls' in European
fashion, join tennis clubs and debating societies. The
majority of the inhabitants come sooner or later under
the influence of one of the Missions and Church activities
absorb a certain amount of their energies, but one still
hears talk of 'second burials', of trials by ordeal, of the
clerk who misses promotion because of 'a white powder
strewn by jealous colleagues upon his blotting-paper', of
the woman who miscarries because of 'the medicine an
enemy put upon her path as she returned from church'.

The Ibo women have a modified counterpart of the
Owerri Union in the Church Meetings. The races
mingle rather more freely in church matters than elsewhere but the language bar still keeps them apart (I
have heard Bible instruction given in three different
languages to the members of one class) and the women
naturally tend to fall into groups speaking the same
vernacular. These Church Meetings and Bible Classes
are primarily for the purpose of prayer and worship or
for instruction but are at the same time a fellowship of
women for mutual assistance, material as well as moral.
All these meetings and classes are well attended, but as
they are often followed by a sewing-class, one could not
be sure which was the true attraction. Attention and
demeanour were, however, always excellent and the
women's gift for extemporary prayer was astonishing.

It is to be remarked that church congregations consisted, as far as I could judge, of a good many more men
than women, which is the contrary of what one usually
sees, in Europe at any rate. Mrs. Grainger explained this
by saying that the women, being more backward, cannot
enter into the spirit and meaning of the services. Consequently they are very bored and would rather meet in a

small class where personal supervision is given. Also, there being no Sunday markets in Port Harcourt, the women take this opportunity of having an extra rest and of cooking special meals! It is the men also, who, having more intellectual curiosity than the women, are the chief supporters of the smaller sects, so long at any rate as their novelty lasts.

It is the number of these sects, large and small, that the outside observer of life in Port Harcourt views with dismay and some apprehension. In one street alone, the inquirer finds the Methodists, the Niger Delta branch of the Church Missionary Society, the Roman Catholics, the Faith Tabernacle, the Baptists, the African Church, the Salvation Army, the African Methodist Episcopals (Zion branch), the African Methodist Episcopals (Bethel branch), the New Church (Swedenborg), the Apostolic Mission, the Seventh Day Adventists, the First Century Gospel (an offshoot of the Faith Tabernacle), and up a side street, a Mohammedan mosque.[1] Other sects come and go, showering badly printed pamphlets as they pass, generally produced in the United States or in South Africa.

The adherents of the smaller sects are generally seceders from the Protestant Missions, seldom from the Roman Catholic. The latter occasionally join the Church Missionary Society or leave the Church altogether but they do not seem to be attracted by the more individualistic doctrines of the ultra-evangelical congregations.

I attended Church Missionary and Methodist services

[1] I have never found an explanation of the curious fact that Ibo converts to Islam, from all I can hear, are unknown. It is true that they are not in such close geographical proximity as say, the Yoruba, where converts are numerous and are still being made, but all the same there are more or less important Hausa settlements in almost any Ibo town of any size and Hausa traders are frequent visitors, either bringing down convoys of cattle from the North or sitting trading in the larger markets. The one and only exception I have known was a young man who had adopted a Hausa gown and a smattering of Islam so that he should not be called upon to work on a *mbari* house!

and the Salvation Army. (To hear Swedenborg expounded in pidgin English would have been edifying, but the leader of the group was unfortunately away.) Both at the Church Missionary and the Methodist services, one could not but be struck by the large congregations, the excellent behaviour, the attention given alike to prayers and sermon, the heartiness if not the harmony of the singing. The buildings are good but entirely unimaginative. Their tastelessness shows how alien they are, like objects portrayed in a catalogue written in a foreign language. Yet the building of some of these churches—one fairly new one cost for example £3,000—must represent a considerable effort on the part of the congregation and probably real sacrifices on the part of many. The sermons were good, not very clearly reasoned, and inclined to be diffuse, but eloquent and in good English (the preachers I heard were mostly Sierra Leoneans) with occasional telling descents into pidgin or slang. To hear God quoted as saying: 'Shut your mouth!' was somehow extraordinarily convincing.

Other experiences were not so happy: the Salvation Army held its Harvest Festival while I was there, in a well-built hall said to have cost £850 or more. To those who admire the Salvation Army, the spectacle offered would have been distressing. To those who could forget what the Army really stands for and what it accomplishes, only one exclamation would have been possible: 'What humbug!' I have a clear memory of the 'Harvest': a small heap of oranges (they cost ten a penny), five yams, two corn cobs, a few tomatoes, two eggs, and several embroidered tray cloths; of the performers at the 'sacred concert' with their piping voices, silk dresses, twisted stockings and high-heeled shoes; of the congregation which consisted of well-to-do Coast people; of the 'Captain', a smug and shifty buck nigger. Once more the lack of sufficient discrimination in the first place and of adequate supervision in the second were apparent.

Relations between White and Black

Distressing as was the whole occasion, one cannot help but feel that we do wrong to put such heavy burdens of initiative and responsibility upon individuals whom we neither know how to choose, so little are we yet able to judge them, nor whom we are able to guide and sustain once we have chosen them. It is true, as one often hears, that the Nigerian 'must learn to stand upon his own feet', but it should be remembered that this is just the point: it is not his own feet we expect him to stand on, his own African feet firmly planted on the tribal path, but on newly made, insufficiently balanced, uncomfortably shod, semi-English feet.

In a town such as Port Harcourt where the white community is comparatively large, it is natural to ask what are its relations with its African neighbours of whatever race they be. As far as the women are concerned, these relations are very few.

At first sight, one is inclined to blame the white woman, especially the Government officials' wives, for such a lack of interest and ordinary human sympathy, but the more one sees, the more one realizes the difficulties. Even apart from the language bar, which in Port Harcourt with its many English-speaking Africans, is not a very serious one, it is curiously difficult to find any common ground for conversation or to devise any form of entertainment which will be natural and pleasant. A little energy, a little initiative and imagination would assuredly overcome these obstacles but the first two of these virtues are hard to come by and without them, the third is of no avail. Unless the emotional drive is very strong, the Nigerian climate destroys all the surplus energy which would enable one to undertake a task to which one is perhaps not naturally drawn. Initiative is handicapped by: 'Is it worth while?' 'What will people think?' 'My husband does not seem specially keen on my doing it.' Or by the ever-recurring thought, 'I may

253

be going home in a few months' or 'We may be moved to another station, it is not worth while beginning something I cannot go on with.' The sense of impermanence frets and discourages the stronger natures who are trying to do something and forms a valid and reasonable excuse for the weaker ones who are content to do nothing at all.

The third necessary virtue, imagination, by which I mean the perfectly ordinary process of occasionally putting oneself into another person's skin, of visualizing the possibility of another range of interests and methods of life than one's own, of taking vicarious part in another's joys and sorrows and thereby enlarging tenfold one's own existence and experience, all this seems sadly lacking in the majority of white women I have met in Nigeria. Again, the constant lack of physical energy probably lessens the mental energy needed for even such a simple effort of the mind as curiosity, but all the same such complete lack of interest in one's surroundings except in so far as these surroundings consist of the local club or the golf-course, is almost startling.

I once asked the very charming wife of a senior official an obvious question about the women of the area in which she lived and which I did not happen to know. She could not answer. I asked her how long she had lived in Nigeria. 'Sixteen years.' Laughingly, I asked: 'Have you ever seen Nigeria?' She was quick enough to follow my thought and frank enough to admit: 'I don't suppose I ever have!'

Nevertheless, even those women who at least begin their Nigerian life with zest and curiosity hardly know how to achieve their object of 'getting into touch with the native'. In a town like Port Harcourt, there are material impediments: the European reservation is some distance from the township, either the white woman or the black must have the use of a car. It is only in the mornings that the white woman is free—in the afternoon, she rests, then her husband comes back from the office, then comes the tyranny of games; while the black woman has her children, marketing and household to attend to in the mornings and can more easily be free in the afternoons. Conversation, especially at the beginning, lacks topics. The white woman, afraid of appearing patronizing, talks with unnatural brightness, the black woman remains tongue-tied. She lacks the small change of conversation and though loquacious on her own topics, the white woman does not yet know enough of her life to realize what these topics are. Both are ill at ease and soon the hampering thought drifts through their respective minds: 'Is she never going?' 'Is it time for me to go?' If both persevere long enough and if both are ready to see each other as likeable human beings, there will come a moment when their mutual womanhood breaks through and then laughter and gossip will ease the stiffness of their intercourse and the white woman at least, more conscious of what she is doing, will know the wild joy of breaking into an unexplored land, the dizzy effort of trying to follow new paths of thought leading through strange landscapes. But this joy is rare and its attainment depends a good deal on circumstances. More often, no closer contact is obtained than what can be found in a sewing-meeting or a church bazaar or at an official garden party.

Even at an official dinner, the host has got to be a little careful whom he asks to meet the members of the African community. There is—and one can never be sufficiently thankful that it is so—no violent colour prejudice in Nigeria except in a few individual cases. Good manners on the part of the white man, good manners, marked discretion and a fine sensitiveness on the part of the black man make social encounters perfectly possible and often most enjoyable, but not all the white men and especially not all the white women will take the trouble to lift the conversation along, to make the effort to turn a formal social event into something a little more alive and fruitful.

255

Women

An official with whom I was talking said that 'there was no use forcing the social intercourse between white and black. They meet now on committees and talk and smoke and that is better than a stolid ring at a garden party or a strained bonhomie at dinner.' He was quite right in so far as the men are concerned. Between the women, however, one would wish for something a little more individual, a gesture of social equality and potential friendship. This is all the more true as the African woman, both rich and poor, is increasingly faced with the problem of what to do with her leisure. Up till now, the Ibo woman especially has hardly known what leisure is: farm or market, house and kitchen, claimed her from morning to night. In Port Harcourt, she has no farm and in any case the educated girls would not go to it. Her house requires none of that lengthy rubbing of mud walls to which the good bush housewife devotes so much time; her food is often bought half-prepared from the market and in any case she herself has no need to walk to farm or ɔba to fetch it; water comes from the near-by pump. As occupation, there remains either the market; or the mischief that Satan still finds 'for idle hands to do'; or, quite simply, sleep, the refuge of the mentally destitute.

As with us, the occupation of leisure will be one of the main problems of the future and one in which the white woman might help, though it will not be easy even to guess along what lines one could guide the African woman.

Very few women read. This is partly due to the lack of suitable material: the educated, though they may find no difficulty with the actual language, will not understand the English background and numberless allusions; the semi-educated will tire of floundering through idiomatic phrases and descriptions of alien scenes. Neither have sufficient curiosity concerning the white man to want to know how he lives and thinks. Girls at school will read a certain amount under the stimulus of their white teachers or goaded thereto by the approach of exams; married women may read a few local newspapers and take in an English house or needlecraft publication. Talking with the highly educated Sierra Leonean to whom I have already referred, she said that women were anxious to read even though it were nothing very serious, and that she regularly passed on her own books and papers. She took in the *Sunday Express* and the *Daily Mail* and had just begun subscribing to the *Manchester Guardian*, *West Africa*, and the *West Africa Review*, and also took in two local papers, but when she said 'women were anxious to read', she was referring to her own compatriots and to a few Lagosians. I have not myself seen any book other than the Bible, except, once, *Pilgrim's Progress*, in an Ibo woman's hands nor have I ever heard any desire expressed for another form of literature. Her practical mind takes in reading for profit, spiritual or material, but reading for pleasure is still an unknown and unimagined satisfaction. Mrs. Grainger's experience has been the same and her efforts to provide something better than the sensational stories found in fashion magazines have met with no response. Needlework, apart from the dressmaking already referred to, is gaining ground. The term 'fancy' covers embroidery of such things as tray- and tea-cloths, handkerchiefs, pillow-slips and nightdress-cases. The two latter are very popular, especially when embroidered with embarrassingly scriptural texts. The designs are European, though the colouring is often native, and, as when the Ibo dress in European fashion, their taste is sometimes at fault. This is a pity as the actual needlework has greatly improved in the last few years and the *uri* patterns (see p. 94) which are to be found in the greater part of Ibo-land would make new and lovely designs, in which the Ibo colourings would be at home. A woman missionary at Aro

Women

Chuku has already made use of these patterns with great success.

Games have hardly taken hold yet. I have seen a few girls playing tennis in Lagos but do not remember any in Port Harcourt. Netball seems the most popular game in girls' schools. Halma, ludo, draughts are seen but the widespread *chacha* played by the less sophisticated led to so much gambling that Government has done its best to suppress it. One woman gave me a graphic description of how *chacha* sharpers would play, with a great show of *naïveté*, by the doors of their houses, hoping to attract the passers-by, or on the edge of the road near the lorry stops. The game looked so easy and innocent and so much money could be gained thereby that women 'climbed down from their seats in the lorry and gambled and gambled until they had lost their goods and then their head-ties and then the very price of their lorry fare'. Though it was an Ibo woman who spoke thus, I do not think *chacha* playing by women was very widespread, even before the days of the Government ban, except perhaps around Onitsha.

One may hope that gardening as a hobby might appeal to the Ibo woman as another channel of expression for her farming instinct. There are already flickers of interest on the part of the men—in the heart of the bush one will find a little crookedly set flower-bed containing a few zinnias planted by a schoolboy, even in Port Harcourt a variegated shrub or a blue-flowered creeper grows beside the house door. One's own servants often show real artistry in the arrangement of vases and mingle colours with incredible but successful audacity. So far the women do not seem to have shown much interest but here is a way in which the European could give real and pleasing service. In whatever way the white women in big stations such as Port Harcourt may fail to do anything for the country, they nearly always succeed, against every possible opposition of soil and

258

climate, in making excellent gardens. If they could pass on a little of their enthusiasm and knowledge, they would provide a healthy occupation to counteract the evils of 'sitting around', they would destroy the idea that if you are educated, you must not soil your fingers, and they would help to make not a desert, but an even more dreary township, blossom as a rose.

Social service, in our sense of the word and with all its innumerable openings and opportunities for making use of the most diverse talents, hardly exists, nor, so long as the family bond holds good, will it be really necessary.

There are, broadly speaking, no poor, though in considering either native communities or individuals, it is practically impossible to define what, to them, is poverty or riches. To the white observer this is perhaps one of the most baffling questions. How assess their needs or their desires? How decide by what standard to measure them? Can a population which has always food in its stomach, a roof over its head, a fire to cook by, a bit of land to farm, and which does not suffer from cold nor want of clothing, be called poor, as compared to our own unemployed, our tramps, our slum-dwellers? The fact that a man has no actual cash in his pocket (and no pocket in which to put the cash) inclines us to consider him as 'poor' but he is only poor by artificial standards, not by the basic standards of hunger, cold, and homelessness. It is true, of course, that the African himself, long before the white man came, looked upon his neighbours as rich or poor but, for the freeman at any rate, poverty was only relative. The man with fifty wives was considered rich but the man with only one was not a pauper by any means when one compares him to our own homeless and destitute.

Nevertheless, changing conditions and the slackening of the family ties may produce in time a class of 'the poor' and obviously it is in the towns that this class will first appear. Up till now, every member of a household was catered for in some way or another, every member was somebody's responsibility and public opinion saw to it that that responsibility was not shirked. Old people past work may not have been very popular but I think they seldom lacked a hut, a handful of food, and had at least the knowledge that they still 'belonged' somewhere and that their fading eyes could rest upon familiar scenes. Now they are not so secure, nor, as has already been seen (see p. 97) can the Christian widow be sure of her future. Children escape from the never very strict supervision of their parents and become vagrants and juvenile offenders. Wives are deserted and should they fall sick, far from their own people, who will care for them? Here it is that church members, through their women's classes and guilds, have the great advantage of belonging to a fellowship independent of race or locality and thus will not be left entirely alone.

The fact remains, however, that up to the present, 'good works' have not been needed because every individual has, unlike individuals in our own country, belonged to some specific person or group of persons whose responsibility he or she is. Under normal circumstances I do not think one could find anybody who could say of himself: 'I am alone in the world', excepting perhaps a few freed slaves who have no memory of their own country[1] or a few casual labourers drifting from

[1] It is surprising how some of these ex-slaves find their way back to their own people. I know of two cases which sound like a fairy tale, especially that of an Okigwi man, carried off as a child 'as he was going in the dark to fetch a brand from a neighbour's hut to light his mother's fire'. A tornado was raging and so his cries were not heard. He was taken down to the coast and eventually found himself in Fernando Po. There he somehow made much money, farming. He remembered nothing of his own country save that his village was near a glade of enormous trees with twisted roots. He felt driven to find it. Led by some homing instinct, he got as far as Eziama where this rich looking man, dressed in European clothes and followed by carriers bearing tin trunks provoked much excitement. Wandering round the forest, he came suddenly upon the remembered glade (it was the shrine of Ajala near the Mission church where I was staying and its

town to town. The Ibo does faithfully practise 'Charity begins at home', and so admirably has he carried out this precept that, so far, there is no scope for wider and less personal charity.

In so far as the sick are concerned, Port Harcourt possesses a very popular African hospital with a staff of one European and one or two African doctors. It has a ward for abnormal maternity cases and the Church Missionary Society have a recently opened Baby Welfare Clinic in the town.

The question of native medicines has never been properly gone into though everyone agrees that valuable discoveries might be made, but as far as the nursery medicine cupboard is concerned, its Ibo equivalent in terms of leaves and peppers, chalk and camwood, does not seem very satisfactory. The women themselves confess that on the whole they 'no have savvy' as regards their children's ailments and even a clever and conscientious woman *dibia* like the one I met in Nguru seemed more concerned with bringing children into the world than in keeping them there. All the same, the care taken of the woman in her first weeks of motherhood is very noticeable. Though she may often be working at her accustomed tasks till the day, even the hour of her confinement, as soon as the child is born all responsibility and anxiety are kept away from her. As will have been seen, in some parts such as Nneato, the woman actually remains in retreat, so to speak, until

gigantic trees could never be forgotten). He knew he was near home but how find his house or people, whose very name he had forgotten? A few words of Ibo had come back to him. He put his case before the senior men. They said: 'His mother will know him.' All the old women of the village walked past him in single file. One sprang forward: 'My son!'

'So glad was everyone that they never stopped feasting, night or day, for fourteen days.'

I met the man in question, a fine-looking, vigorous fellow. He still preserved his Spanish passport and spoke with regret of Fernando Po, but 'I wished to marry a girl of my own country'.

the child's naming day, but even when she is not
isolated to this extent, yet she is served by others, given
special food, etc., and has no household tasks to perform
beyond looking after the new-born baby. This custom
may be due more to the desire to give the child every
chance than to consideration for the mother, but the
result is equally favourable to both. Doubtless, infant
welfare centres with voluntary workers and home
visitors are useful both to those who receive and
especially to those who give; but the utmost wariness is
needed in planning any scheme so that the modern
parent should not lose her sense of responsibility and
should not learn to lean too comfortably on Government
or outside charity. The fear of pauperization, whether in
material or moral ways, can of course be exaggerated but
as the Ibo woman has shown herself so peculiarly apt at
looking after herself and her belongings, it would be a
pity to undermine that sturdy independence by proffer-
ing help which, however enthusiastically given and
perhaps greedily snatched at (for who would wish to be
left out of anything?) is not actually needed. In dealing
with a native society there are, alas, such innumerable
opportunities for the best friends to do more harm than
the worst enemies.

Whether the Ibo woman will see the pleasure of doing
voluntary work for others is another matter. At present,
all her values can be said to be money values and if
not mercenary in our own derogatory sense of the word,
she is so money-minded that she might find it almost
inconceivable to do anything for nothing, not through
lack of generosity or kindness but because she has not yet
met anything in her life to which the idea of money was
not attached in some form. Even her religion, whether
pagan or Christian, is a continual asking and collecting
and counting and reckoning. It will be remembered how
the polygamist Christian was considered a member of
the Church because 'he takes part in all money matters'.

Voluntary Service

Money is, as it were, the hall-mark of true value, the touchstone both in material and spiritual things. Voluntary service may seem an unreal or unsound thing (this latter opinion appears to be held in some English circles to-day), just because it bears no hall-mark save that of moral worth, and has no touchstone save that of a dim ideal.

XV

Sophisticated Woman—in Port Harcourt

How far have the women been influenced by constant Western contacts. Modern morality again. New love of idleness versus old love of independence. The call of the land.

Against this shifting and colourless background must now be set the Ibo woman herself. How does she comport herself in such strange new surroundings? The consensus of opinion, both black and white, is that she has not benefited by her transplantation. Honesty, industry, morals, have all suffered, and Mrs. Grainger, whose close experience of the bush women had made her love and admire them, was discouraged by their rapid deterioration and found it hard to like this new, sophisticated, grasping, celf-centred type.

On the whole, she has agreed with my statements regarding Port Harcourt. She even adds: 'In this cosmopolitan town, the women will need the most careful handling and guidance if they are to become something more wholesome and sane. Even the daughters of the intelligentsia, educated at Lagos or in other boarding-schools, are a problem. We have several here, just spending their days in idleness and getting fine clothes in whatever way possible. Those who marry in church run themselves or their parents into debt by sending home

264

for expensive bridal frills, cakes, etc., and are thus handicapped by money difficulties at the very outset of their
married life.' She notes too the 'deep-rooted jealousy
among the Ibo and Efik towards the strangers in their
midst; and how often, like spoilt children, they sit back
and will not take responsibility, feeling that they would
always be outshone by their better-educated neighbours,
yet neither will they go in and learn from them.' This
attitude of 'sitting back' is so marked that I had the
greatest difficulty in piecing together the life of the Ibo
women and then only from random glimpses and conversations. Admittedly less educated, except in a few
instances, than their foreign sisters, they did not play any
leading part in the life of the town and it was rare to find
any whose cpinion was worth having. Practically all the
outstanding feminine personalities were strangers and as
such were biased informants. The Ibo women who
attended Mrs. Grainger's Bible and sewing-classes were
of the inarticulate type and were inclined to relapse into
silence as soon as a more imposing or more vocal Yoruba
or Sierra Leonean appeared. The Efik women were more
akin to the Ibo and mingled more freely with them, with
the result that in my notes I have not always been able
to distinguish whether my information concerns the one
race or the other.

My most interesting male informant was a Methodist
catechist, an Efik, but one who knew Ibo-land well and
liked the people because 'they are better tempered than
the Efik and laugh a lot'. He may not always have been
quite accurate about his facts but he had reasoning
powers and objectivity. His main theme was that of
educated girls, a question which apparently both he and
other educated men considered the most pressing one at
the moment and one with which I had so far not come
into contact, except on a very small scale. My notes give
almost his own words: 'Girls come home at the end of
their schooling no longer in tune with native life, cannot

put up with the lower standard of living, are bored with farming, which anyhow they do not know how to do, and petty trading with their mothers. They do not marry at once as the educated young man is: (*a*) shy of taking an expensive wife even though he prefers a literate to an illiterate one; (*b*) has no money wherewith to pay the enhanced dowry and, as was the case in Nguru (see p. 154), the parents have none either, having spent it all on educating their son. Thus the girl may have to wait two or three years before getting married. She has no job—there are long waiting-lists of nurses and uncertificated teachers [this I know to be true]—she wants money for finery and there is only one way of getting it. And as young men are badly off too, she cannot get enough from one man and so goes to several. The mothers are discouraged about sending their girls to school, seeing it brings no material [and even less spiritual] advantages. On the contrary, the uneducated village girl has more chance of marrying, as she is ready to take anyone, will be an asset to a young man instead of an expense, and will not demand a higher standard of living.' The girls, he affirmed, who had been to a boarding-school are even worse than those who have not—perhaps the repression of the school years suddenly removed impels them to express themselves all the more freely. He wished that some way could be found in which girls leaving school could have some work by which they could earn enough money to satisfy their superficial need for finery and their deeper need for independence, and thus turn away from immorality. He advocated a properly run dress-making establishment, but was ready to see girls any-where, in shops, or offices, or posts and telegraphs.

When I asked him whether it was not a pity, especially in this time of unemployment, that girls should take men's jobs, seeing that it was psychologically more important for a man to earn money than for a woman, he quite understood my question but did not agree with it, and I was once more struck by the fact that quite obviously our idea, or at least our old-fashioned idea, of man as the breadwinner does not hold good here. He was quite clear that both among the Ibo and the Efik the woman is considered, and moreover considers herself, as much the breadwinner as the man, and her self-respect demands that she should earn by her own efforts. She needs to feel to a certain extent financially independent and that this is no new outlook, due to altering conditions, is proved by the number of times the same sort of remark has been heard both in town and in the bush. All the same, the woman will stand no nonsense on the part of her husband. It is difficult to gauge exactly how far a man is responsible for the maintenance of his wife and family but when I inquired what happened in the case of the husband being unable to find employment, another male informant said: 'When a man cannot find a job, his wife by her petty petty [i.e. by mixed trading on a small scale] or perhaps by dressmaking supports her household, but *should she think the husband was not really trying*, she would not bother.'

The pastor's wife whom I have already mentioned and who was one of the few Ibo women to speak with authority, confirmed what the Efik catechist had said, and then, on her own initiative, brought up the question of what she biblically termed 'harlots'. As she was an Ibo-speaking Onitsha woman herself and had now lived for sixteen years in Port Harcourt, her double experience gave her a good understanding of her own people's reactions to changing conditions. She said (in her conversation she was referring more especially to married women than to girls, as the catechist had done) that in olden days prostitution was rare, as it was severely repressed, but when, in these later days, the Ibo women saw how easily Lagos and Gold Coast women made money, they did not want to be out of it. She gave the impression, which I have often had myself, that it was to them merely a new calling like any other and they became prostitutes as reasonably and as self-righteously as they would have become typists or telephone girls. They knew their own old laws were against it, but times had changed and it would be foolish and unprogressive not to take advantage of this new opening, just as it would be foolish not to take advantage of free sewing-classes, or welfare clinics, or to refuse to buy those new Indian cloths which had just come on the market and which one could sell retail with so much profit.

Bored and impatient with the little money they made at home, it is choice, not necessity, which counsels them to abandon their husbands and their children and come to Port Harcourt. And, being honest, self-respecting women, they do their best to repay their dowries as soon as they possibly can, so that their husbands should be able to get other wives and they themselves should be set legally free. Also it brings them added importance: 'See that woman. She has earned so much money that she has herself paid back her dowry to her husband!'

Sometimes the women bring their children with them as, though by native law and custom these belong to the husband, he may be too poor to keep them, and the mothers would not like to think of their little ones suffering. But now, what with (*a*) trade depression[1] and (*b*) stirrings of conscience through listening to 'church', the women are beginning to find that this new trade does not pay as well as they had expected and the rush has stopped. At no time was it more than a voluntary trade, either in the case of girls or women. There may be a certain woman in Port Harcourt who is considered as their headwoman but this is more a courtesy title than anything else and though she may receive presents, there is nothing like regular exploitation.

[1] These notes were written in 1935, before trade had begun to improve.

Monogamy and Polygamy

My informant did not think that the spread of monogamy had as yet increased the number of young single women who might tend to become prostitutes through lack of potential husbands. The sexes appear to be fairly evenly balanced as regards numbers, and even among non-Christians there have always been monogamous marriages, either through choice or because the man could not afford a second dowry. On the other hand, Christian marriages are frequently monogamous only in name. She affirmed that women prefer monogamy. 'No woman wants to share a husband's love'—or did she rather mean 'No woman wants to share her power', for she went on to say that she would not mind so much if she herself had given the second wife to the husband, 'for then this woman would be under her'. The one argument she advanced in favour of polygamy was a novel one: it was that in the event of a husband ill treating his wife, she would like to have a co-wife to be a witness and to help her to bring a case against the man. But when we came to monogamy and child-bearing, she was no longer so sure of her ground. Public opinion is still strong against women having babies too frequently; the husbands would be severely blamed, the mothers would feel that their daughters were being weakened and their health endangered if they became pregnant more than every two and a half to three years, and the children themselves should not be weaned much under two years. There is also, I think, a feeling that there is something indelicate[1] in having babies too frequently, much as the parents want to have large families. My informant herself, educated, travelled, and broad minded as she was, admitted that she would be upset if her daughter was made to conceive every year. When questioned as to the husband's attitude, she remarked tersely: 'He must just

[1] Vanity also may play a part, as suggested by Mrs. Thurnwald, who quotes a native saying: 'A bitch who gives suck has not a smooth coat!'

overcome temptation!' though she went on to say that she knew of good Christian men who secretly got themselves a substitute, and even of loving wives who themselves provided one.

Whatever one may think of the moral aspect of the question, there is no denying that the Ibo woman's views on certain points in relation to marriage are broad, wise, and generous. Take for example the childless household. One knows this question of children looms large in all African societies but one is inclined to think that nowhere does it count for so much as among the Ibo. It is therefore no wonder that the absence of children causes more heartburnings than anything else. Although the parents know quite well that their son, by marrying in church, undertakes to have only one wife, yet, when after two or three years the latter still proves barren, they are adept at making insidious remarks: 'Your wife is no more than a piece of furniture in your house!' 'Your wife eats and sleeps, and sleeps and eats. Is it for this we paid dowry for her?' The husband probably pays no attention at first but constant pressure from the one side and his own desire on the other, undermine his resistance. The wife herself, tired of the reproaches of her family-in-law, and moved by her own deep grief and genuine sympathy for her husband, may, if she has the means, herself provide a second 'wife', that is to say a wife married according to native law and custom, for the husband she has disappointed. Should this second wife have a child, she will rejoice as much as anyone and would feel towards it as if it were her own. When I asked, no matter how sincerely she had wished to comfort her husband, whether she did not feel a pang of jealousy when she saw another woman actually in the house and bearing a child to her husband, I was told 'no' because, my informant argued shrewdly, 'she had done it of her own free will, she was the benefactress; if it were not for her, her riches and her generosity, neither woman nor child would be there'. The only stipulation she would make would be that the woman realized her position, that she did not 'swell up with pride' and that she never forgot the debt of gratitude she owed her. As it is the first wife herself who seems generally to have the choosing of this second wife, it is natural to suppose she would use her discrimination and choose someone of a quiet and retiring disposition!

This same generous attitude and philosophic acceptance of human nature are shown when the wife either tolerates or herself provides a substitute to fill her place while pregnancy or the lactation period separate her from her husband. In each case, stress was laid upon the fact that it would only be loving and high-principled couples who would come to these arrangements, after frank discussion.

Perhaps the most illuminating conversation I had, because so spontaneous, was a symposium held in a luxurious saloon car kindly lent me by the Sierra Leonean wife of a local financial magnate and which was attended by Grace, a lovely young Ibo woman, a Methodist Mission catechist, and the magnate's driver, a Bini man, eloquent in pidgin English. We drew up by the side of the road in the pouring rain and discussed women, marriage, education and morals, earnestly and, till we became personal, dispassionately. The catechist was convinced that educated men liked educated wives, even if they were more expensive. Grace, who had been to school, preened herself demurely. 'Yes,' said with sombre significance the Bini driver, 'but it was bad for a woman to have more education than her husband.' 'Indeed,' sighed the catechist, 'it was difficult enough as it was to get wives to obey.' All agreed that only those who meant to be teachers or nurse should go up to Standard VI, the others should only learn to read and write and take a course in domestic training. This the Bini driver especially emphasized and though I had often heard the same opinion expressed by others, I wondered at the vigour of his convictions until he let fall that his own betrothed whom he had sent to school at his own expense had so far outstripped his ambitions that she had risen to Standard VI and now, puffed up with so much scholarship, refused to marry him as, good driver though he was, he could neither read nor write!

All agreed as to the present looseness of morals in Port Harcourt, but I believe one and all would have condoned the morals if the lack of them had been compensated by other useful activities. The Ibo's purest scorn is reserved for the lazy, the incompetent. 'What did the girls do', I asked, 'to fill their days and take the place of the farm work they used to do in their old homes?' 'Do?' said Grace, turning up her pretty nose, 'they just walk up and down the market!' 'Or sit at home making fancy,' jeered the catechist. 'Or more likely doing nothing at all,' growled the driver. They nodded assent, lips tight, brows bent. ' *Yes, many do nothing at all.*' And one knew that the last word had been spoken, the final, merciless judgment had been passed upon the womanhood of Port Harcourt.

Setting this conversation alongside the one I had had with the Efik catechist, they seemed further proof of what was increasingly noticeable: the existence to-day of two distinct strains in the Ibo woman's character—the old love of independence which drives them to work hard to make money for themselves; the new love of idleness, ministered to by domestic facilities. The change was summed up in a rueful sentence: 'In the bush, my wife fetched wood and water, rubbed the house, farmed and marketed and never asked me for a penny. Now she goes to the pump, buys wood in the market, barely sweeps the cement floor and expects me to provide even the children's castor oil!'

Nevertheless, the married women have one stabilizing factor in their lives, their periodical visits to their husband's home for the purpose of either supervising or actively helping in the work on his farm. The bulk of the women pay such visits at least twice a year, staying away for several weeks or even months at a time. Though they may not regret their land 'yet they often think of it, save money to send home for the hire of labourers, and anxiously wonder how the crops are doing.'

When I asked the pastor's wife already quoted whether the women did not miss the farm work which in their old homes so absorbed them, she said they were quite pleased to live in a town and not to have to fetch wood and water. Nevertheless, when talking and making merriment together, they would recall their childhood, their games, their mother's care, their food, and would tell each other how 'there was a special kind of food my mother made for me; it was a poor man's food, if I gave it to my friends here they would laugh at me, but my heart holds to it'. Homesickness could hardly be expressed with more exquisite simplicity.

Again, while still at Owerri, I had asked Salome the same question. She had numerous relatives who had gone to Port Harcourt and knew the conditions well. Her answer was almost the same in that, behind the woman's material anxiety regarding her farm (I often noticed that a woman speaks of 'her' farm even when it is her husband's, thus showing how much she herself feels responsible for it), coupled with an appreciation of the greater ease of town life, lay an unvoiced and probably unconscious nostalgia. Salome said: 'Should she have a trustworthy mother-in-law, she would not worry; or, if she were a lazy woman, she would be only too glad to escape the heavy work of the harvest and the trudging to and fro with loads of newly dug yams from the farm to the *ɔba*. But when the time of the cutting of the new yams and of harvesting comes round, her heart is not at rest. She is wondering whether everything is being done as it should be, knowing the proverb: When a man is not at home, his things are not at home either.'

Women

Often she asks leave from her husband to go home for two or three weeks and he allows her, giving her money to hire labourers so that she can get through more quickly. But if he refuses, then: 'When next she comes home with her husband on a visit and calls on her women friends, she will immediately look up at the roof to see how many corn cobs are dangling from it. She will see the same women selling baskets of corn to the Mbieri people and to the Hausa people and will say to herself: "See, I have no corn for myself. Why did not my husband let me come and see to the planting of it?" She will go to the farms and compare hers with the others, the yams, the calabashes, the gourds, the pumpkins, and will be disappointed that the other women have so much more than she has.'

The disappointment is doubtless partially caused by the fact that the other women will make more money out of their farms than she will, but only partly so. Deeper than that, is her sense of loss, her shame that she should have no crop, almost equal to the shame that she should have no child. 'See, I have no corn for myself!' is not merely a cry of greed but the voicing of a real hunger.

Part III
Men and Women

XVI

Men and Women

Women's modern mindedness equal to that of men.
Racial unity and subversive factors. Taxation. The land.

In the three following chapters it will be necessary to
take a rather broader outlook on subjects which up till
now we have only looked on parochially in relation to
the special area under discussion. This will naturally in-
volve a certain number of digressions which will appear
irrelevant to the lives of the women but, as has already
been said in the Introduction, neither in a fully civilized
nor in a comparatively primitive society can one sex be
studied without reference to the other. And in Ibo-land
where the equality of the sexes is so marked, in fact if not
in theory, the penetration of Western ideas will influence the one almost as much and as quickly as the other.
It is true that by force of circumstance, it is generally the
men who receive the first direct shock but the women
stand so close beside them that they feel the reverbera-
tions very soon.

Here again it seems to me that the Ibo woman does
not conform with the usual theory that women are the
guardians of tradition, the last to give up those strong-
holds of faith or custom which men, more adventurous,
or more far-sighted, or more ambitious and eager for
change, abandon more or less readily. In other tribes I
have known in Nigeria, I would have said that this was
so, but not among the Ibo. The older women do hold to

277

their old customs, but more as they would keep to old habits than as fierce reactionaries guarding a menaced faith. I have already referred several times to the older woman's readiness to let the young go their own way, almost conceding them the right to go their own way. Only on certain points such as their intolerance towards the childless daughter-in-law, their impatience of monogamy, their upholding of the custom of the circumcision of girls, are they intransigent. The fact that their children abandon their ancient faiths seems hardly to cause them a pang so long as they themselves can follow the rites of their own childhood. Whether this attitude is caused by sheer indifference or by a philosophical toleration or by an intuitive understanding that no *status quo* can be maintained for ever, that no amount of disapproval can be an efficacious and lasting obstacle to the development of the social unit once it has received the impetus of a vital contact, I do not know. I would almost be ready to maintain that the last explanation was the truest one. In any case, in speaking of the future of the Ibo race, there will be no need to differentiate very much between the men and the women. Naturally, the spread of education will be much slower among the latter but the fundamentals that go to make up Ibo characters are independent of education and the influences that will affect them will be more intangible than what could be classified under that heading.

Perhaps the subject we should take first is that of racial unity. It is true that what is said to-day will very likely not be true to-morrow, or at least the day after to-morrow, but it may be of use to stress the point that *to-day*, there is very little racial unity either in a wide or in a narrow sense, that is to say there is neither a feeling of unity between the various West African races nor between the members of a single race. Under normal circumstances, neither Pan-Africanism nor Pan-Iboism exists.

Absence of Racial Unity

This may be too sweeping and dogmatic a statement but *under normal circumstances* one sees daily proof of its truth. Even such a dramatic occasion as the spoliation of Abyssinia would, I think, have passed unnoticed by the great majority, including literates, if 'ideas had not been put into their heads' by the newspapers, the intelligentsia and the Missions. It is true I heard some native pastors, sincere men, speak with heartfelt sorrow and indignation on the subject but even at the time I could not help wondering whether, had they been left to themselves, hearing only bald accounts of the facts, they would have felt any sympathy for, or kinship with, a people so remote from their own interests.

The Africans themselves know very well how great the differences are between them, and indeed, in Nigeria, it is only in very recent years that I have heard the word 'African' used at all, a reaction probably against the term 'native' which they thought carried a contemptuous sound and against that of 'black man', which after all was only a very natural counterpart of the 'white man' they used in speaking of us. Now we politely call each other 'African' and 'European' and all the savour has gone out. Perhaps even in the back streets of Kano one would no longer be dubbed a Nazarene.

But there is more lip-service done to the ideal of unity than a real acceptance of it, whether this unity be between races or between members of one race. To the rural Ibo, even the man who comes from the next village-group is a stranger and in consequence almost surely a rogue and a thief. This is natural and an attitude not unknown even to-day in rural districts in England; but the same applies, and almost in the same degree, to the more advanced members of what are considered to be the more advanced races, races that at least have been in longer contact with European civilization. Take Port Harcourt, for example, a town so modern and so artificial that one would think the idea of tribal barriers and

279

distinctions would appear as anomalies. Yet it is not so. The races hardly mingle. The Efik amalgamate fairly easily, but the Sierra Leoneans, the Gold Coasters, the Lagosians, are sharply divided among themselves and only unite in their contempt for the Ibo, whom they still consider as little more than barbarians. A highly educated woman from Free Town married to a man who had made a good deal of money in Port Harcourt, and had lived there for sixteen years, said she had practically no contact with Ibo women and had never attempted to learn the language. She mixed rather more freely with the Lagosians, especially as she had spent some time in Lagos, but on the whole the women keep narrowly to their own racial circles. The men must necessarily more often go outside them, mixing with the Ibo—'the older men for business purposes, the younger for immoral purposes'!—but never on a footing of social equality. The Ibo are quite aware of this general attitude and are annoyed by it. They especially resent that of the Yoruba, whom they readily allow to come and trade in Ibo-land but who make it impossible for an Ibo to trade in Yoruba-land.

Not only do these 'foreigners' despise the Ibo but they often actively fear him. An educated Lagosian, obliged as a barrister to do a good deal of travelling, had just returned to Port Harcourt from an up-country trip and described how anxiously he had driven along a certain stretch of road, his revolver beside him, fearing his car might break down and he would be at the mercy of these naked savages. It happened that I had just spent a happy week among the hills overlooking this same road, naturally unarmed and unescorted. This incident, typical of many I have heard recounted, makes one wonder how the educated Nigerian will fill the administrative posts to which he aspires. One can visualize him at a secretariat desk, but not in some bush station, casually fearless of whatever few dangers there may be, casually interested, amused and kindly, such as one finds the average

Tribal Distrust

Assistant District Officer to be. Above all, the latter has the invaluable asset of taking it for granted that he will be obeyed. Though the educated African considers himself immeasurably superior to the bush man, he yet lacks the authority that the more subtle sense of superiority which does not even trouble to take cognizance of itself, gives to the white man. It is true that the barrister quoted above was a Lagosian, a 'foreigner', but when I said, in conversation with two Ibo teachers whom I had met in the bush, that it would be so much easier for them to do the sort of work I was doing than it was for me, a stranger to all their ways and customs, they gasped: 'But we would never dare go into the houses and talk to the people as you do! If a black man tried to, they would kill him!'

Outside influences are of course constantly at work undermining little by little this attitude of superiority of one African to another. Yet perhaps undermining is the wrong word. The foundations of the dividing walls go down into unknown depths, it is only the visible part of the barriers which may get worn away. And even that will take time. Quite recently, having been listening to much talk about the proposed founding of an African Club open to Africans of any race, it was suggestive to hear, in answer to a question of mine put to a non-Ibo as to what the Yoruba thought of the Ibo, the classic reply: 'Ibo they chop man plenty too much', although, my interlocutor being a senior member of the Education Department and also a prospective member of the club in question, it was expressed more elegantly: 'To tell the truth, we believe the Ibo to be cannibals.' A little later on the same day, a native of Benin, resident for many years in Ibo-land, a rich man, owner of cars and lorries, cameras and a brass band, gave exactly the same answer.

An observer might distinguish two types of influence at work in this process of removing at least the outward signs of racial barriers, one beneficial, the other harmful.

281

Men and Women

Under the first category comes Christianity and education. Within the walls of the churches, within the men's Bible classes or the women's guilds, there is bound to be a certain solidarity, a certain need for understanding each other's feelings which will result in a greater readiness for mutual comprehension and give and take. Pastors and catechists are appointed to their parishes irrespective of their home of origin, so long as difference of language does not constitute a bar.[1] Church members can count on the goodwill of their fellow members as they travel through the country. Schools also, especially boarding-schools, come under this head and are bound to accustom the boys to each other's racial characteristics. At a later age, practically all work, except it be farm work, will bring different races together, and in the same way the clerks' tennis clubs and debating societies and the African clubs which are springing up in the bigger centres will mingle Ibo with Yoruba, and Efik with Bini and Sobo, and what is almost more difficult, will bring together the Ibo-speaking people themselves.

Naturally the women will not feel these influences so much but, as has already been pointed out in the Introduction, the Ibo woman does not seem so innately suspicious of her sister Ibo as the man does of his brother Ibo. The Onitshans, however, stand apart. Though Ibo-speaking for centuries—the date of their migration is variously placed in the fifteenth, sixteenth, and eighteenth centuries—they are of Bini origin and though the men married freely with the Ibo women of the surrounding country, they still look upon themselves as immensely superior. I remember two Onitshan women, wives of clerks, who came to see me in Okigwi. They had been to school, wore their head-ties and cloths with an air, spoke of Okigwi Town as if it were the depths of the

[1] At one time, when Christianity was only beginning to spread through Nigeria, West Indian and Sierra Leone pastors were the white missionaries' chief co-operators. Now they are being replaced by Nigerian-born men.

bush and when, wishing to compare customs, I told them about some Nneato ones, the tone of pitying contempt with which, lips shot out, they said: 'These Ibo!' could not have been surpassed by the most prejudiced Englishman voicing his disdain for the 'dam' nigger'. I am told that even in girls' schools there is a certain amount of cleavage. The Ibo girls naturally band together according to their home towns or village-groups, but will readily join together when occasion demands it; the Onitshans, however, keep apart, and the Warri and Brass girls also, though in their case it is more understandable as their mother-tongue is Jekri, not Ibo.

All influences of this type, be it church or school or office or playing-field or club or workshop, work slowly and inconspicuously but lead to an ultimate unity, or at least to an ultimate federation which would be normal, workable, durable, and for the greater good of the people. But there is another type of influence, more rapid, more dramatic, and more noisy which can lead only to a temporary unity and to an artificial and unhealthy federation.

No sort of politics come into my sphere of work but one could not read the local newspapers nor listen to some of the educated men without realizing that there was a small but vocal party which was ready to sink momentarily their racial differences for the sake of a common grievance against the Government. Too nebulous to be formally called Nationalists, too keen to get what they can out of the white man to wish sincerely for his immediate departure, too undiscriminating and illogical to be of true value to the country in the way of voicing its real needs or exposing any just grievance, these men merely criticize for the sake of criticizing and have no sound scale of values by which to judge between the essentials and the non-essentials.

From my own very small knowledge of this side of affairs, I should think the only risk—danger is too big a word—of these men getting hold of the mass of the people lay in the possibility, with its attendant demoralization, of another big rise followed by a sudden fall in European market prices. The rise, mysterious, irrational, feeds the imagination of the people and fulfils their childish belief in the possibility of the 'miraculous solution'; on the other hand, the fall, though equally mysterious, is not irrational, for it must necessarily be the work of an 'enemy'. Still lacking almost completely a logical comprehension of cause and effect, all disaster, whether it be hailstorms or drought, illness, death, or a failure of crops, is ascribed to some angry or jealous agency, be it natural or supernatural, Government or one's neighbour, God or gods. Even if there were no violent repercussions in the way of distress or unemployment, yet the moral effect would be bad and once again, as in 1929, bewilderment, suspicion, anger and a sense of frustration would undermine confidence in the good intentions of the white man and make the people, suggestible and undiscriminating (in realms which are not peculiarly their own) as they are, ready to follow unworthy and self-seeking shepherds.

It is true that the bulk of the Ibo population is landed and therefore can never starve nor lose its head completely—politics would have little import in the bush when the time came to plant the yams—but the educated and the semi-educated are an incalculable quantity, amenable and unthinkingly loyal so long as things go well but possible material for a conflagration if economic distress pushed them too hard against the wall and if agitators, with their background of false rumours and twisted information, upset the precarious balance of their minds, already swaying on the tight-rope stretched between the old and the new. But even if this section of the population became restive, it would not be likely to have much influence in the bush districts other than those directly and deeply concerned in the palm-oil trade and therefore the most immediately sensitive to economic changes, unless the ever-present and always resented question of taxation became, for one reason or another, prominent again.

I know I shall be thought to be exaggerating, I know many districts pay up quickly and freely, but I am sure the bulk of the Ibo of the Owerri Province still resents taxation to a degree out of all proportion to the hardship it may very occasionally inflict—at its very highest and in the richest oil-producing districts, it never went beyond 7s. per adult male per annum as compared with the £1 and more levied in East Africa—but because it is, for some curious reason, especially distasteful to Ibo mentality. This distaste will disappear—or rather it will be reduced to the normal dislike all human beings have of paying their rates and taxes!—if Government never ceases to handle the question with care, never takes its eye off the working of the machinery, never takes its eye off the reactions of the people to increase or decrease in the incidence of tax, never takes it for granted that the idea of payment of tax has now been accepted, never ceases to explain and re-explain the theory of taxation, both to the men and to the women. For the women's interest in tax is as vital as the man's. Here, in Ibo-land, it is no question of a long envelope laid by master's plate at the breakfast table and quietly slipped into his pocket while the mistress asks with detached interest: 'Have they put up income-tax again this year?' but it is a question of burning importance to the wife who has to calculate quickly: 'Is it better to sell the new yams or pull some of my cassava or shall I try to get my husband to cut down some more *banga* so that I may make another tin of palm-oil?' I have heard as much talk of and around 'tax palaver' from women as I have from men, some of it shrewd and reasonably critical, some of it childish and based on misinformation, but all of it charged with personal feeling and, in some parts, warm

285

with animosity. Whether the women will ever rise again as they did in 1929, no one can guess. From what I saw of the Nguru women at least, I should think they had it in them. And if tax no longer troubled them, they would find other grievances: they would rise in defence of sex equality or demand votes for women; they would be capable of importing sets of railings so as to have the satisfaction of chaining themselves to them. But I doubt whether even the Nguru women, in spite of their veritable lust for spectacular discomfort, would move to defend their sisters of another tribe, or that even the thorny subject of taxation would so overcome prejudices that it would bind two races together in a common movement. One cannot think that the Ibo farmer would rush to the rescue of the Yoruba trader though he were being ground to dust beneath the heel of the tax collector, nor would the Jekri or the Bini rise up in arms to protect the pockets of the Ibo. It is more likely that sporadic, even though synchronized, troubles would spring up all over the country than that there would be a concerted anti-British movement, with a single aim and a single leader. Unity within a people may come fairly quickly, but unity between the peoples is still remote, even in the relatively small section of Nigeria known as the Southern Provinces.[1]

There is one more point, apart from taxation, concerning which the Ibo is susceptible beyond reason and prone to accept the wildest rumours. If you were to ask an Ibo man or woman what was the most important thing to him and his people, he would probably, and quite rightly, answer: 'Our land!' and, ever suspicious, his immediate reaction to any new move on the part of Government, no matter of what nature, is one of fear lest this land should be taken from him. It is never:

[1] The Southern Provinces have an area of only 89,515 square miles (excluding Lagos and Colony) and a population of 8,138,418 as compared with the Northern Provinces with an area of 281,778 square miles and a population of 11,303,476. (*Nigerian Handbook*, 1936.)

The New Value on Land

'Shall we be beaten, or killed, or enslaved?' but 'Is the white man going to take our land?' This Government has never done, except in rare instances and in small quantities (for railways, townships, etc.) and against payment. On the other hand, the Administration does its best to carry out the maxim: 'Make ye sure to each his own, that he reap where he hath sown' but it is not easy. Before each farming season begins, there is a sudden surge of disputes and wranglings, sometimes between two villages, sometimes between individuals. As a District Officer comprehensively put it: 'This is now the bloody season.' The ever-ready matchets swing out, there is much wounding and even an occasional killing. The absence of well-marked boundaries already referred to, the number of different plots each village must own so as to allow for long fallows, the absence of any written proof of tenure, all make the land question one of increasing difficulty, especially now that in some areas at least the growing population makes it a deeply serious one. Government is doing its best to get out some sort of large-scale survey but with such extensive afforested and till now ill-mapped areas and with a still only partial understanding of what the system of Ibo land tenure really is, one feels a certain apprehension as to its result. Moreover, a change is already taking place in the situation. Land has now a market value apart from its food-producing value. It tends, at least in some instances, to lose its almost sacred nature and to take on a lay one. The soil that was pregnant with the crops-to-be, which was the abode of ancestors, the habitat of spirits, protected by 'medicine' and sacrifice, may now represent merely a potential building-site, a possible deal in real estate. These instances are still rare: the peasant himself is not yet affected, but he will have to beware, not of the white man, but of his fellow African. At a dinner given in the house of a missionary in Port Harcourt, I was astounded to hear four educated natives bitterly deplore

287

the fact that the Nigerian Government, some years back, had refused, in the face of great pressure, to approve the alienation of land for large-scale oil-plantations. When I tried to point out the evils resulting from a divorce between land and people in a country so essentially agricultural and so wedded to its own interpretation of the small-holding system, they would not listen. There would have been large sums paid down in cash, there would have been wage-earning employment—what else mattered? And then these men, who were upright, worthy people, but educated by exclusively Western methods and coming from Sierra Leone and the Gold Coast, burst forth against the Government which, so they considered, seemed to delight in upholding the peasants and the illiterates and to be bent upon protecting them at all costs. 'Government seems to mistrust us and not to wish us to have anything to do with the bush people,' they complained. I could not help saying, as tactfully as I could, that from my own experience, the educated coast people I had met knew less than nothing of the bush and were, therefore, not able to represent the peasant. Generally speaking, they forgot his very existence. When they did remember it, it was to speak of him as a 'barbarian'.[1] This they denied, but every word of the subsequent two-hour argument went to prove the truth of my assertion.[2]

[1] I actually heard this term being used at a meeting of the Legislative Council in Lagos by a Member of the Council when speaking of his illiterate fellow countrymen.

[2] In my notes, I find the remark, 'Good tempered, and not too Indian, though a tendency that way.' What I meant was that it is most happily possible to have heated discussions with Africans in a perfectly cheerful and friendly spirit. Voices are raised, fists clenched, but laughter is ever near the surface and, given the certitude that the white speaker is sincere, he is able to say what he likes upon all but a few subjects. Where wordiness is present, it is the wordiness of a child loving to hear its own voice, proud of all the new words it knows. It is not the metaphysical meanderings of the Indian windbag, though one fears that species will soon arise, thanks to politicians, lawyers, and journalists.

Government and the Native

Nigeria is so fortunate in not having to cope with the problems of white or coloured settlement, so fortunate in having had a government which has resolutely stood out against any cession of the land, that it would be a thousand pities if these advantages were lessened or nullified by the shortsightedness of Africans themselves. I would like to see lectures given in every secondary school, every teachers' training institution, and every village-group on such subjects as the potential evils of alienation of land no matter how great the immediate profits might seem, and on taxation, considered, not as an unwilling tribute and a symbol of servitude to a conquering race, but as a free return every self-respecting man should want to make for benefits received and a symbol of the adult status of the community.

All the same, referring again to the attitude of Government towards the educated coast people, is there not a danger that the Administration should think too exclusively in terms of the bush man, forgetting the still small but growing number of semi-educated, whose semi-education makes them all the more sensitive, more suggestible, more unstable? The bush man, that is to say the farmer, is the mainstay of the country, he is still in an overwhelming majority, he is, in the long run, the most reliable element, the one we understand the best and sympathize with the most. Yet as it is we who have directly and indirectly created the educated class, with its virtues and its faults, its strength and its weakness, we must not, and indeed cannot, ignore it. It would be imprudent to do so, but what is much more important, it would be unjust to do so. It would also be wasteful, for there is good material here, often hidden under a mass of mannerisms and commonplaces and copybook maxims; there is idealism, no matter how childish and unpractical; there is a stretching out towards the orderly and the seemly, be it only shown in the careful crease of the trousers or the immaculate gloss on the shoes.

Men and Women

We must not forget how varied, inconsistent and imperfect are the examples we ourselves set to the native, how bewildering our different modes of life and conduct must appear to him.

I have wondered what the African means when he uses the word 'civilization' as he so often does? Does he see civilization symbolized by the white man he happens to meet? Does he get his conception of it from the *First English Reader* or from *Gems of English Literature*? Or has he, outflung beyond any visible horizon, some intuitive perception of a world of altered and resplendent values?

XVII

Men and Women

Missions and the christianized native. The double life. The educational bait. Multiplicity of sects. The black man's response. Emotional resistances.

The next subject, that of Missions, is one of immediate and ever-growing importance. It is far too vast to fit into the résumé which is all a book like this has room for and at the same time the position of missionary work is so constantly altering that it would be practically useless, even if one had the space, to try to say the final word concerning even one of its minor aspects.

In dealing with any modern native community, Christianity,[1] or rather the work of the Christian Missions, is a question which one cannot leave aside, so far-reaching are its effects, and yet one which one hesitates to approach, so complex is the matter in itself and so varied are one's own reactions. As one who has invariably received the greatest kindness from both black and white members of all Missions, whose work has been

[1] It is to be borne in mind that the whole of Ibo-land is in process of being christianized, the normal and necessary stage before individual and practising Christians appear out of the mass. Thus the words 'Christian' and 'convert' are used in a purely relative sense. Again, so-called mass movements occur when depressed classes, as in India, conceive that they can better their lot by becoming nominal Christians or when, as in Nigeria, the adoption of nominal Christianity opens the door to education with, on the immediate horizon, a lucrative post under Government.

materially helped by the facilities so freely offered, who
has made lasting friends with men and women worthy
of all praise and all affection, I would consider myself as
having a pro-Missionary bias. As one who, by virtue of
her neutral position, has been confronted by aspects of
the results of Mission work not always seen by them, has
heard the guileless and revealing remarks which are
made when the native knows he has no need to adapt his
words to his listener, has occasionally got behind the
orthodox exterior and has seen the incredible muddle of
old and new which represents the average convert's
mind and the almost laughable contradictions and innocent hypocrisies which constitute the average convert's life, I would expect myself to have an anti-
missionary bias. Could I but find a balance between these
two positions, I could perhaps express opinions of value.
Were the subject under discussion any other, were it
entirely of this world, as agriculture or trade, could one
judge it by reason or experience alone, it would be comparatively easy to do so. But it is the one subject where
reason does not suffice and the acutest judgment, the
sanest criticism, must still make room for the mystery of
grace.

Were it not for the hope that grace is at work in ways
unseen one would often be ready to say that Mission
work was a failure. This is a hackneyed phrase which one
hesitates to repeat, connoting as it does either a personal
prejudice against Christianity itself, a sentimental view
of the virtues of the untouched savage, or the too-ready
acceptance of one-sided information. But in my case,
whenever I have been inclined to make this statement, it
has been the result, not of conversations with a die-hard
pagan nor of what I might have heard from a malicious
backslider, but of seeing and hearing the devout church
member or well-meaning catechumen.

As often, Christianity is betrayed by Christians; but
betrayal is, of course, far too condemnatory a word. Such

a tremendous load has been suddenly put upon shoulders
not yet ready to carry such a mixed burden that it is no
wonder the bearer falters, turns back, or rests awhile in
the familiar world of his own customs before resuming
the Christian path. The only real surprise is the fact that
he does not seem to know that he is doing so, so that,
with no strain nor conflict, he can attend Communion
and believe in 'medicine', keep, until he is found out, a
'church' wife and several 'native marriage' wives, tie
up preciously in the same corner of a handkerchief his
rosary and the shaped bit of 'iron for juju' made for him
by an Awka blacksmith, plant side by side in the garden
round his new cement and pan-roofed house the hibiscus
of 'civilization' and the *ogirisi* tree of pagan family rites.

One wonders sometimes whether the Missions realize
to what extent the lives of their members are double.
They know the backslider who has defied the laws of the
Church or whose life is an open scandal to the congregation but do they know the hundreds of well-meaning
men and women who transgress with cheerful equani-
mity every rule and teaching? From the missionaries'
own statements, one often thinks not. What they assert
never does, never could happen, one knows from personal experience does happen, and that not among sin-
ners and renegades but among upright and sincere men
who lack merely a clear idea of what it is all about and a
compelling conviction that the 'all' presented to them
by the Missions is the real and only all. And in any case,
the term 'double life' is misleading for that implies a
recognition that there is some sort of opposition of view
or aims, that one life is in some way different from the
other, while in fact the Ibo's genius lies in his capacity
for interweaving them with such facility that it is impossible either for him or for others to see the joins. He
has no sense of incongruity. If such things were still
possible, he would see nothing strange in going off on a
bicycle, or in a sports car if he had one, to take part in a

cannibal feast; he would make out a cheque on the Bank
of British West Africa for the purchase of a victim for a
human sacrifice. He is bafflingly unable to see any clash
in modes of living or in modes of thought, and just as his
own customs and organizations fade and reappear, melt
and solidify in never-ending sequence, so do his thoughts
easily embrace any and every mode of outlook in an effortless fusion of old and new, of the indigenous and the
extraneous. Of course, one does not expect him to slough
off in one generation the beliefs and customs of centuries. It is not this inability that puzzles one: it is rather
this amazing ability to hold both sets of customs at one
and the same time without a shadow of conflict or bewilderment.

With this ease of adaptation goes, of course, the
inability to conceive that religious convictions matter
very deeply to anyone else. For example, I think it would
be true to say that I have never met an Ibo who had any
realization of what impels the missionary to come to
Africa. They see that he lives in fairly comfortable
quarters, has servants, a car, plays tennis, so they con-
clude that to be a missionary is a job like any other, as
readily taken up and for the same reasons as the job of
Assistant District Officer or that of a Public Works
engineer. That the missionary needs something more
than a material incentive to enable him to face his heavy
task, that he has ever felt the call of love or pity, that he
has made sacrifices, given up home and friends, accepted
quite inadequate remuneration, so as to obey that call,
never enters his mind and, if presented to him in so
many words, is beyond his comprehension. The fact, if
one is able to persuade them of its truth, that the men
and women belonging to the Roman Catholic Mission
have given up the last penny of their worldly possessions
and are vowed to celibacy does impress them, but the
equally valuable if less spectacular sacrifices made by
others, leave them untouched or sceptical. No one would

desire less to be praised or admired than the missionaries themselves but the outsider cannot but feel that not only is the Ibo attitude an unjust one but that it would be good for him to admire somebody other than himself, to know that rush of gratitude which is of so much greater value to the giver than to the recipient, to realize the existence of another set of values and of motives than his own.

Another factor which tends to make him think that religious convictions have no very profound significance is that of the indifference, or seeming indifference, of most of the white people he encounters. His judgment is not yet sufficiently developed to be able to discover the possible true Christian behind the non-churchgoer nor to discern the spiritual outlook which does not necessarily express itself in the conventional religious gestures. This factor undoubtedly hampers the work of the Missions a great deal and lends an air of unreality which is hard to explain away. I have known numberless officials whose lives have been as upright, whose devotion to the native has been as great as that of any missionary, who have quite literally sacrificed themselves for the good of the country (though they would be the last to admit it!). The native has seen this and has appreciated it. When you hear it stated: 'He be good white man', you know he has stood before the hardest tribunal in the world, he has been observed and weighed and judged with all the cunning and the shrewdness, the intuitions and the perceptions of the primitive. The verdict is final and astonishingly accurate; but in giving it the native does not consider whether Christianity has played any part in the development of the man he admires nor does he in any way connect his virtues with his religious beliefs. He has not seen him go to church nor keep the Sabbath nor abstain from drink; that, nevertheless, he may be inspired by the Christian spirit does not strike him.

One of my most disheartening conversations,

disheartening because it gave in ingenuous, cheerful, indifferent words what I had myself caught glimpses of in elusive ways and from casual observations, was with an educated, high-principled and thinking man whom I knew well and who belonged to the new generation, though in his case he was more consciously loyal to old customs and beliefs than some of his contemporaries. He had been brought up a Roman Catholic but I think he had attempted to grasp too many modes of thought and had drifted away from Christianity; personally indifferent but still intellectually interested and by no means hostile. I had asked him why his people became Christians? After a long pause, he gave as a reasonable and carefully weighed answer: 'They become Christian before they get sense.' The damning nature of this statement he never realized. He merely explained that the boy who goes to a Mission school takes it for granted that becoming a Christian is a corollary to becoming a scholar and will automatically and unreasoningly go through the requisite forms without thought or question. Pursuing the subject, he stated that some girls, other than schoolgirls who would pursue the same course as their brothers, would also become Christians for the unexpected reason that it was 'less trouble'. Questioned more closely, he reminded me of the innumerable family and social obligations a pagan girl is under. She must take part in the girls' dances, which, with all the rehearsals, represent a good deal of physical exertion; she must pay the proper visits, at the proper times, help cook at festivities, condole with the bereaved. The Christian girl says: 'I am a Christian. I have nothing to do with this,' and sits quietly at home. It is true she has to go to church on Sunday but there again 'she can sit down, then she comes home and her duties are finished'.

I asked him point blank how many turned to Christianity because they searched for the truth and wanted more than their pagan beliefs could give them.

Conversion and Education

At first, he shrugged his shoulders. The question hardly required an answer, there were so few. Then, more gravely, he conceded: 'Some old women.' At the end of a long life, seeing the vanity of all earthly things, they turn towards the heavenly, and the respect in his voice proving that he knew what the acceptance of Christianity meant, he added: 'They really surrender their hearts to God.'

I would by no means assert that this man's statements could be taken as generally true, but that they are very often true, I have no doubt, and how can it be otherwise? The missionaries came, bringing salvation in one hand and education in the other. The people had no hunger for salvation but they were hungry for education which they saw would benefit them. Apparently education was indissolubly bound up with 'church'. Some of the Missions even insisted that literacy was necessary to baptism. The Ibo was nothing loath. Provided he acquired literacy, he did not mind being baptized: to the missionary, education was the handmaid of religion; to the heathen, religion was the means to education. They felt no need for another faith but they had great need of a new way of attaining wealth. The parents themselves often did not bother to change, but they willingly offered their children to this new God who was able, not only to unlock the gates of Heaven and Hell but, what was much more important, to open the doors of European trading firms and the desks of Government offices.

I think it is true to say that only among the Ibo, the most ambitious of the peoples of Nigeria, has there been what could be called a mass movement towards Christianity. It would be obviously unjust to claim that the only motives behind this movement were mercenary ones but they bulk large all the same and even to-day I do not think that it is uncharitable to say that the reasons why a man deserts one form of Christianity for another

297

are generally more material than spiritual: 'If a man wants to join C.M.S. and wait too long for baptism, he tire, he go R.C.M.' If lucrative posts seem, for the moment, scarce in one Mission, he will try another. If the high class-fees of one church cannot be got together by the end of the year, there is a hasty search for a less costly one. If little Kanu sticks too long in Standard IV because his teacher says he is not bright enough to be moved into Standard V, let him see what luck he will have with the Fathers or with the Seventh Day Adventists.

It is true that in becoming Christians, the Ibo were expected to give up a good deal to which both their hearts and their senses clung, but they trusted they would find some sort of compromise and though running with the Western hare, they could still hunt with the pagan hounds. Their trust was not misplaced. Easily, airily, they slide out of one skin into another, or rather, by some miracle peculiar to themselves, comfortably wear both skins at once.

If I insist so often on this Ibo capacity for leading a double life, it is not because I regard it as a sly or contemptible or hypocritical trait. It is none of these. In a sense, their guilelessness, one might almost say their good faith, is what makes it all the more surprising. It approaches the attitude of the child who, quite naturally, wants to get the most he can both out of his own world and the adult world and has no scruple in conforming for the time being to the adult's view while keeping unaltered his own childish mode of thinking. It is, however, important that one should realize the existence of this capacity. Missionaries especially, I think, need to do so, so that they should not be too elated over a convert nor too cast down over a backslider. The Ibo himself sees nothing in such clear terms of black and white. It is the white man, not the black, who, after a conversation on religion or ethics, unconsciously makes the gesture of dragging his feet out of a bog and, with a deep breath, tries to shake off the clinging mud of so much confused thinking. The black man emerges untouched, unweary, not even knowing the bog is there.

It is not only the Ibo's own limitations that hinder his better understanding of the missionary's aims: the Missions themselves help very often to obscure a true view.

Reference has already been made in a chapter on Port Harcourt to the multiplication of sects. Though Port Harcourt is so artificial a community that it might be argued that nothing of general import could be deduced from it, though one is inclined to take for granted that the religious hotchpotch one finds there is but the product of an artificial agglomeration of different races leading an artificial life and that the often ephemeral existence of these 'Churches' will have no influence on the rest of the country, yet it is not altogether so. That same artificiality is spreading and is being introduced to a greater or a lesser degree in all parts of the country where roads, lorries, schools, and Missions have broken up the ground ready for the sowing of any seeds the wind may chance to carry there. Branches of the various sects open with astonishing rapidity, doctrines spread, converts, each hoping for material or spiritual perquisites, appear. The responsible Missions such as the Church Missionary Society, the Church of Scotland, the Methodists, the Kwa Ibo, have formed a union, have mapped out individual spheres of influence and have undertaken to care for members of each other's Churches in all places where the member's own Church is not represented; but smaller Missions, such as the Seventh Day Adventists, the Salvation Army, have not felt able to belong, nor of course will the Roman Catholic Church agree to any bounds being set to its sphere of work. And still further from any thought of union or co-operation comes the mass of fancy religions, often originating from America, which prey upon the native, his suggestibility, his vanity, his generosity.

Men and Women

If the West African were grown up, really adult in his capacity for distinguishing, judging, making a mature decision, it would not matter so much. He would make his choice according to his own temperament, his own cast of mind, his own intuitive perceptions. In full possession of his reasoning powers he would have the right to choose the form of religion which convinced him most; but he is not adult, he noticeably lacks discrimination when faced with objects or ideas which are new to his experience. He is naturally religious, he is naturally attracted by novelty, he is naturally inclined to get all he can. He is ripe for outward, if not inward, conversion to any creed. If it is one of the more reputable Missions that first comes his way, well and good, he joins that without pausing to weigh the claims of the other rivals, but his allegiance so easily gained and thoughtlessly given, will not bind him very securely. Not only will his traditional beliefs call to him insistently in moments of private trouble, fortified by all that is precious to him in the way of family ties both with the living and the dead, but he will be ready to try any new thing that promises him a quick return in both material and spiritual goods, any sort of miraculous solution of his difficulties and which, above all, while offering Heaven to himself, decrees Hell for his enemies.

Apparently nothing can be done to stop new 'Churches' setting themselves up where they please and issuing any literature they like, so long as it is not openly libellous or seditious, nor would it be wise to draw too much attention to them or to make them feel, as they quickly would, that they were being persecuted for conscience' sake. Nevertheless, it seemed to me that both the Administration and the Missions looked upon them with perhaps too great an indifference. The class of semi-educated which would be likely to join them is rapidly increasing, so their chance of raising more recruits will increase also, and though it is difficult to gauge their political importance,

300

some of their teachings are openly anti-Government (and by Government I do not mean only the existing form of Nigerian government but what we take to be law and order in general); the others are insidiously so. And all of them are spiritually dangerous in that they minister to what is most childish, not childlike, in the human mind. I do not doubt that some of their adherents accept the doctrines with a simple and beautiful faith and so, by their own virtue, turn the dross given them into gold, but the majority see only their own advantage, their own importance—the country is full of 'bishops' and 'primates'—and the snap of belonging to a 'peculiar people'. To those who love both God and the African such travesties are painful and an insult both to the Creator and to the created. I do not think the Ibo has asked for bread—he is too well fed by his own self-satisfaction—but if we insist on giving it to him, let it be true bread and not a stone. Unfortunately, it must be remembered that the long-established Missions have already given an example of a diversity of doctrines. The would-be convert can already listen to at least four publicly recognized forms and sees no reason why there should not be a few more, equally credible. As Professor Westermann in *The African To-day* admits: 'It is unfortunate that Christianity comes to Africa split into sects!' No outsider, however respectful of Mission work and however cognizant of his or her reprehensible fluidity of belief, can help regretting, over and over again, that some self-denying ordinance had not inspired the various Missions to leave the Nigerian field to one single form of Christian faith.

Again and again I tried to guess what the ultimate Church of Nigeria would be. One fact was very noticeable, at least in the Owerri and Onitsha Provinces: as both policy and finance dictate the lessening of the European staff of the Church Missionary Society, so does the European staff of the Roman Catholic Mission increase.

Old stations are being enlarged; new stations are being opened up (sometimes in rather unnecessary proximity to the Protestant station!); vast and durable buildings of stone or cement are taking the place of the old rickety dwellings; girls' schools, hospitals, dispensaries, symbolize that the pioneer period is over and the occupation of the country has begun. Of the relative merits of the two missionary bodies it is not for me to speak. The only phrase I have heard which, to my mind, sums up the situation, was uttered by a Government official, long in the country, a practising member of the Church of England, and liking the native. In casual conversation, I had asked him which Mission he considered the best. His reply was: 'The Roman Catholic.' I asked him why. After a moment's thought he answered: 'Because they see things as they are. . . .'

Whether, apart from or in conjunction with recognized Missions, the Ibo will ultimately evolve a Church of their own is still too early to say. In the meantime, one cannot but regret the absence of any native features in buildings, music, ceremonials. Though there are sincere efforts on the part of some modern missionaries to allow native inspiration a place in acts of worship, yet one is always conscious that at the back of their minds there are so many reservations, so many objections, so many 'buts' and 'ifs', that one can hardly hope for any result. Very deep down, often denied, still lurks the suspicion that everything 'native' must be 'evil'; that nothing that is not Western, I would almost say British, can be Christian. With illogical haste the Protestant Missions entrust the black man, almost unsupervised, with all the responsibilities of priesthood, with the propagation of new doctrines, the imposition of alien discipline, and yet will not trust him to sing a song or dance a dance which will express his own idea, in his own form, of the glory of the Lord.

Revelations

Only thrice, under widely varying circumstances, have I felt a real uprush of worship and joy. The first occasion was some time ago in Lagos where, with one of the Roman Catholic Sisters, I had been to see a strange little body of freed women slaves, repatriated from Brazil years ago, now destitute and cared for by the Mission. The oldest of them all, fabulous in her age and her emaciation, was near death. She knew it. Smiling gladly at the Sister, she pointed to a little framed engraving of the Virgin and Child (the lettering was in Portuguese, so she must have clung to it all the way from Brazil), and said in strangely mixed Portuguese, pidgin English and Yoruba: 'I will see Her soon. I will see Her seated on Her throne, and I will dance for Her.' She half raised herself. 'I will dance and dance and *dance*!' Such a blaze of ecstasy ran through her that one half-expected her body to shrivel up and burst forth anew in a dancing flame. The nun smiled down at her. Two days later she was dead.

The second time was in a hill-top village just over the northern border of the Okigwi Division. It was Easter morning, radiant after rain. My interpreter Mary and a native teacher called the few Christians and some pagan 'inquirers' into the little mud building that served as church and school. The village was poor and almost unknown. There could be no Sunday finery, indeed there was practically no clothing at all. Though the members of the congregation may not have understood a word of the service, they were at home in it, their naked bodies sat easily on the low mud benches, their children squatted, noiseless, on the floor beside them; through the doorless openings, they could see the tops of the palm-trees, and across the valley the golden cone of Imoago's sacred hill. They had learnt by heart an Easter hymn. 'Alleluia' was a fine word. They shouted it with joy and exultation, bare bodies tense with the effort, and the pouring sweat testified to the strength of their convictions. Heaven knows what image they had in their minds

of this crucified and risen Saviour but it was an image
of their very own, their own personal creation and
possession, and they delighted in their treasure. Alas,
some time later, returning to the same village, I chanced
to be there at the same time as a missionary who was to
give Communion to the two men and three women who
made up the baptized membership of the church. The
service was conducted with all reverence but was profoundly disappointing, and with (or so it seemed to me,
perhaps made over-sensitive by my affection for these
village folk), no realization of the people's thoughts and
needs. The opportunity was exquisite in its implications,
but no advantage was taken of it. Before them they had,
not the Shepherd come to feed his flock with leisure and
with care, but the white man with his wrist-watch, in a
hurry to get on. Would they not think 'as servant so
master' and see God with a wrist-watch too, alien in
voice and gesture, hurrying past? It must be quickly said
that the calls upon the missionary's time are so great that
it is often a physical impossibility for him (as it was on
this occasion) to do more than pay the shortest of visits to
many of his flock. But then would it not be better to
leave them quite alone than to feed them so hurriedly
that they mis-digest?

The third time was near Inyeogugu. Down a broad
forest glade came a band of children, boys and girls, led
by two young teachers. The boys walked in front, making shrill music upon their native flutes, the girls followed behind, bright kerchiefs upon their heads. As they
came, they sang 'Jesus is born! Jesus lives!' They were
going to visit an ex-schoolmate who had had a baby and
evidently thought this a suitable refrain. So true and
glad was their news, they had to declare it again and
again and as they swung swiftly along, with a flutter of
coloured handkerchiefs beneath the arch of trees, flutes
and voices rising high and clear, they looked the embodi-
ment of joy. All faces were alight, all heads thrown back,

all feet moved to the quick rhythm. They were no longer boys and girls, but a shout of happiness passing lightly through the forest.

Though the Ibo has no difficulty in reconciling pagan and Christian modes of thought, or Western and African modes of life, though he readily accepts Western institutions and abandons with alacrity old ways for new, all the same there are occasions when the white man's influence counts for naught and he finds himself faced with a depth of feeling and strength of conviction against which his arguments are of no avail. One meets what Miss Monica Hunter[1] aptly terms 'emotional resistance' chiefly in those spheres of thought and custom which have to do with family life, taking, as one must always do in Ibo-land, the word family to include both its living members and its dead. Thus the custom of 'second burial' is not likely to die out for generations; nor is that of 'title-taking', as, apart from their more material aspects, they both form links between the world of flesh and spirit. The payment of dowry will also endure, for it is more than a mere money transaction, it partakes of the nature of a contract between two families and has, therefore, a far-extending social significance. Polygamy, too, perhaps the most important of the Ibo social customs from the women's point of view, is deeply rooted and though among the educated lip service is paid to monogamy, one soon comes across the many rocks, deeply embedded not only in custom but in the Ibo's whole conception of life, on which it strikes and so often breaks.

One could wish the Missions had not been quite so uncompromising in their attitude towards certain of these customs—or rather that they could have been understanding first and uncompromising afterwards, if they still felt that they had to be. What I think really angers the anti-missionary native is this sweeping

[1] *Reaction to Conquest*, by Monica Hunter.

condemnation of what in many cases the missionary knows nothing of; what really hurts the pro-missionary native is this lack of interest in what for generations have been the main features of his life, this lack of respect for what he and his fathers have held to be true and important since time immemorial.

Ceremonies, dances, have a great deal more 'to' them than what the average white man sees in them; silly, pointless, ugly, they may occasionally be, yet they are in some dim way expressions of the spirit and it is that one should look for, not the outward show. Behind every 'religious' manifestation I have seen, however trivial or possibly repulsive, there is a faint hovering flame of something which bears no apparent relation to the actual manifestation itself. It is this we must look for, and if we do not see it, it is our own eyes that are at fault. The most frequent and the most reasonable complaint one hears against the Missions is: 'They do not know' or 'They do not understand' or 'They have not seen'.

In his preface to *La Religion des Primitifs*, the late Mgr Leroy, writing already in 1909, had the wisdom to say: 'If there is one elementary principle to be followed by every man who proposes to bring others to his own faith, it is to know what they believe themselves; there might perhaps be points of contact at which one could meet and instead of endless controversial discussions, always a little irritating, mutual explanation would suffice for mutual comprehension.' And he goes so far as to say: 'The study of the beliefs of these primitive peoples is in itself extremely interesting, not only because . . . it is one of the necessary elements of ethnography, history, philosophy, not only because it is a new and fascinating exploration of the depths of the human soul, but also and above all, because it reveals surprising points of comparison with the highest forms of religion, so that, one can say, the theologian who ignores it, ignores a part of theology.'

Destruction without Reconstruction

Surely should it not be the Christian's pride to discover even the faintest indication of a universal kinship created by the universal working of the same Spirit; and would it not be his shame to pass by or even contemptuously reject any element which might enrich his own faith?

In how far native customs and beliefs can be carried over into Christianity and into Western civilization in general, I do not know. It is an attractive theory, but in practice curiously difficult to carry out. But I am sure a more patient understanding of and a more respectful attitude towards native institutions would help immensely the work of christianization. Not only would it be more just but it would be more expedient. Though written in a quite different context, the words: 'The prime fact about modernity . . . is that it not merely denies the central ideas of our forefathers but dissolves the disposition to believe in them',[1] are relevant. By denying too crudely and carelessly the old beliefs, one is liable 'to dissolve the disposition to believe' in the new ones, be they never so fine nor so true. To quote Walter Lipmann again: 'The more recent reformers . . . frequently betray a somewhat similar inability to imagine the consequences of their own victories. For the smashing of idols is in itself such a preoccupation that it is almost impossible for the iconoclast to look clearly into the future where there will not be many idols left to smash.'

This one often feels: has the reformer considered what will be the result of his reforms? Does the iconoclast, before he raises his hammer, stop to think what will replace the idol he so indignantly destroys? Take the question of marriage once again, a question almost more complex and more delicate in a primitive society than in our own. 'Christian marriage is a prison. . . .' These words might well have startled a reformer, coming as

[1] *A Preface to Morals*, by Walter Lipmann.

307

they did from an elderly Christian woman, a church member of long standing. She had been telling me a number of stories all ending in matrimonial disaster, and when I asked her to explain herself further, she said that the very stories she had been relating showed that her people were not yet ready for monogamous and indissoluble marriage.[1] She advocated marriage according to native law and custom with, if they so desired it, a simple service of prayer and blessing before the bride went finally to her husband. If after five years or more, the couple had remained in monogamous and happy union and—important point—the woman had had children, then they could present themselves for marriage in church according to full Christian rites. By then they would know their own minds, they would have shown that they realized the sanctity of marriage and the man would have proved that he was able to be monogamous, not such an easy task when the rules concerning intercourse during pregnancy and the subsequent long lactation period are remembered. Such marriages would be a credit to the church instead of bringing scandal and disgrace as they often do. I could not help but agree with her. Only in exceptional cases are either man or woman ripe for the huge responsibility and weight of Christian marriage. They do not grasp its implications and its possible consequences, neither one nor the other can foresee the long years tied to a cruel man or a slipshod woman. Noticeably unable to visualize more than a very limited future, they are not yet capable of assessing what a life-long bond really means; nor has the man yet enough strength of character to withstand family pressure urging him to polygamy in the event of his 'church' wife being childless. Men and women hear the churches exhorting them to a Christian marriage; they are dazzled

[1] Divorce can be obtained but only through a lengthy and costly legal process. The Roman Catholic Church does not of course admit divorce at all.

by the importance of the ceremony and the opportunity for display; the woman knows that to be a 'church' wife confers a certain status (she may possibly also know that it enables her to inherit property from her deceased husband, a privilege she would not have if married by native law).

Shrewd enough, as I have already said, along his own lines, when dealing with problems arising in the normal course of tribal life, the native is at sea when faced with situations belonging to another order of thought and conduct. He loses his perspicacity, his judgment, his sense of proportion and of reality. I know that teachers and pastors tell him what a Christian marriage means and what it entails. Doubtless he listens and even understands, but again, as with so much of his education, it is only a little portion of his brain that understands, and the knowledge remains there, uncommunicated to the rest of his being. Once more we are cruel in that we expect too much and unjust in that we blame him when he disappoints our expectations. When the native through education, experience, and mental development has acquired discernment in the new realms to which we have led him and is honestly capable of weighing and judging alien modes of life and thought, then let him by all means bear the full weight of Western codes of conduct and take on the full responsibility of Christian morality but till then let us go gently with him and make sure he is having a fair deal, not only in the realm of the material but in the more subtle one of the spiritual. Let him not be trapped for the best of reasons and for his highest good, but trapped all the same. Though there was exaggeration and personal bitterness, yet there was also a good deal of truth in old Christina's spontaneous cry: 'Christian marriage is a prison!'

Take the question of native songs and dances. This is one of the regions where the iconoclast has most furiously raised his hammer. The scant references I have made to dancing (dance and song almost invariably go together) give no idea of its importance in the life of a Nigerian community.[1] The very fact that the dance forms such an integral part of the African's existence is perhaps the explanation why I have made so little mention of it, any more than I have made mention of the air one breathes or the soil one stands on, for it is as much a constant accompaniment of life as sun and rain, wind and heat. It escapes all definitions, defies all analysis. It is, in some elusive way, Africa. Although I have been so often in closest contact with the country and the people, although I can remember scenes and looks and words which opened up whole worlds of new understanding, I have only twice been able to say with complete conviction, 'I am seeing Africa', and on both occasions I was watching girl children dance. These were supreme occasions, causing a veritable shock of insight, but even apart from these two moments, it has always been the dance which has enhanced the 'African-ness' of the African. The dances may be dull or strange, grotesque or beautiful, but always they transcend themselves. I know of no European equivalent, nothing which gathers up into a single activity every possible range of thought and emotion, and then leaps beyond them. (Of course I am only speaking of dances performed under natural conditions, those one meets haphazard in a market place or near a forest shrine or within the compound walls, not those which are performed out of due season as a spectacle for the white man.) I doubt whether the Western mind could ever be at home in an African dance, not because of any difference of step or rhythm or tune, but because it belongs to a region unknown to us, to another dimension one might almost say, which we have either

[1] 'The most obvious difference between modern and primitive music is that of function: ours merely, or more usually, an emotional appendage, theirs an integral part of everyday existence, in which both instruments and music are wrapped up in ritual and tribal life.' Douglas Varley, *Man*, September 1937.

left behind us long ago or to which we have not yet
attained. The African—the Ibo at least—in his new-
found eagerness to copy us, will gradually draw away
from it into the puerile gyrations of a half-caste jazz;
but I hope it will be long before the women abandon
altogether the vast chanting circle, the stamping feet and
upthrown arms or the grace of slow precise movements,
the hardly moving hands and feet and delicately droop-
ing head.

Why is it that all African dances have so often been
declared to be wicked and obscene? Is it because they are
looked upon as being essentially sexual in tone and therefore demoralizing? The more one sees of the Negro,[1] the
more one is inclined to think that sex does not play such
an important part in his life as one is led to believe. Pro-
creation does. Are there two male types, one whose chief
interest lies in the possession of women, and the other
whose chief interest lies in the possession of children?
And if a man belongs to the latter type, as does the Ibo,
would his sexual desires be quickly and easily satisfied, so
that he has no need to 'run after women' or to think
about them except as potential mothers? It is true that
native songs and dances can on rare occasions be common
and vulgar—as vulgar as our own can be—but I think
that what is seen in them as purely sexual in its narrow
sense is in reality a glorification not of 'sexuality, but of
fertility, which is respectable and even beautiful. Or
is it only because we cannot understand these dances
and what we cannot understand, cannot be 'nice', and
so the legend grows? But it is impossible not to feel
angry impatience with those who spread this legend,
based on the evidence of their own prejudiced or evil-
seeking eyes, or merely upon hearsay, and who wish to
destroy instantly what is often both a rare form of
beauty and an age-old means of expression. The dances

[1] I specify 'the Negro' as the statement would not seem to be so
true of other Nigerian people, especially those of the North.

gone, what will take their place? Where will that fire
and energy go to? Because we in England have no
single activity such as this into which we throw all
that we have and are, is it a reason for taking it away
from others, simpler and more direct than we are? Let
us also remember how the elders of Owerri Town banned
Western dancing because of its impropriety and how
observant natives will naturally ask why dancing in the
Western fashion, man and woman tightly clasped together, probably indoors in a hot and crowded room, and
in the middle of the night, should be more seemly than
his own dances, with dancers of one sex only, out of
doors and, in the case of the 'best' dances, in broad daylight?

Take the question of 'second burials'. In how far
native ceremonies and customs have been carried over
into Christianity *without* being christianized is hard to
determine, the native himself often not knowing or not
wishing to admit that he could not do without his old
beliefs and, rather than lose them altogether, has hidden
them behind a Christian symbol, not transmuted them
into a Christian truth. My suggestion that the memorial
services with their sonorous list of relatives published in
the newspapers and all the pomp of black-bordered
notices posted on the walls, were substitutes for second
burials was not altogether denied, and the wakes frequently held (and known, curiously enough, by that
almost obsolete word) are, to some degree, a replica of
the pagan funeral feast with its crowd of lamenting
relations and friends, its drummings, songs and dances.
The drummings are banned, the songs in praise of the
deceased are now turned into hymns, the dancing into
praying, the palm-wine and the baked meats into lemon-
ade and biscuits, but the gesture remains the same, and
one can also see connections between the visits of condo-
lence paid to a bereaved Christian woman by her Bible
class-mates or by fellow members of some 'Ladies'

Christian Association' and those paid to a pagan woman
by her age-grade companions.

The wrath of the iconoclasts against the *mbari* houses
of Owerri is more understandable, though even here we
should go slowly lest in pulling down the gaudy shrines
and obscene figures, we pull down some valuable mental
edifice merely because we have not yet the key to it, or
block up some channel of expression which we have not
the ability to replace. How one would love to be able to
transfer their delicate patternings of walls and roofs to
the bare, dull churches, to capture for better and more
durable ends all that minute and conscientious skill, and
if there were still some artistic energy left over, why
should not every village-area in turn have its Madame
Tussaud where we still could see the District Officer, stiff
and starched, the Giant Policeman, the lady doctor with
her patients, the tailor and his sewing-machine, the
legendary elephant and tortoise, and whatever of pleasant ribaldry the people's own humour, purged by their
own good taste, chose to portray?

XVIII

Men and Women

---

*Education and other Western developments; courts of
law; house building and home making; general facilities.*

Education is a subject almost as important as religion
and in the case of Nigeria, so interwoven with it that
what is said on one subject applies with almost equal
force to the other. Here again we have the cheerful
fusion of Western knowledge with African ignorance.
The native 'knows' with a little fragment of fragile
brain that the earth is round, but he knows with every
conviction of his heart and the whole strength of his
body that it is a flat plate. Here again as in the religious
sphere, we have the outward acceptance and the inward
disbelief, here again we have the precept without the
practice and, here again especially, we have the material
motive at its crudest.

The more one sees of education and its results, the
more displeased does one feel with the educational
methods employed; but unfortunately the rut has now
been worn so deep that it will be almost impossible for
the educational machine to be lifted out of it. This
machine was originally designed on strictly British lines:
the readers were illustrated with robins and snow scenes;
the arithmetic problems dealt with trains and wall-paper
and water-taps; history taught the Wars of the Roses
and geography the height of the Chilterns. Then came
the era of jobs: Government and mercantile firms

Western Standards of Education

clamoured for clerks and accountants, schools for teachers, hospitals for orderlies. The supply was met and, gradually, was over-met. Examinations had to be introduced so as to weed out the competitors. The examinations were British too: School-Leaving Certificate, Cambridge Local, College of Preceptors. The curriculum could not be altered to something more African and better suited to the bulk of the people because there would always be a few boys who would wish to sit for these exams, and would, therefore, have to be taught certain subjects in certain ways. And in any case, by that time, the native himself did not want any change and would have hotly resented any attempt to make his son's school more like his father's home. If education was not strictly in terms of slates and pencils and primers and blackboards and later in terms of copy-books, rulers, satchels and school caps, if it was restricted so as to teach only those subjects which would be of honest worth to the pupils or altered to give a more African bias and atmosphere, he was not satisfied. Reference has already been made (see p. 58) to the native's attitude towards the vernacular: the same attitude persists all through. It is now the native himself, in his overwhelming multitudes, who, through his vocal Unions and his newspaper editors, holds grimly, fanatically, to the robins and the water-taps. Should an African hornbill be substituted for the robin, it would be a brutal proof that the white man wants to thrust the black man back into his place among the primeval swamps and forests; should a calabash take the place of the water-tap, it would show that the ruthless conquerors mean to deny to the conquered even the simplest advantages of civilization. There will be a swing back of the pendulum in time and more especially there will be a growing appreciation of education for its own sake. Just now, it seems as if one could only let the muddle take its own course, trusting that time will clarify it and knowing that in the meantime the Ibo has

315

the good digestion of the cheerful man and can swallow almost anything we give him without lasting harm. What the people need most at present, I think, are neither teachers nor preachers but explainers. Explainers of all the new words that pour so torrentially round their heads, words like money, exchange, world markets, Government, democracy, law, taxation, censorship, hypnotism, gravitation and the American debt. In the depth of the bush, I have been asked about all these things and have had to answer questions as difficult as that of a suspicious teacher: 'Does the King pay taxes?' or Mary's guileless and reasonable interrogation: 'As you white people know so much about hygiene, there can be no sick children in your country?' or a Nguru woman's sharp query, arms akimbo: 'This shortage of money [she was referring to the fall in oil prices], is it from God or Government?'

If we turn to girls' education, there is more to be said and to be done. It is profoundly disappointing that Government has not created the post of Woman Director of Women's Education in a country where women play so great a part but one of which the average white man necessarily knows almost nothing. It seems an obvious step and one which would have meant much for the future of Nigeria. With the best will in the world, how can a Board of Education composed entirely of men have any practical views on the upbringing of little Fatima of Kano or young Mbafɔ of Okigwi? Even later when a woman member was appointed to the Board she could only advise and had no executive power. Questions relating to girls' education tended to find their way to the very bottom of an already overloaded agenda and even the most kindly disposed education official, wearied by the insistent demands of the boys' schools, was apt to brush aside as unimportant something so far from his experience or interest as the best educational policy for girls. Though the subject is still of manageable proportions at the moment, it will not remain so for long in the eastern provinces. Girls are flocking to the ordinary mixed day schools and all the girls' boarding-schools I know of are full. Wherever I went, I found a demand for training-homes such as already described (see p. 189). The Roman Catholics are pushing forward, and here also their large European staff gives them an immense advantage over other Missions. In and around Onitsha especially, girls' education is active and the idea has permeated even to the remotest bush districts.

As in the case of the boys' schools, one wonders sometimes whether the quality of the education given is of the right kind. I have already expressed (see p. 133) my mistrust of co-education. My criticism has been countered by the affirmation that experience shows that girls in mixed day schools are brighter, more ambitious, have more initiative and character than those educated in a girls' boarding-school. This may very likely be so, but it may be due to the faults of the boarding-school rather than to the virtue of the day school.[1] And if the present curriculum is unsuitable for the majority of boys, what of its unsuitability for girls? Here again the tyranny of examinations impedes its freer interpretation: girls too want jobs and although they seldom aspire to more than a Standard VI pass (which incidentally has been modified recently in a right, or at least a much better direction), even that amount of formal book-work is beyond, not their powers of acquisition, but their powers of assimilation. Feeling certain that the instinct for family life and the love of children were the finest and most stable things in the Nigerian women, I had always hoped that their education could have been kept free of all formalism. I had seen it bound together with the care of home and babies so that a school should have been a crèche and a dispensary, a class-room and a kitchen all in one. It

[1] Mrs. Hilda Thurnwald has very interesting comments to make on girls' education in East Africa.

might have kept the women back a little but it would have prepared them for a real and safe forward move when the natural time came. It would have served to waken them, to accustom them to some new habits, to some new ideas. It would have corresponded to that quiet period of 'gentling' a wild animal before it can be trained.

Instead, we have pushed them forward out of their own world, out of their own natures, one might say. Once more, in our excess of kindness, we have been cruel in expecting far too much of them. Some just sit back, stolid beneath the lash not of any material whip but of our own ambitions for them. We complain of their inertia, their indifference, of their inability to put their backs into their work, having lost sight of, or never having seen, that the one dominant interest in their minds is to get married, and even more, to have babies. Others outwardly respond, quote poetry and know about vitamins, but the knowledge is so little assimilated that it creates, not a fuller and more contented mind, but merely a restless one. They do not want to get married, not just yet. They want to see life first, 'to drink the breeze' as a young teacher said to me, and the life they want to see has nothing to do with poetry nor with science.

Our European women teachers have perhaps all had the fault of being too 'nice', too refined of mind, too civilized. I do not for a moment suggest that the Ibo woman, or any other primitive woman, is coarse or common; on the contrary, she often reveals marvels of delicacy and modesty, but she has a robust sense of the rock-bottom things of life, of the things that matter: sex, with very special emphasis on child-bearing, the soil as provider of food and therefore the great sustainer of life, the stomach as the constant companion whose wants urge men and women to endless and wearisome labour but whose satisfaction gives also delightful moments of pleasure and well-being. The European teacher believes also in the sanctity of marriage and the desirability of having children but with a touch both of sentimentality and of intellectuality which separates her from the girls. The soil she knows is that of the garden, refined and handled, weighed and measured, not the fat red earth that has to be wrested again and again from the bush, drenched with rain, heavy with crops; nor yet the poor sands of the uplands where the women's bean crops flourish valiantly beneath the widespread sky. She rejoices over a budding rose or a bougainvillæa that has 'taken', but few feel the wonder of the slow growth of the yam tubers or care for the well-hoed mounds or the cunning curves of the ridges. As for the stomach, it is taken for granted and as little attention is paid to it as possible, so food can give no pleasure since it arouses no interest. Here are three worlds where the black and the white mind do not meet, three sets of experience they do not share.

The teachers have an ideal not far removed from what they would wish an English girl to be, forgetting the latter's centuries of background, the million diverse influences that have moulded her, the thousand minds that have considered, and planned and reflected upon her training. They think this ideal girl should have new interests and take it for granted, not only that she will be eager to have them but that they would be good for her. I think the majority of girls are not eager; the minority are eager but their new interests are not exactly what their devoted, anxious teachers wished them to be.

I was talking with a young married woman, brought up in a very good missionary boarding-school, well married to a Christian husband. I had met her several times, we had a number of mutual acquaintances, our relations were easy and pleasant and I had no difficulty in following either her English or her train of thought. But the last time I happened to see her, her sentences seemed occasionally to have no meaning and I found myself every now and again held up as if, in speaking, she had missed out or misused some vital word. At last I discovered what was baffling me: she used the word 'civilized' as synonymous for 'immoral'. And this in all good faith, with no hint of bitterness or sarcasm. It was merely the result of her own experience and observations: when a girl was civilized, that is to say, educated, she very nearly automatically became immoral. For once, cause and effect were clearly related in the Ibo mind and the fact was there, plain, taken for granted. The white man or woman must be prepared for some bitter moments when he or she tries to see what form the European idea of a fuller life has taken when reflected in the native mind.

One must not stress this aspect of education unduly; on the other hand it should be faced, even if it were only for the purpose of mitigating any complacency on the white man's part, any sense of patronage and of benefits conferred in the realm of morals. More especially, perhaps, should the women teachers give more thought to the background of their girls, so that the seeds they sow should be adapted to the soil in which they are to grow. But this will be difficult. Not only have they practically no time for acquiring a knowledge of this background, but all their training has been against a comprehension of it. They cannot any longer simplify themselves enough to stand upon the same level as their pupils nor visualize a world which contains husbands, babies, hoes, cooking-pots and little else, and which yet is an important, amusing, busy, satisfactory and satisfying world. The girls *must* want something else, they *must* long to know more, they *must* yearn for a wider life! Now, having been told so often that they ought to be dissatisfied with the old conditions, they have become so, not quite knowing why or wherefore or what they want instead. It is true that eventually they would have become dissatisfied whether we had taught them to be so or not, dissatisfaction being an ingredient of growth, but at least they would have had time to find the reason for their unrest and possibly a way out. At present, their characters are not equal to the strain we have put upon them.

The new developments in trade, are, both by scope and nature, a factor of considerable importance in the education of the native. Though the Ibo were never traders on the heroic scale of the Arabs or the Hausa who took their caravans back and forth across the desert, the Ibo must nevertheless have covered a good deal of ground on their rounds, especially the members of those groups, such as the Isu, who were pre-eminently traders and who had their definite trade routes up and down the eastern provinces, though they do not seem at any time to have ventured far outside. This local trade, as has been seen in the preceding chapters, still continues, but it has also been seen how a new form has sprung up beside it, that of trade with the Europeans and the marketing of a crop which up till recently had only been a food crop.

The purely economic value of this trade is outside my scope but its psychological value is curious: it has stirred imagination in a way which little else could have achieved, thereby engendering a motive power which had long lain dormant. No recital of wars, of brave defence or gallant conquest could have moved the Ibo. Tales of heroic deeds, martyrdom, self-sacrifice, would have fallen upon deaf ears as would the achievements of art, the grace of poetry, the power of music, but the saga of trade enthrals them and it is to the sound of clinking money, of lurching lorries, of oil-casks grating as they are rolled down to the beach that they become alive. Yet I would not wish to accuse the Ibo of being mercenary in a purely derogatory sense. His desire for money is a vital need, an expression of himself. Finance may be his form of creative art and when he has perfected himself in that art, he may turn to others of a more aesthetic nature. Could one perhaps compare him to the Jew who concentrates narrowly upon the acquisition of wealth but who, having gained it, so often turns it to such good purpose both social and artistic? One could almost risk the statement that the Ibo will make a good millionaire (and that is a rare compliment). It is only in the process of becoming a millionaire that he may grate on us.

The pursuit of trade has also had the useful result of serving as a lesson of interdependence: almost forcibly the Ibo is brought (*a*) into contact with distant neighbours or with strangers and (*b*) to the realization that the modern economic system cannot work without the co-operation of these neighbours and strangers, to obtain which he must study them, humour them, and eventually learn to trust them.

As to the role of the women in the more modern forms of trade, this will be described in the next chapter when speaking of careers for women.

Of minor importance at the moment, but of major importance as signs of what the future will hold for this vigorous race are the varied ways in which the Ibo shows himself a potential man of the world rather than a reactionary bushman. His unhesitating acceptance of, even often his insistent demands for, such Western institutions as hospitals, post offices, courts of law, is surprising. His readiness to jump the enormous gap between the dark, tiny, mud-floored hut and the spacious cement-block, storied house, his taste for European clothing, his fearless confidence in the white man's car or lorry, are all indications of his alacrity to abandon old ways for new. Here, except in a few exceptional cases or in relation to certain exceptional spheres of thought and custom, there is no wall of prejudice to break down, no fear of the unknown or reluctance to make use of new methods and facilities.

On the whole it can be said that Western medicine is

appreciated throughout Ibo-land. The fear of being left out of anything that is going on overcomes what suspicion there is. What are termed 'African Hospitals', of which the staff is paid by Government, while buildings, etc., are paid for by the local Native Administration, are nearly always well attended. The bush dispensaries which are maintained entirely out of Native Administration funds and supervised by Government Medical Officers are popular. The patients may very well attend their own medicine men at the same time as they receive the white man's zinc ointment or cough mixture, but the possession of a dispensary is looked on as a distinct step upwards in the social scale and in time its medical value will be equally appreciated.

The Missions have been strangely backward in medical work. There is only one outstanding example in Iboland, the Church Missionary Society hospital at Iyi Enu, near Onitsha. It is staffed by women doctors and nursing sisters for whom no praise can be too high, handicapped as they have been by indifferent buildings (these are now being improved), constant shortage of staff and the necessity for training their own African nursing-staff.

The Roman Catholic hospital at Emekuku already described will also be a great asset to the country but it is disappointing that schools should not have taken a more active share in the simplest forms of first-aid. To see a teacher giving an elaborate lecture on hygiene to a class of pupils some of whom are suffering from craw-craw, others from suppurating cuts or possible ulcers, makes one doubt the value of his teaching. I believe that since the time I was in close touch with schools a little more has been done, but it is an enormous field and one in which teachers' wives, if given a minimum of instruction, could play a useful part.

Of course it is true that it is primarily the business of the parents to carry out what in England would be regarded as the most rudimentary kind of home nursing, but here in Nigeria one must remember that practically

all the apparatus is lacking: the clean bowl, the warm
water, the little bit of lint or cotton wool, let alone such
things as iodine or vaseline or sticking-plaster. Even the
rag-bag of every English mother from which is drawn
the wherewithal for bandages or poultice covers, polish-
ing-cloths or emergency dusters, pieces and patches, is
lacking in the Nigerian household and twenty times a day
domestic hazards make its absence felt. One sometimes
thinks that an even greater contribution to the civilizing
of Nigeria than roads and bridges, prisons, secretariats and
electric light, would have been the gentle distribution
of clean rags, brooms and dusters, needles and thread.

As for the post office, one could wish it were not so
appreciated an institution so that one would not always
find its counters besieged by an eager, clamorous throng.
The Ibo, even those who can only laboriously print a few
scrawling words, have a passion for letter-writing; tele-
grams are also sent on the slightest provocation in spite
of their cost, and of course all absent relatives in Government or commercial employment are expected to send
part of their earnings to their families. Though one does
not see in Owerri as one did in Kano post office, a Hausa
trader nonchalantly telegraphing two or three hundred
pounds to Tunis or Tripoli, the aggregate amount of
small sums sent in money orders must be considerable.
Every new postal development is made use of immediately: one's steward boy discusses the merits of C.O.D.
and a woman trader begs the European agent not to
forget to order her next stock of cloth by air mail. The
savings bank is the only branch which up till now has not
been patronized as fully as it might be,[1] though ordinary
banking accounts are held by the richer people.

[1] On the whole, as Mrs. Thurnwald points out with reference to
East Africa, even educated natives regard money as having a fictitious
value and quickly change it into real value as exemplified by, say,
European goods.

The Law Court

Unfortunately this most laudable zeal for such excellent things as medical services and postal facilities extends to such mixed blessings as the various forms of courts of law which have been introduced as supplements to the Native Courts and which bring with them a small host of native lawyers[1] and their touts and the whole paraphernalia of litigation, all the more attractive to the black man when dressed up in alien phraseology and sonorous obscurity. Also he now has the hope that a clever lawyer will find some possible quibble and so, protected by the law, he will escape from justice. Such cases, when talked over in the bush, rouse far more bitterness than did the unjust sentences which in the old days a District Officer might have given through inadvertence or insufficient information. In the latter case, the people took it for granted that, within his limitations, he had done his best and knew that on the whole he was out for justice. If he occasionally failed to give it them, they bore no special grudge against him. But in the former case, they are astonished and indignant, and each time the law, in these trick cases, triumphs British justice is, in their eyes, defeated. They do not yet hold with us that a man is innocent until he is proved guilty and they cannot understand our passion for giving a prisoner every chance of defending himself, and when an obviously guilty man escapes purely, as they think, because of the length of a lawyer's tongue and his capacity for bewildering the poor white judge, the whole system is brought into disrepute.

As for the penal system itself, the bush is eloquent in its condemnation. Till the coming of the white man, the practice of making the punishment fit the crime was carried out to an admirable degree, especially in those cases when the administration of justice was left to the women. Certain of the punishments which they carried

[1] Lawyers in Nigeria are all members of the English Bar, trained in England at their own expense.

out in Eziama—or used to carry out—were possibly a
trifle unrefined, but they were without doubt real deter-
rents,[1] while the sentences given to-day by semi-British
justice are none at all. One of the chief grievances of the
women, heard on many occasions and in different parts,
is this matter of sending men to prison rather than
allowing local custom to deal with them according to the
nature of their crimes. They say, and with much truth,
that short-term sentences only make the men 'strong-
headed', by which they mean that, seeing what an easy
thing prison is, they are indifferent as to whether they
are sentenced again or not; the food is so good that when
they come back 'their skins are smooth as silk', and
when I asked whether the women at least did not feel
the shame of having 'done time', my only answer was
a hoot of laughter. They also very rightly point out that
the sentence really tells on them more than it does on
the man: he may be taken away just as the farming
season begins and though this might cause him much
anxiety and thus be a form of moral punishment, nevertheless it is the women who will have to do the extra
work, or eke out enough money wherewith to hire labour,
or run the risk of having insufficient food for the next
year. Some forms of native punishment such as the death
sentence (or often the suicide sentence) for minor—or
what appear to us minor—crimes, mutilation or selling
into slavery, had of course to be abolished, but other
ones, short and above all swift, and often aimed at hurt-
ing the culprits' pride by ridicule rather than his body or
his property, seem much more suited to the native's
mentality and circumstances than the impersonal and in
his eyes, illogical 'prison'.

No Prison Reform League in England could disapprove

[1] If a man has offended his wife's modesty and, to avenge her, all
her townswomen pour into the compound and dance round him,
lifting up their kirtles and yelling: 'Look! Look! Look!' till he hides
his face in his hands and cries for mercy, he is not likely to commit
that particular offence again.

of these short-term sentences more definitely and for better reasons than these women. An alternative acceptable to British ideas is not easy to find: probation means supervision which would be impossible to provide; fines, though often imposed as an alternative to prison, fall again upon the women as much as on the man and fines are one more road leading to debt, that curse of primitive communities who have risen above—or fallen below!—the daily need provided for by the daily work. One could wish that some task of immediate utility to the man's own community could be imposed upon him —if of a slightly ridicule-making nature so much the better.

Long-term sentences are not understood but at least the training the men get in the convict prisons turns them into useful citizens. It was impossible not to laugh when some bush women tolerantly remarked: 'We cannot see *why*, because a man has killed another, he should be given a free education but since it is so, it is a good thing.' Women convicts, though humanely treated, decently housed and well fed, do not yet share in the educational benefits of the males, but their numbers are very small. Boy delinquents are admirably trained and handled in a 'school' at Enugu under the personal supervision of the Director of Prisons but quite apart from the convict prison itself.

Allied to the subject of law and prison, is that of bribery, a question which should be raised again and again, in place and out of place, until public opinion, for no other authority can deal with it, has pronounced its sentence. Bribery is by no means a new product for which Western civilization must be held responsible, for it is only another form of the 'dash' of olden days, but that there is a difference in more than name is, I think, real. The 'dash' was comparatively innocuous: the Ibo gave or accepted it as a matter of course. It was custom and therefore legitimate, respectable. It was done openly and it was safeguarded by well-known rules and etiquette. That there could be an ethical aspect of the question never struck him. But now he has been told that it is a bad and immoral custom; he sees how heavily the white man disapproves of it, he has become, so to speak, dash-conscious. The custom in its old and comparatively innocent form is driven under and reappears in a new and infinitely more harmful form as hidden bribery by the rich, of ruthless demands upon the poor, without the safeguards and limits of custom. It touches every section, falsifies every situation and baulks many of Government's efforts for the well-being of the people. Hot words came from the bush women on this subject, and I inclined to believe them when they said: 'We women, we do not take bribes.'

The newly developed ambition for better housing is a happier theme. Except very occasionally, this ambition is not yet well served by the local builders, at least around Owerri. Poor construction, bad proportions, an ornamentation which is neither African nor European, spoil many of these new habitations and make one wish that skilled guidance were immediately available to check the spread of this poor type and give the country an architecture both more pleasing and more suitable. The Government specifications according to which all dwellings in the townships must be erected, are perhaps admirable on paper but produce the most unsightly, uncomfortable and inconvenient results when translated into fact by a native contractor. Indeed, the townships in places of such recent growth as, say, Enugu or Port Harcourt, where the authorities had practically *table rase* are most disappointing. It is difficult to understand why stricter attention has not been paid to this question. Not only is it politically important that the more advanced members of the community should be satisfied in such elementary ways as by the provision of good sites, good lay-outs, good homes, and that they should see, in the most concrete form possible, the benefits of our much talked-of civilization, but it is also educationally—taking education in the wider sense—important that wherever white supervision is available the very best type of architecture should alone be allowed. And by the best type, I do not of course mean the most expensive or the most akin to Western patterns, but that which is the most suitable and—why not?—the most pleasing, the most likely to harmonize with the people, the land, and the climate.

It is true as I have already pointed out when describing Port Harcourt, that a native seldom regards a township as his permanent home; nevertheless a good portion of the lives of many traders and Government employees will be spent there and, since it is we, the white men, who have introduced the need for urban planning, it is our responsibility to see that such planning should be of the best. Once more, as in education, we have had the inestimable advantage, the almost unique opportunity, of standing in front of a blank page. It is discouraging to realize how often we have covered it with meaningless scrawls and ugly smudges.

Apart from the townships, the educated Ibo, in general, will not long remain content with the normal type of native dwelling which, in Owerri Province at least, is admittedly poor as compared to the solid mud houses of the Hausa or the beautifully roofed huts of the Nupe. It could naturally be improved upon as is already done in individual cases, but it seems an idiosyncrasy of the native that he would rather adopt a completely alien method than adapt his own, or profit by a good example set nearer home, say by a neighbouring tribe. It is also unfortunately true that the white man in the southern provinces has rarely tried to show what could be done in native style and materials. The day school, if of any importance, or the boarding-school

329

or the church are all definitely, and usually uglily
European. Even if the original aim has been to preserve
and improve upon native architecture, one feature after
another is allowed to disappear and to be replaced by a
Western substitute. It is true that the native dwelling
needs constant attention and repair: the overworked
principal or missionary suddenly tires of hearing that the
roof needs patching and sends for a lorry-load of corrugated-iron; a mud wall begins to bulge and, impatient,
the white man has it rebuilt with imported cement.[1]

Whatever the major cause may be, what may be
loosely termed Western architecture, whether based on
entirely Western or on a mixture of Western and native
materials, has come to stay and its diffusion will be comparatively rapid if the present good economic conditions
continue. The development of the house instinct as apart
from the land instinct will be one of the most interesting
by-products of civilization. As far as I know, a dwelling
has never meant anything to the Ibo man or woman
beyond being a shelter and a sleeping-place. The hearth,
the roof-tree, have no symbolism nor half-mystical significance. Yet the semi-European houses, when suddenly
met with, as sometimes happens, in the depths of the
bush, do take on a symbolic value which one tries in vain
to interpret. Against the ancient background, rising

[1] It is interesting to note how seldom the white man or woman has
the patience to carry out his or her theories on this subject of the preservation of native conditions or habits no matter how warmly they
advocate it. A boarding-school which prided itself, and very justly, on
training its girls under improved but purely native conditions so that
there should be no break with their own homes, has now only one
mud building left; the others are still on simple lines but quite non-
native. A woman missionary, devoted to the country and the people,
deplored the passing of old days and the Westernization which was
spreading even in the bush, driving away the old simplicities, yet the
photographs I saw of her native girls showed them all dressed in
'frocks'. Once more, all unconsciously, the Westerner does not, cannot
perhaps, accept or approve of the existence of other standards than his
own.

The Modern Home

from the ancient soil, appears this new creation of the black man's mind, this new assertion of his wealth, his power, his pride. What form will it take, what shape and colour will translate his own idea of his own greatness? It will necessarily be founded on the white man's pattern, but, curiously enough, not on the white man's pattern of to-day as seen, say, at Lagos or Port Harcourt, the light, airy, wide-verandaed bungalow. No, the black man turns to an older pattern, the more secret, shuttered, thick-walled style of some old houses still found in Free Town but more especially perhaps in Cape Coast Castle and Elmina. Yet I doubt whether this represents the final pattern. At Oguta, for example, a 'rich' town of big native traders, a few new houses were being built which had an upward soar, awkward and uncertain but betokening an obscure aspiration after a still unformulated but dimly conceived ideal. In how far a more permanent dwelling will awaken any deeper emotions than that of vanity or self-advertisement remains to be seen. I think personally that the Ibo has it in him to create good houses, not mere shells of cement and pan, but real expressions of himself which in their creation will be an outlet for his artistic gifts and in their possession will be a stabilizing factor. Up till now the soil has been his anchor; more and more will he let that anchor go. It would be well if the virtues of the farmer could be translated into those of the householder. But for the full development of that healthy and enriching love of home, the woman's co-operation will be necessary, and so far, I think from my own observations, she lags behind. The house-proud wife is often found in the bush, but in the townships it seems more often the man who takes the active interest. Several times educated men have complained to me that their wives were glad enough to have a European house but cared nothing for the proper running of it. They were pleased when their husbands ordered in a new set of chairs or fine sideboard, but once the furniture was there, they never touched it. 'They do not care to make it shine as does the white woman.' Here, again, the schools, though inculcating cleanliness and order, have somehow failed to awaken any deeper sense of beauty, taking beauty in its most simple and humble sense.

As with education, so with clothing: the *mauvais pli* has been taken, thanks to those first heroic but unimaginative missionaries who decreed once for all that clothing was necessary to salvation. The desire for dress is now a mixture of this old conviction that nakedness is sin, of superficial vanity or snobbery, and of a deeper and more respectable feeling that it is one of the symbols of civilization.

On hygienic, economic and aesthetic grounds, one is sorry that the Missions laid, and in many ways still lay such stress upon the necessity of being clothed. To take but two instances: must schoolboys in the bush spend their parents' hard-earned money on singlets and shorts which are of necessity usually in rags, often not too clean and which in the rainy season cling damply to shivering bodies which, naked, would have quickly dried, warmed by the contact of other naked bodies in the crowded school-house? Must girls plague their hard-worked mothers because they 'no get frock plenty like other girls' at the boarding-school? And more especially, must the Christian girl, compared to her pagan sister, unselfconscious and therefore unremarked, appear in the full immodesty of badly cut satin stretched over high-set breasts, curving tightly over heavy buttocks, an object made to attract the lust of men instead of evading it? In the town, the pace has been set and nothing can be done except to develop the girls' own tastes towards a better use of European fashions, but in the bush there is surely no need to hurry on the process of hiding those charming bodies, nor of depriving them of the benefit of sun and air and the rapture of the first rain on bare skin.

'Westernization'

As to the wearing of shoes, one knows all the arguments in favour of using some kind of protection for the
feet. If the women and girls would wear some sort of
open sandal, well and good, but instead one finds them
groaning because their tight rubber-soled tennis-shoes
draw their feet or their high-heeled walking-shoes rub
and pinch. It is difficult to know whether the corn of
civilization is better than the jigger of barbarism, but in
any case children might be exempted from wearing
black button-boots.

The Ibo has two great enemies, himself and his best
friends. He will gleefully pull down his own house about
his own ears thinking that somehow it will be miracu-
lously rebuilt for him with all the Western improvements; he will sell his birthright of land and the right to
till for a bowl of ready money; he will drive his sons to
schools from whence they come back estranged from all
he lives by. As for us, his friends, do we not always tend
to think for him along Western, or more often narrowly
British lines? Should we give more importance, because
of our European set of values, to a question than does the
Ibo himself? In dealing with the women, even while we
are pouring out our sympathy over what we think they
ought to be suffering, that is to say what they would be
suffering if they were white women brought up with our
own background, our values, our type of sensibility, do we
not see that we are preparing for them sufferings and
dangers, cruelties, hardships and degradations beside
which their present disabilities and discomforts will be as
nothing?

There is nothing really relevant in an incident which
took place some years ago, in Lagos, and yet it has
remained in my mind as the symbol of much that we are
doing to the native: a bishop's wife told me how hard put
to it were many of the native pastors' wives to appear in
decent European apparel—would I send her any of my
cast-off clothes? Here, in Africa, in a wide land of sun

333

and air, where poverty had been unknown and charity unwanted, through our doing, our stupidity, our conventionality, our wrong emphasis, our incapacity to transmit the Word except wrapped up in English fashions, we had introduced that most excellent but piteous of charities, the Poor Clergy Relief Association. Standing under the palm-trees bent double by the wind blowing up the harbour, watching the sailing canoes scurrying before it over glinting ripples, I had memories of a house in a Bloomsbury square, the low doorway, the dark passage, the linoleum; the rows of hangers with their coats and dresses, the summer frocks, the widows' black. 'Will you send me your cast-off clothes for the native pastors' wives?——'

The Yoruba woman, when uneducated, is proud, reserved, perfectly capable of looking after herself; have we already reduced her to the ranks of a beggar, deliberately creating for her an artificial and undignified need?

Part IV

Conclusion

XIX

Conclusion

The future. Careers for women. Men as home-makers; women as town-makers.

The more one knows the Ibo women, their old customs, their present lives; the more one understands their status and the character and qualities which have enabled them to attain to that status, the more anxious does one feel about their future. After the first startled recognition of their importance as members of society, one is constantly asking: where are they going to? what will become of them? what use will be made of this rare and invaluable force, thousands upon thousands of ambitious, go-ahead, courageous, self-reliant, hardworking, independent women? The answer they give themselves is not really worthy of them. They can do more than make money, be more than 'rich' women; but to accomplish this, openings must be made for them which will give scope for their startling energy, their powers of organization and of leadership, their practical common sense and quick apprehension of reality.

Let us first see in what ways they can attain to what they themselves so much desire and which, as we have seen, is in a greater or a less degree, expected of them: that is to say, some measure of economic independence, either (*a*) as independent money-makers, or (*b*) as salaried workers.

M

Conclusion

(*a.*) In general, throughout the country, one can say that the woman's universal money-making occupation is that of farming with its resultant local marketing of surplus produce such as yams, cassava, fowls, etc. Neither she nor her husband deliberately 'grow for the market' except in a few cases, but anything over and above the requirements of themselves and their children is naturally turned into cash; or should the family, for any reason, be in immediate need of money, a portion of the crop is sold notwithstanding the risk of a possible shortage of food later on. The quantities disposed of are small and variable, but with no wages to pay nor rents to meet and with only a tiny expenditure on farm implements—a couple of hoes, a matchet, a basket—the profits are clear and are just enough to enable the woman to engage in trade, that is to say in the buying and selling of other people's goods as distinguished from the sale of her own or her husband's produce. The simplest form is when, going from one market to another, busily comparing prices as any good housekeeper should, she sees that the price of, say, cassava is down in one locality and up in another. She hastily puts together what money she has received for her own surplus produce and invests it in a basketful of cassava which she carries off for sale on the next market-day at the locality where the cassava is scarce. Simple as the transaction is, bringing only the smallest profits, it yet necessitates a certain trade sense. The woman must have an accurate memory for prices— in the bush, a mistake of a halfpenny counts as a disaster —and she must know the market-days of all the surrounding villages.[1] She must foresee how many other women will have noticed the disparity in prices and seek to profit by the same opportunity or when she gets to the market where she expects to find a cassava shortage, she may find it already swamped by her competitors.

[1] These are fixed, as already mentioned (see p. 75) by the command or in honour of the local spirit.

338

The Woman Trader

The next step upwards is when the woman is able to buy a few non-local products of European origin such as soap, matches, leaf tobacco, cigarettes, salt; or non-local products of native origin such as pots or mats. The profits on the first are of course a little higher, but also she has to buy them at an enhanced price from the middle-woman, unless she herself has the opportunity of getting them direct from the European firm. This necessitates a journey to a town perhaps some twenty or thirty miles distant. Nowadays she can probably do part of the jour-ney by lorry but if she is well enough off to afford the fare, she will probably also be well enough off to invest some money in the purchase of European manufactured cottons, the backbone of the women's trade. From now on, however much farming she may do in the intervals, she ranks as a real trader.

There are, broadly speaking, two methods of trading in cotton goods:

(*a.*) The woman, if her introductions and recommen-dations to the European firm are good enough to inspire confidence, is allowed to take away with her, say, up to £20 worth of pieces (these pieces are of six to eight yards).[1] The pieces are priced by the firm and anything she can get over and above these prices belongs to her. At the end of every month, she brings back any pieces she may have left over, provided they have not been cut into, and hands over the price of the sold pieces as marked by the firm, keeping, as already mentioned, any profits she may have made on them. She then chooses another consignment and starts off again. If she trades in a very big way, taking a consignment worth several hun-dred pounds, she employs other women to take some of the goods to sell in other towns or in the bush markets, though in the latter there would be a readier sale for cottons by the yard than by the piece.

This method, which is practically that of 'on sale or

[1] The picturesque measurement by fathom has almost died out.

339

return', has the advantage of requiring no capital and of entailing few risks. On the other hand, the profit is smaller as the firm's profit must be paid first before the vendor can take her own; there is the hindrance of not being able to cut into a piece, and often customers do not wish or cannot afford to buy the whole length when all they require is enough for a head-tie; and the obligation to return the unsold stock on a fixed monthly date when it may happen that trade has just woken up and an absence of several days will be a great inconvenience.

Some women, if they live in a town where there are European firms, deal regularly with these but others prefer to go to another town, either because it is nearer the coast and goods are therefore a fraction cheaper, or because they hope to get the very latest thing in fashions or some *nouveauté inédite* in the way of design or colouring.

(*b.*) The second method is not so common: the woman buys her stock outright, only a very few pieces at first, till she has established a connection and got together a little more capital. This method gives her greater freedom and, if she is lucky, a larger profit, but it also of course entails a greater risk, as if she has not gauged correctly her customers' changing tastes, she may have to sell her stock at less than cost price or put it up for auction. But in trade as elsewhere, what is one man's poison may be another man's meat and the cottons that the Okigwi woman will not look at may be the success of the season at Onitsha, or what the townswoman considers dowdy may be the essence of refinement in the bush.

Many of the cotton goods sold are very attractive. Some are of the freak variety, introducing patterns made up of the letters of the alphabet, or numerals, spiders' webs, or footprints, or Royal portraits, but many are founded on adaptations of Indian patterns and are printed in deep rich colours most becoming to dark skins. There is no distinctly prevailing colour among the Ibo as blue is distinctive of the north and also of the more northern Yoruba. Brown, red-brown, blues and yellows, are popular but this year (1937) there is an increase of materials of a definitely European type, dots or spots or stripes in lighter or pastel shades, which are unbecoming. Fortunately, the women themselves are not much attracted by them.

The designs for new materials are often chosen by the women themselves. The European firms call together their best clients among the women traders and submit to them the patterns they have received from England. The women study the samples and recommend those they think will meet the public taste of the moment. Some women are even so ready to back their taste as to order, say, a hundred pieces in advance and thus hope to have exclusive rights over that particular pattern. Great are the heartburnings if it is discovered that the firm has played them false and that they have not the monopoly of purple fish on a green background or of the interwoven palm-fronds in maroon and yellow, or whatever the coveted pattern may be. Customers are equally anxious to have something exclusive and the best way to sell the more expensive materials is to be able to murmur: 'There is not another woman in this town who has so much as seen this bit of velvet!'

Though they are remarkable saleswomen, the Ibo woman trader is not expansive nor loquacious, nor does she seek to entice her customers by any wiles or graces. There she sits in her market-stall, her wares spread out in front of her, surveying the passers-by with unconcern. Should one stop, she waits impassive till he or she has fingered every piece. When prices are asked, she answers shortly. Another price is offered. She shrugs her shoulders, pulls down the corners of her mouth, turns away. If the price offered has been very low, she spits disdainfully, but with reticence. The price is increased. She turns back towards her customer. Quick loud words fly between them, ending with a mutual: 'Last price!' hissed out in English. Either the customer puts down his money and walks off, his length of cloth beneath his arm, or with a last look of enmity, moves on to inspect the next stall. In both cases, the woman straightens her disarranged wares, goes back to her stool, and recommences her unconcerned survey of the passers-by. Not a frown nor a smile betray whether the deal has been lost or won.

Apart from the women employed by other women as distributors of goods in other towns or in bush markets, one hears occasionally of trade partnerships between two women. For example, the excellent yams grown round Onitsha will be bought by a woman residing there and sent down by lorry to her partner living in Port Harcourt. The latter will easily dispose of these yams in the local market and in her turn will send up a load of cloth to be sold in Onitsha. Again, an Onitsha woman will buy up the best fish that comes to Onitsha waterside and send it, again by lorry, to her partner in Enugu, who sells it in the market to the white men's cooks, returning the money she has made to Onitsha for her partner to re-invest in a fresh supply of fish.

When one remembers that most of these women are illiterate and yet keep without effort and with few mistakes the most intricate accounts, one wonders why the schools spend so much time and labour on teaching them 'mathematics'.

Another form of women's trade is the sale of prepared foodstuffs such as *gari* (ground cassava) or of cooked food (little bits of fried fish, or a sort of bean cake, etc.), which will be bought by labourers who have no homes of their own, or strangers passing through, or lorry passengers waiting for their transport. These latter appear to form a lucrative clientèle. Having been once asked in the Okigwi Division to beg Government to build a road to Onitsha which, owing to the nature of the country would have necessitated the employment of a whole body of engineers and an expenditure of thousands, I inquired why this road was considered so desirable. The answer was: 'Widow women could stand by the roadside and sell bean cakes to lorry passengers.' The assurance that the benefit to the finances of widow women hardly justified the enormous expenditure convinced nobody.[1]

The palm-kernel trade also belongs to the women, but I know of only one town where palm-oil is bought and sold on a large scale by women. This is Oguta, where a remarkable figure, Madam Ruth as she is known, dominates the community. Some years ago, just at the time of the boom, she launched out into the palm-oil trade, buying from the bush farmer or the small middleman and selling direct to the European firms. A veritable Amazon among traders, she now sweeps through the market-place like a ship in full sail; stands, in rose-pink velvet and purple head-tie, on the bank above Oguta Lake, shouting commands to her women bent low over the paddles as they shoot the oil-cask-laden canoes across the lake; or weary after the day's work climbs the steep lane to her home, dangling her Yale latch-key. There are others like her but she is the acknowledged leader and nowhere else in Owerri Province did I meet any such outstanding feminine figure in the world of commerce.

It will be seen from the above short survey that trade provides many varied openings for women, adapted to their varying circumstances and personal capacities. These openings have also the advantage that they can be made use of with the minimum of capital, at any rate in the initial stages. In the bush markets, a fowl or three or four yams given to the juju priest in charge of the market gives the right to the few feet of ground necessary for the farmer's wife to display her produce; in the

[1] Another reason for the perfectly irrational demand for roads in certain parts is snobbery. When one is asked: 'Have you a motor road?' and are obliged to answer 'No', you 'feel shame too much'.

Conclusion

towns, till the embryo trader has made enough money to rent her own stall in the market, two petrol cases up-ended by the side of the road provide the necessary shop window in which are grouped the one square of carbolic soap, the half-tin of cigarettes, the few lumps of Reckitt's blue and the neat bundles of matches that go to make up her stock-in-trade. No shop assistants are required beyond the women's own children or her various trainees, who thus acquire their commercial aptitude at an early age. Even literacy is by no means essential, the remarkable memory of the native being equal to remembering the most involved transactions.

Another opening of recent origin, which has already been mentioned (see p. 245) is that of dressmaking. The demand for 'frocks' grows apace. Strictly speaking, the 'native dress' of a girl before marriage consists of her own lovely skin. The next step leads to the coloured cotton cloth wound round the waist and falling well below the knees with a top piece like a loose sleeveless blouse. This is simple and becoming but has been super-seded in the schools by the overall type of garment or, in most of the convent schools, by a plain white dress slightly waisted, or in some unfortunate instances by a hybrid garment consisting of a white top reminiscent of a chemise, tacked on to a khaki skirt of uncertain length. One could wish that all girls' schools should lay an almost extravagant emphasis on the art of dressing, as their pupils when they leave school will almost surely aban-don cloths and head-ties, which they manipulate with such skill, and keep to what they imagine to be European fashions which they unfortunately put on with such lack of taste. This would also have the effect of improving the products of the dressmakers which at present are care-lessly cut and quickly run up by machine with no attempt at neatness or accuracy of detail. My dressmaking acquaintances tell me it is not worth their while to try and do better: it would take more time and therefore

344

more labour and the Ibo girl or woman would not be willing to pay more money just for the sake of getting well-stitched buttonholes or a well-turned hem. It is curious how often one comes up against this indifference to the standard of work. I had already noted it in the bush and various sensible informants complained of the same thing.[1]

At present, trade in some form or other, or dressmaking seem the only two openings for the independent woman money-maker. I have heard of some licensed women pawnbrokers and of one licensed woman money-lender but neither of these careers can be considered ideal ones. A few energetic women have even been prison contractors. So far there are no Ibo-speaking women barristers or doctors but there may be some registered midwives, Government or Mission trained, working on their own; and of course there are the medicine women whose profession must be a lucrative one so long as they can keep public confidence.

(*b.*) Wage-earners have never formed part of the Ibo social system. In olden days, slaves and pawns provided the additional labour in farm and house which would be represented in England by wage-earning labourers and servants. In Ibo-land nowadays farmers hire labour, both men and women, or more especially girls, at certain seasons but they are paid by the day and can only be counted as casual labour. The boys and girls I have called trainees (see p. 240) work for their temporary guardians but *au pair*. Occasionally one hears of a girl who is practically a servant in our sense of the word in a native household and who gets a present of money from time to time but there is no conception of a regular monthly or weekly wage. Salaries and wages are Western introductions.

[1] The standard, for example, of carpentry is generally very low, though every now and then one sees an excellent piece of craftsmanship which shows of what the people are really capable. Here again I was told no one would pay enough to make better work worth while.

345

Conclusion

The salaried work available for women is thus necessarily dependent on Western institutions and the variety of openings now available is limited. Teaching stands first; then comes nursing; paid welfare workers in a few of the large towns; midwives in charge of small maternity homes dotted about the country and supervised by the Church Missionary Society. In all these careers, the proficiency which comes from experience is sadly lacking. Although the marriage age is later than it used to be, few girls will go on working after they are twenty-three or twenty-four if a suitor is forthcoming. The conception that any given form of work of social value, like teaching or nursing, could constitute a vocation, a lifework, is still foreign to them. They take it up more often to fill in time before marriage, or because they want to earn a little money of their own so as to be more independent in their choice of a husband, or because they want to see a little more of life before they do marry.

This shortness of the period during which the trained girl is actually available for work is a great handicap but has to be accepted until the spread of stricter monogamy reduces the number of potential husbands and increases the number of unmarried women, who, it is to be hoped, will find that vocations such as teaching or nursing will not only protect them from the gibes of public opinion which for a long time still will look askance at the husbandless, but will also sublimate their intense and admirable maternal instinct. In this connection, the experiment the Roman Catholic Mission is making in opening a novitiate for native women is of the greatest interest. On the face of it, such an experiment, in West Africa, seems doomed to failure, but there is something extreme in the Ibo woman's character which might make it possible for her to sacrifice all she now so ardently desires and turn her face towards a life the exact opposite of what she had most hoped for. The very completeness of the renunciation would attract her. Because she so

346

passionately wants 'all', she could equally passionately give up all.

Among the lesser-known professions for women are posts such as prison wardresses.[1] There are, of course, not many such posts vacant and the Prison Department will never be able to absorb more than a few women. There were only fourteen female convicts in the big central prison of Enugu when I was there (1937). Posts and telegraphs have also a few vacancies. So far, the European firms seldom employ women shop assistants in their showrooms. Although the old type of shops, long known as 'factories', and consisting only of a large, cement-floored, pan-roofed shed with miscellaneous goods piled high on every side, is being slowly replaced in such centres as Port Harcourt and Enugu by something more like a departmental store, they are still few and far between. In Port Harcourt I know of only one where a girl is employed in the ladies' department (she happens to be of a well-known Owerri family).

Domestic service in European households is, except in a very few instances, confined to 'boys'. I know of two or three white women who have employed girls or women with varying results but the number does not seem to increase, so one cannot describe domestic service as an opening. In Mission homes where it is possible to

---

[1] Prison matrons or wardresses, imposing as they now are in khaki uniform and brass badge, are irresistibly comic (but then the whole Nigerian prison system belongs to the realm of Gilbert and Sullivan). I remember a short figure in a white frock, a cheerful head-tie and a stout umbrella (this was before uniforms came in) supervising the feeble attempts of a gang of women to sweep with long unwieldy brooms a rest-house yard. The umbrella, always open, was large. The more wily of the prisoners gathered behind it and squatted in secure repose. In another place, the matron wore elastic-sided boots and gave me a pink rose, while all her prisoners smiled approval. Work finished, they moved off, waving their hands to the white stranger. The matron, limping painfully, followed a long way after. In another, the day being hot and the wardress far gone in pregnancy, she sat upon a bank while one of her women fanned her and the others looked on with respectful sympathy.

have a whole staff composed of girls, they seem to work quite well, but in such cases the girls take domestic work as part of their training and cannot be regarded as servants in the ordinary sense of the word. In a large town, say, like Port Harcourt, I do not see that domestic service would be very appropriate for girls. Accommodation would be lacking, supervision difficult, the surroundings demoralizing. In the more family atmosphere of a small out-station, it would be feasible and should be encouraged under certain circumstances, not only as a source of momentary profit to the girl but as a training for her future home-life.

The careers described above, except those of trading and dressmaking, are whole-time jobs and ones which generally take the girl or woman away from her own home and can, therefore, only appeal to a small section of the community, quite apart from the fact that vacancies in these careers are limited. What of the great bulk of the women? Many will say that they are already engaged in the best career of all, that of marriage. From the many references already made to it, it will be seen that the Ibo ideal of marriage (all questions of polygamy or monogamy apart) is a very different one to our own— or rather to what it was till, say, before the War. This idea of marriage as a business partnership, this appreciation by the husband of his wife's powers, this expectancy that the wife will contribute to the family exchequer, and her own sentiment that her self-respect demands that she should do so, have no counterpart that I can think of until the most recent times and in the most advanced among European countries. But even this standard of activity is not sufficient for her. She has qualities of organization and of initiative for which she finds her home too small. In the bush, in the Women's Councils, there was room for her but, as I have already pointed out (see p. 109), what is the status of these councils to-day now that they are no longer allowed to enforce their rulings in their own way? In the remoter parts, I think their old prestige will uphold their authority for some time to come but they will not long survive too close a contact with Christianity and sophistication.

At present, the qualities the women show in the management of their local affairs have been transferred to the spheres of church or trade. As to the former, from what I have seen, I have learnt rather to mistrust the little cards, the badges, and the promises which bind the women to membership of the numerous Christian Fellowships, Guilds, Unions, Ladies' Associations and the like, just as I have little faith in Girl Guides (although much in Boy Scouts). These groupings tend to cut across normal family obligations and to make unnecessary divisions between Christians and pagans. A missionary woman teacher, full of intelligence and intuition, living very close to her girls' minds, admitted she did not think they had, as yet, any comprehension of 'the old school tie' feeling. Another missionary friend writes from Port Harcourt: 'I am beginning to believe that the numerous church fellowships, etc., among the rank and file fulfil a social function rather than a religious one,' though she adds: 'But I begin to note a change. I was surprised to find on my return the women had done some solid building on their own. Spontaneous bursts of charity and a greater willingness[1] on the part of the better educated to impart knowledge to the illiterate were two of the outstanding features.' This is all to the good, yet so long as the Ibo preserves his almost more than Scottish sense of responsibility towards the members of his family, it is far better that this should be maintained rather than be replaced by more general forms of organized charity, and I would not press the Ibo woman to take up social service in our meaning of the word, especially as it has already been seen (see p. 259) that the need for it is not yet urgent.

[1] Any unwillingness is a variant of the 'bush people are barbarians' attitude already described (see p. 288).

Conclusion

As regards the second sphere, that of trade, we know that it has from all times been a normal and popular one, the only present difference being that it has become more extensive and more penetrated by European influence. This business instinct, so highly developed among the Ibo women, is a perfectly respectable one so long as it does not remain entirely selfish and is carried out by methods which are both honest and far-sighted. Let her only remember what she already knows but sometimes forgets: that her business will not flourish by ruining that of her neighbours, that it is unfair to corner food-stuffs so that the poor suffer, that it is not right to falsify her measures (as is the case with the cigarette-tins in Owerri market!), that the rich woman she aspires to be will be worth nothing if she is not also a virtuous woman so that, dying, she will not need to sigh: 'All my fires have been of grass. . . .'

All the same, more or less useful church interests and purely money-making ones, cannot be the sum total of the Ibo woman's future. In the councils, wherever they are still preserved, she plays an active part for the public's good; in the more sophisticated areas, her activity is also needed for the same purpose and it is to Government that one looks to call it into being.

I do not think that women should be drawn into the sphere of the Native Courts: they are capable of more creative and worthwhile work than that but I should entrust them with the greatest possible amount of municipal organization, a sphere which has some small resemblance to that in which they took a share in their own primitive society. I should like to have in every township a modified equivalent of a borough council consisting only of women, responsible to the Local Authority for general hygiene and cleanliness; I would let them run the markets, settle the water rates and discuss the building regulations (both very sensitive points) and I would give them executive power and their own funds wherewith to purchase materials and hire labour. I would let the women themselves nominate this borough council in the same informal but satisfactory way in which they elected the spokeswomen of their own councils; and I would by no means encourage the election of the 'educated', who seem so often to have lost their native strength and shrewdness, but rather the type of the woman trader. I cannot think that if Madam Ruth had been chairman of the local borough council, the Oguta incinerator would have been stuffed with unburnt rubbish nor the Oguta lanes noisome with stagnant pools.

This suggestion is not made in any feminist spirit nor for the purpose of giving the women undue importance, but simply because I believe they would do the work more sensibly, more painstakingly, more honestly and with more vision than the men and that the sense of importance and of responsibility would steady them. I do not even believe it would cause much jealousy on the part of the men. As we have already seen, the Ibo does not seem to have any feeling of resentment towards the wife who has made herself rich or important, and he is already well accustomed to her independence so long as 'he finds his food ready when he comes back from work'. Once more, the Ibo seem to depart from tradition in that the men would appear to be the home-makers more than the women; on the other hand, as whatever I have heard of civic good sense has come from the women, it is they perhaps who are destined to be the town-makers. In these matters, as in many others, we must not expect the Ibo woman to fit naturally into our own English mould, nor must we try to press her into it. The result is the genteel, boneless, spoilt, hypochondriacal[1] individual we now often see. On the contrary, we must do our best to grasp what is the genius of the race, no easy task and one

[1] This hypochondriacal tendency is distinctly marked in the most educated women I know.

351

only to be accomplished by prolonged and sympathetic observation without preconceived ideas or axes, no matter how excellent, to grind. We must encourage her to make her own path, not to use ours. Much as she loves her children, faithful wife as she often is, I doubt whether her spirit could ever be confined within the narrow sphere of home. I thought at first the women of Eziama were immersed in cooking-pots and babies, that their minds contained nothing beyond the price of yams and the advent of the next market-day. When I saw them gathered in the twilight of Ajala's grove, when I sat with them in the Women's Council, I knew I had been mistaken. There would be no confining these women within the conventional bounds of home life, not unless we wished to atrophy them, to waste their vigour and their special savour. If we think we should refine them, we will either make them colourless or—once the check of our influence is removed—drive them to extravagance of conduct. If we want them to be 'ladies', they will cease to be women; if we expect them to be 'womanly', they will merely become weak. The Nguru women, on account of their psychological history and present material conditions, are in a class apart. The most typical Ibo I know remind me of hard-headed, warm-hearted, sensible, realistic French business women, excellent wives and mothers no doubt but with an innate desire and capacity for *les affaires*, a type which we hardly know in England. So true is this that when, sitting recently outside a café in a small French market town, I saw a Frenchwoman, magnificent in her vigour, blonde hair and flashing teeth, swing down from a lorry, go over to a table and with laughing firmness deal out banknotes to the subservient farmers whose beans and apples she had just been buying, I said to myself, unconscious of any gulf between them: 'Why, there is Eunice of Oguta. . . .' But *les affaires* need not necessarily be mercenary ones. If money she must handle, if bargaining she must enjoy, if organization she must plan and orders she must give, let it be in the name of the community and for its good. She will be dealing with people and things she knows more about than we do, and, curious trait in a primitive race, she absolutely revels in the idea of a great number of people or large sums of money, not with the idea of turning them her own advantage, but as some sort of outlet for her own exuberant vitality, a field worthy of her, a task suited to her powers. At first, she might need a little guidance, or rather an explanation of the tasks she would have to perform and the policies she would have to think out. The way to carry them out she would find herself.

There used to be in Nigeria a post known as that of Secretary of Native Affairs, now, one would think unfortunately, abolished. The duties attached to it were indefinite and formless, nevertheless it brought the native himself before the eyes of the capital, it carried the smell of the burning bush, the sweat of the farmers, the dust of the markets, the talk of the meeting-house into the immaculate offices of the Nigerian Secretariat. One could wish that, instead of the woman District Officer for the Owerri Province whose appointment was suggested after the Aba Riots, there could be created a post of Woman Secretary of Women's Affairs.

XX

Conclusion

---

*The subjective outlook. What do we think of the Ibo?
What does the Ibo think of us?*

Re-reading my notes now that they have been put into something like book form, I am troubled to find how unacademic appears my attitude to the women I lived amongst. I have never been able to look upon them—or upon myself—as other than ordinary human beings, and as such we have liked or disliked each other, bored or amused each other, understood or baffled each other. Again and again I see the subjective has obscured the objective and there is not one chapter that can be analysed nor one set of facts that can be quoted, so little have they been dissected or tabulated. It is true that my notes contain every detail of the process of pottery making, that I have sat side by side with the mat-weavers and the *uri* painters, that I have counted the yam heaps in the farms and followed the price of foodstuffs from one market to another, but somehow these facts seemed unimportant in relation to the process of change, of ferment, of adaptation, that was going on around me. Very probably, in trying to draw a picture of the wood rather than the trees, I have fallen between two stools and my study ends in being based neither upon accurate perception nor upon correctly interpreted intuition.

Be that as it may, I make no apology for the absence

354

Conclusion

of any recognizable pattern or laid-down laws: the more
one studies native life, or rather, the more one lives the
native life, the more does one see that custom is *not* constant, that behaviour is not according to set patterns,
that stimuli do not call forth the same response. Making
a helpless gesture after I had angrily accused her of a
contradictory statement: 'Some do this and some do that,'
said Moreneke, my Ilorin interpreter. Her words sum up
the whole situation and the greater my experience, the
more I recognize their wisdom.

The subjective outlook has one point in its favour: it
does not much matter whether it is fact or fancy that it
views, a lie can be as illuminating as the truth, for the
form of the lie can sometimes give away more secrets
than the truth. Nor need it take itself too seriously for
after all it is only the affair of one person and integrity is
satisfied if one's own eyes have reported truthfully to
one's own self. If others want to share the view or listen
to the report, they do so by their own wish and at their
own risk. Nevertheless, I would be deeply distressed if,
because I have no great liking for a people so entirely
dominated by material values, I had not perceived their
qualities nor helped others to appreciate them.

What the white men think of the Ibo varies considerably. Those who come from the North, used to dealing
with Fulani and Hausa, are often prejudiced against
him. Those who come direct to Ibo-land, often take to
him. 'I like him. He's cheerful and loves his children,'
was one sweeping but human comment of a District
Officer in a bush station. 'It's the women who wear the
trousers,' said the agent of a trading firm who battled
daily with imperious women traders. 'Our girls and
women are reserved and hard to know, but they are
capable of every devotion and sacrifice,' declared a nun.
'The bush woman is lovable and sincere. Some of the
townswomen are not so grasping and self-centred as I

Conclusion

feared—a *very* few, 'tis true!' admitted a Methodist. 'We like them because they are so ready to be converted,' said a Father. When asked why they were so ready, he smiled: 'Because it costs less to be a Christian than a pagan.' 'Modern primitives,' said a clever missionary teacher referring to her girls who alternately delighted her by their simplicity and infuriated her by their sophistication. 'Form without design,' remarked a quick-witted friend who did not know Africa and to whom I was vainly trying to describe Ibo tribal organization. All these labels are accurate in so far as labels ever are, but they represent no formula which is helpful to the understanding of the race. The apt observation of a Political Officer who knew his people well and was one of the few really good Ibo linguists, though negative, is perhaps the best description of them: 'The Ibo abhors a definition.' Perhaps that is why he himself so constantly eludes us.

If the impression the Ibo makes upon us is so indefinite, what of the impression we make on him? One often asks oneself this question, sometimes with amusement and sometimes with despair, sometimes with mere intellectual curiosity and sometimes with profound concern. It has never seemed to me possible to question black men concerning white men, and they themselves, partly, no doubt, out of prudence, but also because of some finer feeling of good taste, seldom discuss one European with another. But one thing is certain: the Ibo does not think very much of us. Disassociated from our inventions, the gramophones, the cars, the rifles, the thermos flasks and the riches he imagines we all possess, he sees little in us. When he strives to copy us, it is not because of the courage or the wisdom, the virtues or the talents he may see in us, but simply because we represent to him Success. In ourselves we do not interest him except in so far as we contribute to his own interests. We cut quite astonishingly little ice unless there is, which is rare, downright

356

Conclusion

fear, or in cases even rarer, true love and confidence. In the ordinary way, I think we are alternately a Punch and Judy show (as I certainly was!), a pleasant young man easy to hoodwink, an over-stern taskmaster, a nuisance that must be tolerated, an easy-going fellow generous with his money, a useful person to know, a self-important bigwig; but never are we what we are to ourselves: the strong man, the just master, the wise leader, the father of the people, the friend and confidant, the soldier or the feudal lord. In the north, where a hundred horsemen shouted 'Lion!' and the crowding throng yelled 'Bull elephant!' when slaves ran before one picking up the pebbles over which one might have tripped and bending back the branches that might have brushed one's face, when 'Way! Make way!' clamoured the red-robed guard and the long brass trumpets blared to heaven, one could have had illusions about one's importance. Not so among the Ibo. I never ceased to wonder at and be a little disturbed by, their lack of any reverence, if I may use so portentous a word, for anyone superior to them. Admiration, respect, prestige, were dead words to them, either when used in connection with the white man or with themselves. True democrats, no one was better than themselves but yet they were somehow better than anyone else. This self-assurance was sometimes a little frightening. The Ibo men and women are so continually in the right and so busy proving that everyone else is in the wrong. They want to learn from us but only such things as may be materially productive as soon as possible. They tolerate us because they need us. They do not look upon us resentfully as conquerors but complacently as stepping-stones. What will happen when they can, or think they can, mount alone and have no further use for the stepping-stones, no one can tell.

357

Glossary

Abomination
A term first used by the Ibo themselves to describe anything which appeared to them unnatural. Their selection of the unnatural seems to us an arbitrary one but was governed by ideas we do not yet fully understand. Twins are 'abominable'; babies born with too few or too many fingers; 'cowled' babies; babies born feet foremost; children who cut their top teeth first; who in play draw milk from a dog or goat; milk from any source except the white man's tin; etc., etc. On the other hand, albinos and dwarfs are not 'abominable'. Animals can be 'abominable' too if they do anything which appears unnatural.

The word itself was undoubtedly brought into use by Protestant converts; cf. the many references in the Pentateuch.

Bush
A term which, when used as a noun, covers roughly what we call 'the country', i.e. any area which is not urban or sophisticated. More specifically, it means forest or scrub.

Used as an adjective by the white man, it has generally a laudatory sense: 'I like these people, they are so bush.' 'A good place, quite bush still.' Used by the black man, it has usually a derogatory sense and has roughly the signification which 'barbarous' had to the Romans.

The 'bad bush' is that portion of the bush which has been dedicated to a certain spirit (though I am not sure whether such a dedication is common throughout the whole of Owerri Province) and where all 'rubbish' is thrown, such as twins, lepers, mothers who died in childbirth, the 'bags of misfortune' described on p. 114, etc. Government no longer allows bodies to be thrown into the bush, but this rule has still exceptions in the remoter parts. No native likes going through the 'bad bush', especially at night, though paths continually skirt it and even go right through it.

359

Glossary

Cassava (manioc)
The roots, soaked, scraped, and pounded, give a starchy flour. Cassava, though of small nutritive value, is increasingly used as a foodstuff, as its cultivation needs less care and space than yams.

Chop
Pidgin-English for food of any kind.

Cloth
The old term for cotton materials, generally manufactured in Manchester, and sold in the factories. By extension, it is also used for native materials, woven from indigenous or imported yarn.

Craw-craw
A skin disease prevalent among children and to a lesser degree among adults. It causes much irritation and discomfort but can be cured by cleanliness and sulphur ointment.

Factory
The old term used for European firms' warehouses.

Fufu
A native term which covers any pounded food which has been cooked until it resembles a thick porridge, or pap, as the natives call it in English.

Gari
Hausa word for meal.

Juju
A totally inadequate term used to cover anything of a supernatural or half-understood nature, or any object representing or symbolizing a supernatural being. Both the white man and the native, when speaking pidgin-English, call the carved wooden representations of spirits 'juju'; electric light is 'plenty big juju', as is castor oil. The priest who serves a spirit is a 'juju priest'; the shrine where symbols of the spirit are kept is a 'juju house'. A stream or a hill or a portion of the bush, can be 'juju', which may mean it is either dedicated to a certain spirit or that it is in some way 'bewitched'.
    The Long Juju of Aro Chuku was the symbol of the spirit which spoke through the oracle.
    I use this term (*a*) because it is the most familiar one to white and black in Nigeria; and (*b*) because it is manifestly unscientific and any more scientific English term would be misleading in the present state of our knowledge concerning the native's spiritual conceptions.

Medicine
Another totally inadequate term used to cover anything which has

360

Glossary

to do with witchcraft, good or bad; or with native medical art,
whether carried out by means of actual drugs, decoctions, massage,
blood-letting, etc., or by the use of supernatural means such as incantations or charms.

A medicine-man (*dibia*) is not a priest, though he is believed to be
the interpreter of the spirit's wishes; he can be a diviner; he is called
in to ascertain what ancestor is re-incarnated in a baby; he can be the
medium through whom a man either calls down a curse upon an
enemy or delivers himself from a curse. A medicine-woman seems
practically always to deal only with curative medicine.

The votive offerings made to the Yam Spirit in the hope that he
may protect the crops are often called medicine, as well as the symbolic bundles of grass and sticks hung over a doorway to protect a
house. I use the term for the same reasons as I use the term 'juju'.

Inverted c (ɔ)

This sign represents an open 'o'. Words like Lɔlɔ, ɔzɔ, ɔba, should
be pronounced roughly like Lawlaw, *awzaw*, *awba*.

Pan

The old term for corrugated iron.

To sit upon a man

A pidgin-English term which describes better than any English one
the punishment inflicted by women on any man who had trans-
gressed their laws. The punishment could include the destruction of
his property but consisted chiefly in ridiculing him by song and dance
and gesture.

Index

Index

Index

Index

Index

OWERRI PROVINCE

Statute Miles

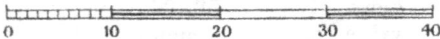

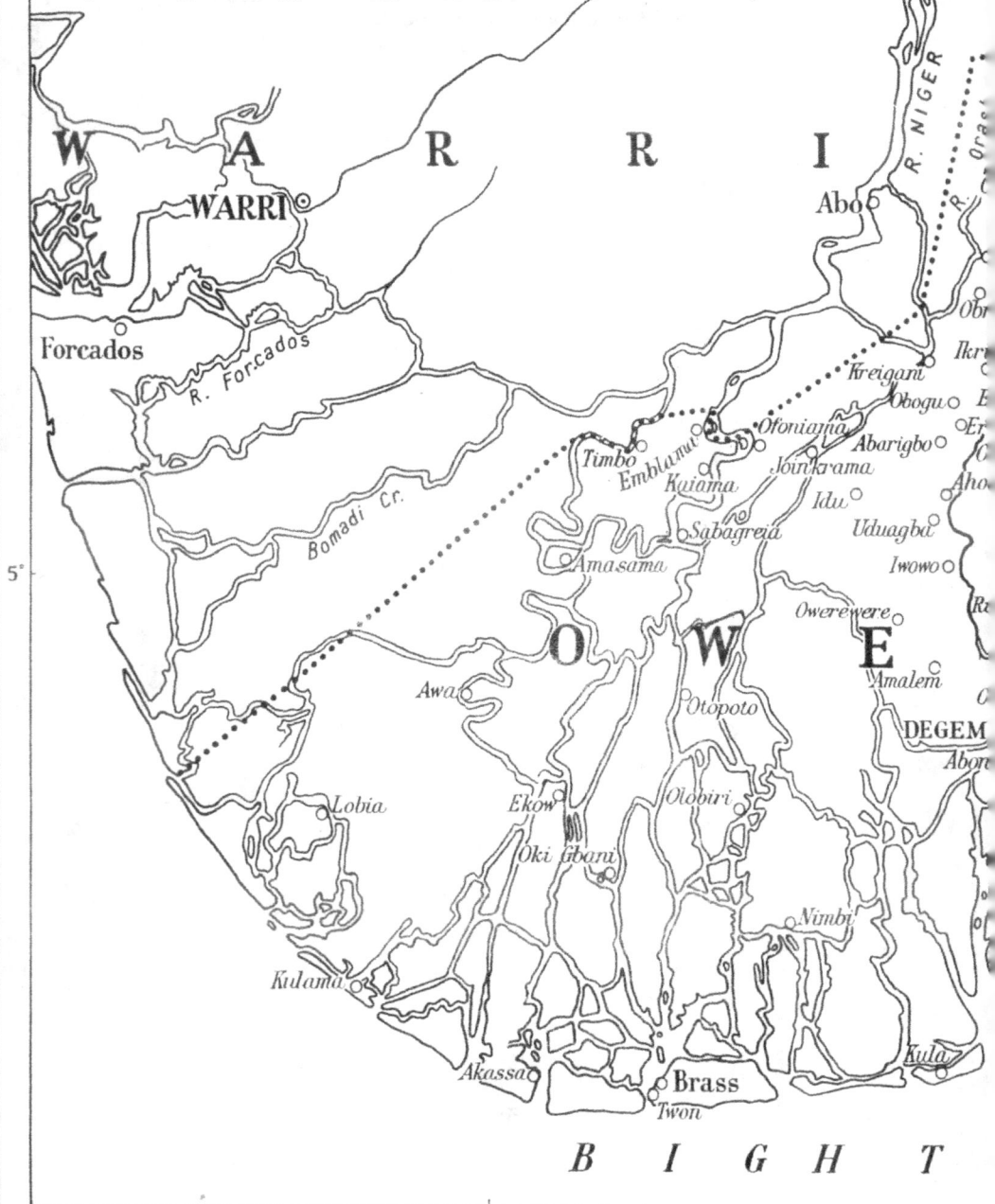

0   10   20   30   40

⊙KWALE

W A R R I

WARRI ⊙

Abo ⊙

R. NIGER

R. Oras...

Obr...

Forcados

R. Forcados

Ikr...

Kreigani

Obogu ⊙   E...

Er...

Bomadi Cr.

Timbo   Emblama   Ofoniama   Abarigbo ⊙

Kuiama   Joinkrama   Aho...

Sabagreia   Idu ⊙   Uduagbu ⊙

Amasama   Iwowo ⊙   R...

O W E   Owerewere ⊙

W   **E**

Amalem ⊙

Awa ⊙   Otopoto

DEGEM

Abor...

Lobia ⊙

Ekow   Olobiri

Oki Ibani

Nimbi ⊙

Kulama ⊙

Kula

Akassa   Brass

Twon

B   I   G   H   T

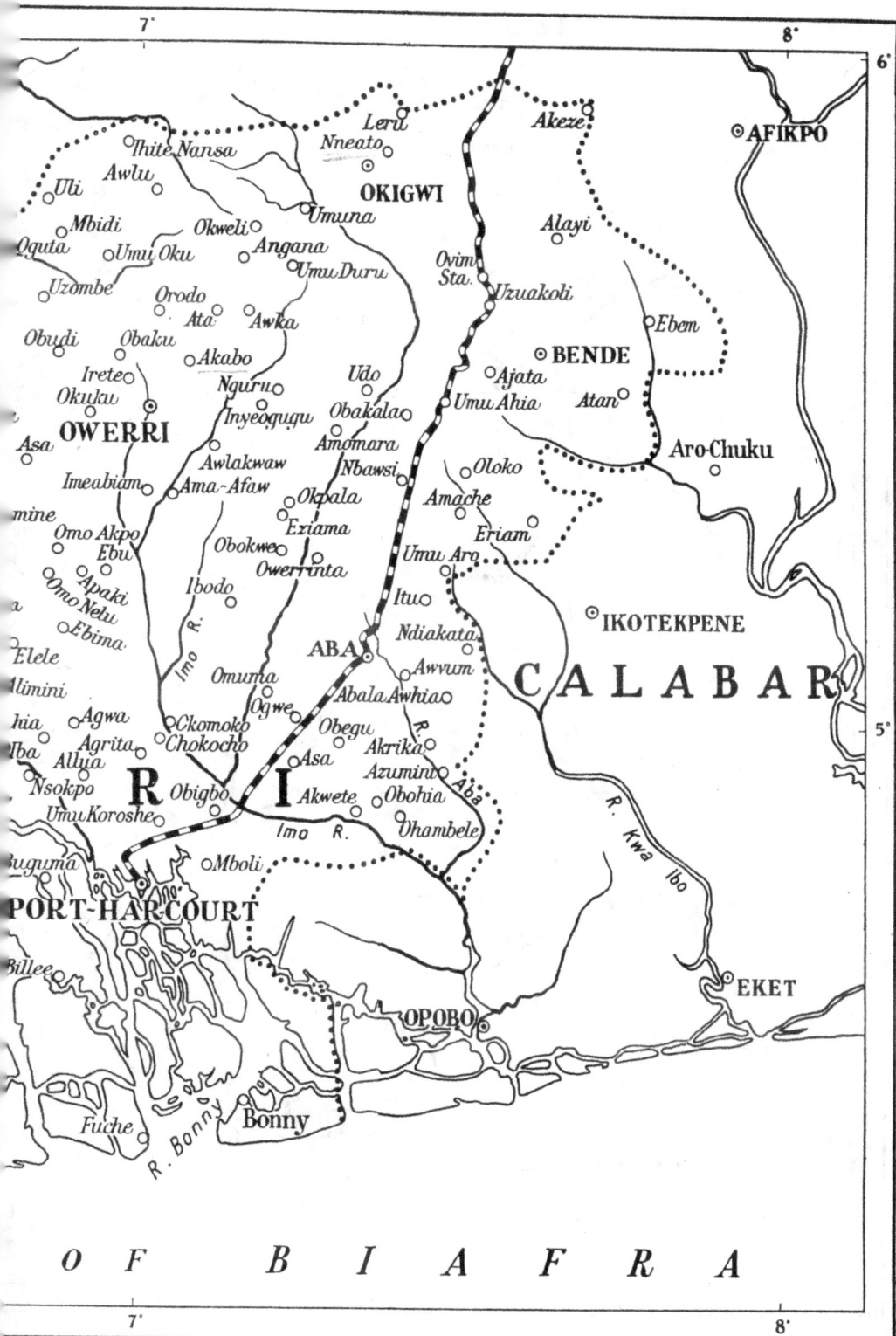

Ihite Nansa
Leru
Nneato
Akeze
◉ AFIKPO
Awlu
Uli
OKIGWI
Mbidi
Okweli
Umuna
Alayi
Oguta
Umu Oku
Angana
Umu Duru
Ovim Sta.
Uzuakoli
Uzombe
Orodo
Ata
Awka
Ebem
Obudi
Obaku
Akabo
Udo
BENDE
Irete
Nguru
Obakala
Ajata
Atan
Okuku
Inyeogugu
Umu Ahia
Aro-Chuku
OWERRI
Amomara
Asa
Awlakwaw
Nbawsi
Oloko
Imeabiam
Ama-Afaw
Okpala
Amache
Omo Akpo
Obokwe
Eziama
Eriam
Ebu
Owerrinta
Umu Aro
Apaki
Ibodo
Itu
IKOTEKPENE
Omo Nelu
Ndiakata
Ebima
ABA
Elele
Omuma
Awvum
CALABAR
Ilimini
Ogwe
Abala Awhia
Agwa
Obegu
hia
Chokocho
Ckomoko
Akrika
Iba
Agrita
Asa
Azumini
Obohia
Alua
R I
Nsokpo
Obigbo
Akwete
Uhambele
Umu Koroshe
Imo R.
Imo R.
uguma
Mboli
PORT-HARCOURT
R. Kwa Ibo
Billee
EKET
OPOBO
Fuche
Bonny
R. Bonny

O F   B I A F R A

Stanford, London.

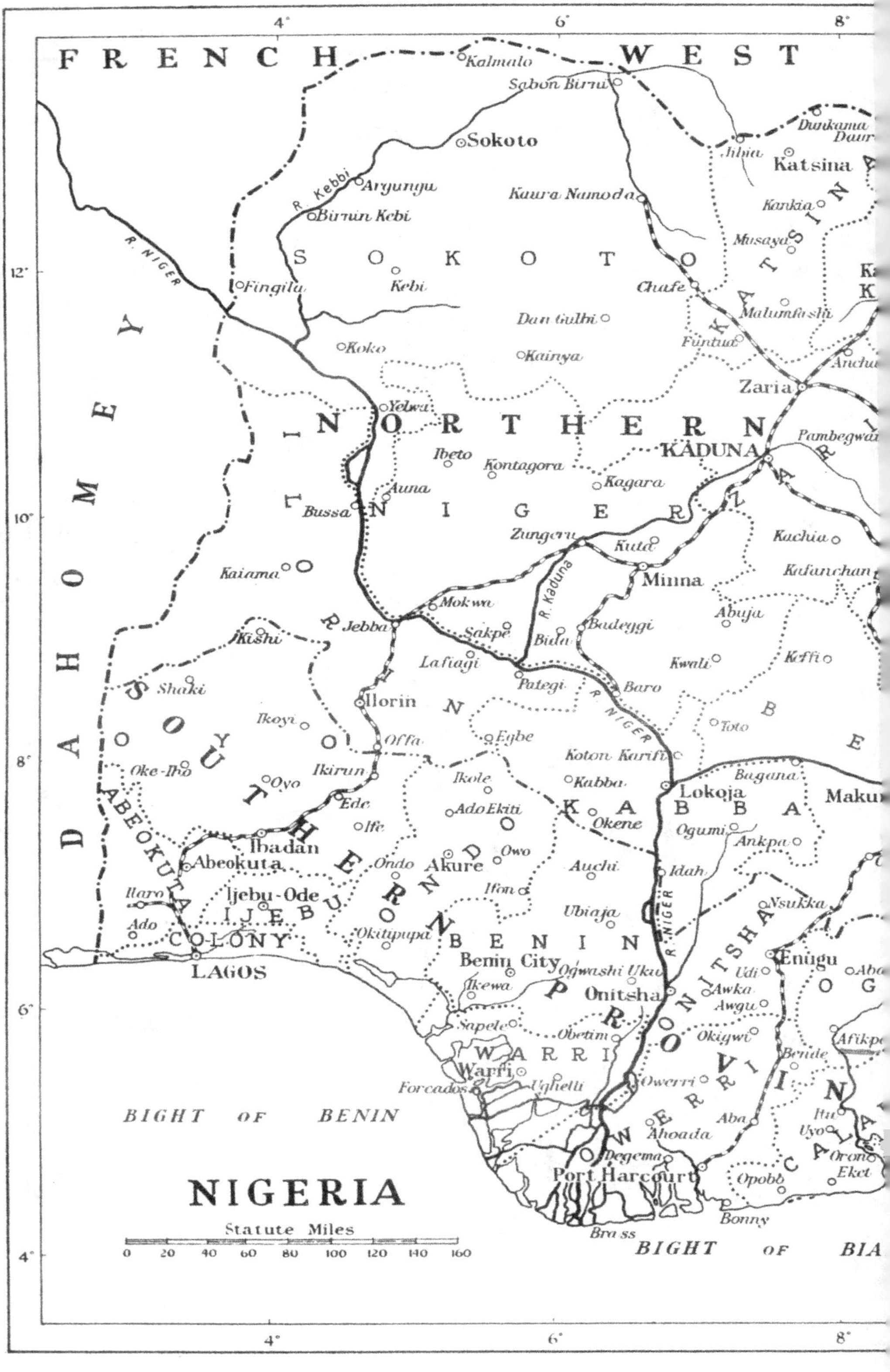
NIGERIA
Statute Miles
0 20 40 60 80 100 120 140 160
FRENCH WEST
DAHOMEY
NORTHERN
SOUTHERN
NIGER
SOKOTO
KATSINA
ZARIA
ILORIN
KABBA
OYO
ABEOKUTA
IJEBU
COLONY
ONDO
BENIN
WARRI
OWERRI
ONITSHA
PROVINCE
CALABAR
R. NIGER
R. Kebbi
R. Kaduna
Kalmalo
Sabon Birni
Sokoto
Argungu
Birnin Kebi
Kebi
Fingila
Kaura Namoda
Jibia
Dunkama
Katsina
Kankia
Musaya
Chafe
Malumfashi
Funtua
Dan Gulbi
Kainya
Koko
Zaria
Yelwa
Ibeto
Kontagora
Kagara
KADUNA
Pambegwa
Auna
Bussa
Zungeru
Kuta
Minna
Kachia
Kafanchan
Kaiama
Mokwa
Jebba
Kishi
Sakpe
Bida
Badeggi
Abuja
Lafiagi
Pategi
Baro
Kwali
Keffi
Shaki
Ikoyi
Ilorin
Offa
Egbe
Toto
Oke-Iho
Oyo
Ikirun
Ikole
Koton Karifi
Kabba
Bagana
Lokoja
Ede
Ife
Ado Ekiti
Okene
Ogumi
Ankpa
Ibadan
Abeokuta
Ondo
Akure
Owo
Auchi
Idah
Ilaro
Ijebu-Ode
Ifon
Ubiaja
Nsukka
Ado
Okitipupa
Enugu
LAGOS
Benin City
Ogwashi Uku
Udi
Awka
Awgu
Ikewa
Onitsha
Sapele
Obetim
Okigwi
Afikpo
Bende
Warri
Forcados
Ughelli
Owerri
Itu
Uyo
Aba
Ahoada
Degema
Port Harcourt
Oron
Eket
Opobo
Bonny
Brass
BIGHT OF BENIN
BIGHT OF BIA
4°
6°
8°
12°
10°

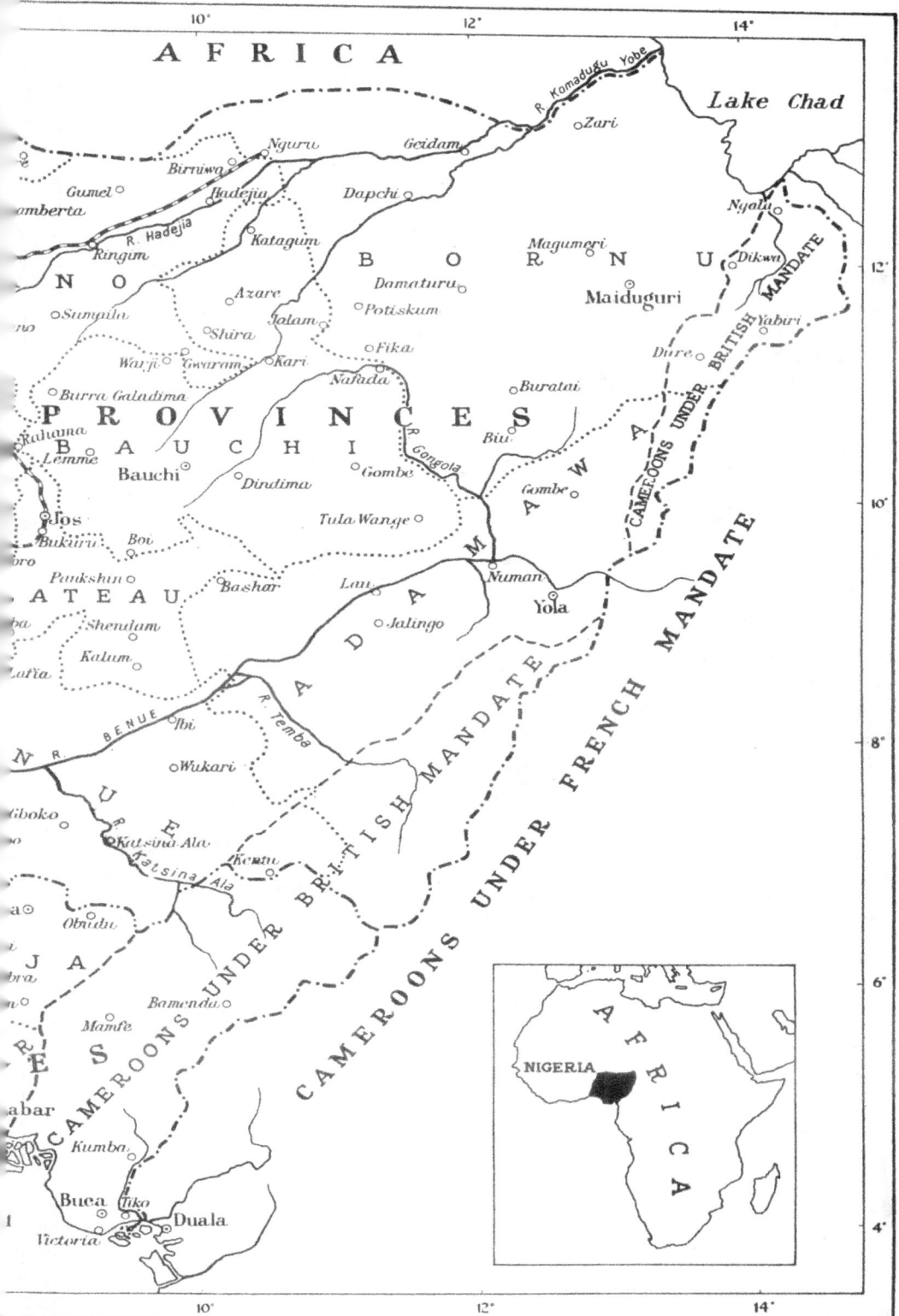

AFRICA

R. Komadugu Yobe

Lake Chad

Zari

Nguru Geidam

Birniwa

Gumel

amberta Hadejia Dapchi

Ngala

R. Hadejia Katagum B O R N U MANDATE

Ringum Magumeri Dikwa

N O Azare Damaturu Maiduguri

Sunyulu Jalam Potiskum Yabiri

no Shira Kari Fika Dure

Warji Gwaram Nafada Buratai CAMEROONS UNDER BRITISH

P R O V I N C E S

Burra Galadima R. Gongola Biu

Rahuna B A U C H I Gombe

Lemme Bauchi Dindima Gombe

Jos Tula Wange A W

Bukuru Boi M

Pankshin Bashar Lau Numan

ATEAU Shendam Jalingo Yola

Kalum A

Lafia D

R. BENUE Ibi R. Temba A

NR M

Wukari A

E CAMEROONS UNDER FRENCH MANDATE

Giboko Katsina Ala

o Katsina Ala Kentu

a Obudu

J A

bra Bamenda CAMEROONS UNDER BRITISH MANDATE

n Mamfe

R E S

abar

Kumba

Buea Tiko

Victoria Duala

CAMEROONS UNDER FRENCH MANDATE

AFRICA

NIGERIA

Stanford. London.

For Product Safety Concerns and Information please contact our EU
representative GPSR@taylorandfrancis.com
Taylor & Francis Verlag GmbH, Kaufingerstraße 24, 80331 München, Germany